*If we want to save the land,*
*we must save the people who belong to the land.*

WENDELL BERRY

VERMONT
ALMANAC

STORIES FROM & FOR THE LAND

*Sugarmaker & Editor*
DAVE MANCE III

*Christmas Tree Grower & Editor*
PATRICK WHITE

*Business Manager*
AMY PEBERDY

*Forester & Editor*
VIRGINIA BARLOW

*Graphic Designer*
LISA CADIEUX | LIQUID STUDIO

*Cover Painting*
SUSAN ABBOTT

*Monthly Paintings*
NICK DE FRIEZ

FOR THE LAND PUBLISHING
BOARD OF DIRECTORS
*Marjorie Ryerson, President*
*Trevor Mance, Vice President*
*Chuck Wooster, Secretary*

BEHIND THE SCENES
*John Douglas, Chris Doyle, Marian Cawley,*
*Giom, Lora Marchand, Tamara White*

What's the difference between a rural and an urban place? According to one US Government definition, it's population. If there are 49,999 people in your town, you're rural. If one more person moves in, you're urban. But of course that's nonsense. The difference is that a rural place has the land at the center of its identity and an urban place has something man-made at its core. We're told that so many of our rural communities are struggling to try to reinvent themselves. Blue Ribbon panels are convened; marketing firms brought in. We'll rebrand ourselves! We'll become a tech hub! Why not just remember who we are and recommit to the things that made Vermont Vermont in the first place?

**WWW.VERMONTALMANAC.ORG**

Volume 1. *Vermont Almanac* is published once a year by For the Land Publishing, Inc., 6151 VT RT 7A, Shaftsbury, Vermont 05262. Copyright 2020 For the Land Publishing, Inc. For purchase inquiries, or to sponsor our work, please contact amy@vermontalmanac.org. Direct all editorial correspondence to dave@vermontalmanac.org. (802) 439-5651. For the Land Publishing, Inc., is a 501 (c) (3) public benefit educational organization. Printed in Springfield, Vermont.

*October 2019–September 2020*

**SUSAN ABBOTT** moved to Vermont almost twenty years ago, drawn to its work-a-day patchwork of small towns, dirt roads, village greens, barnyards, and back fields. She's an active partner with nonprofits in projects like this one that connect art and conservation.

**TANIA AEBI** lives in Corinth, and is very excited about having successfully overwintered one beehive. She is now hoping to get two hives through the next winter.

**VIRGINIA BARLOW** has worked as a forester, writer, and editor in Corinth.

**MEGAN BAXTER** grew up in Hanover, New Hampshire, and worked as a farmer while earning her BFA in poetry. Megan teaches writing at Colby-Sawyer College and works part-time at Honey Field Farm. meganbaxterwriting.com

**GEORGE BELLEROSE** is the author of *Forty-Six Years of Pretty Straight Going: The Life of a Family Dairy Farm*, and the forthcoming: *Portrait of a Forest*, a book about the logging industry in Vermont.

**KATE BOWEN** is a farmer and logger's wife who calls the Green Mountains home and is dedicated to preserving Vermont's rural heritage and agrarian landscape.

A lifelong farmer and agricultural advocate, **DR. TERENCE BRADSHAW** is director of the University of Vermont Fruit Program and Horticulture Research & Education Center. He was raised on a dairy farm on West Hill in Chelsea.

**LISA CADIEUX** was born and raised in Swanton and spent her childhood in the woods creating imaginary wild-life habitats. As an adult, her creative work includes book design, interior design, metalsmithing, weaving, cooking... liquidstudiodesign.com

**JUDY CHAVES** lives, writes, and feeds her woodstove (among other things) in the village of North Ferrisburgh Hollow. She is the author of *Secrets of Mount Philo: A Guide to the History of Vermont's First State Park*.

**MEREDITH COWART** grew up on her family's Christmas tree farm in central Vermont. She earned a Master of Forestry from the Yale School of the Environment and works as a facilitator for the Rocky Mountain Institute.

**DR. HEATHER DARBY** is a Professor of Agronomy at the University of Vermont. She has been conducting outreach and research on industrial hemp since 2016. More information about Darby's research can be found at www.uvm.edu/extension/nwcrops.

**TAMMY DAVIS** is a lover of coffee, a farmer's wife and mama to 6, with one in heaven. She loves to write about farm life and her faith, as well as read and spend time with her family.

**NICK DEFRIEZ** lives in Chelsea and has been painting pictures of the same hillside for the last 30 years.

**JUDY DOW** is a nationally known activist, basket weaver, and teacher of traditional Abenaki culture and native practices.

**CHRIS ELWELL** earned bachelor's and master's degrees in forestry; his applied education includes experiences working in the forests of the Appalachian, Rocky, and Cascade mountain ranges.

**LISA FANTELLI** is a feed, seed, fertilizer, and lime specialist at the Vermont Agency of Agriculture. She lives in Plainfield with her husband and two happy dogs in a house owned by a cat.

**PAUL FREDERICK** was born and raised in Rutland and is a 1982 graduate of the University of Vermont. He and his wife, Diana, live in Hardwick

**AMANDA GOKEE** is a Jewish-Ojibwe writer living in Vermont, where she grew up. She is interested in food systems, food sovereignty, and the connection between people, plants, and places.

**KIM GOODLING** is shepherd to a flock of Gotland sheep at Vermont Grand View Farm. From her family farm, Kim offers farmstay vacations and maple syrup, as well as wool products and online classes to other shepherds. grandviewfarmvt.com

**CAROLYN HALEY** is an author, editor, and reviewer living in rural Vermont. When not at her desk, she enjoys gardening, paddling, riding, and birdwatching, along with autosports and aviation, and spectating the arts.

**PAUL HELLER** grew up in Montpelier. He has been a fish peddler, librarian, innkeeper, and is now retired. He lives in Barre.

**BEN HEWITT** was born and raised in Enosburg Falls, and now lives and writes in Stannard, where he and his family operate a diversified homestead. In his spare time, he can be found exploring Vermont's dirt roads on his bicycle, skiing, and singing to his incredibly tolerant cows.

Meteorological weather consultant **ROGER HILL** of Weathering Heights of Worcester, has 45-plus years' experience in the field watching and forecasting Vermont's "in your face" weather and changing climate. weatheringheights.com

**SHIRLY HOOK** grew up on West Hill in Chelsea. Shirly is a citizen of the Koasek Traditional Band of the Koas Abenaki Nation, and serves on the Council of chiefs. Her first book was published last year, called *My Bring Up.*

**MARY HOLLAND** is a lifelong naturalist/environmental educator/writer/nature photographer who spends her time looking for interesting finds in the woods to photograph and put on her blog, www.naturallycurious withmaryholland.wordpress.com.

**JIM HORST** grew up on a dairy farm in Bennington and has been planting Christmas trees for almost 50 years. For the past 20 years, he has also served as executive director of the NH-VT Christmas Tree Association.

**ANNE HUNTER** is an illustrator, picture book author, and farm wife living in Shaftsbury.

**MARK ISSELHARDT**, University of Vermont Extension, draws on degrees in forest management and plant biology and 25 years of experience in maple to provide research-based education on issues from tree to syrup jug.

**CHARLES W. JOHNSON** is the former Vermont State Naturalist, a 20-year veteran of the US Coast Guard, and author of several books, including *The Nature of Vermont, Bogs of the Northeast*, and most recently *Ice Ship: The Epic Voyages of the Polar Adventurer Fram.*

**KATHLEEN KOLB** describes herself as a landscape painter, working and living along the spine of the Green Mountains of Vermont. The painting of Bill Torrey sharpening his saw was part of the *Shedding Light on the Working Forest* exhibit that toured the state in 2015-2017.

**KATHRYN KRAMER** is the author of several novels and most recently a memoir, *Missing History: The Covert Education of a Child of the Great Books*. She is currently completing a book about Vermont, *The Rise and Fall of the Republic of West Delphi*. She lives in Corinth.

**SYDNEY LEA**, a Pulitzer finalist, recently published his thirteenth collection of poems, *Here*. Shortly ago, Able Muse published *The Exquisite Triumph of Wormboy*, a graphic mock epic in collaboration with former Vermont Cartoonist Laureate James Kochalka.

A Long Island transplant, **TED LEVIN** came north to graduate school forty-five years ago and never left. His most recent book is *America's Snake: The Rise and Fall of the Timber Rattlesnake,* published by the University of Chicago Press.

**DEBORAH LEE LUSKIN** hunts and writes in southern Vermont and blogs about Living in Place. Learn more at www.deborahleeluskin.com

For a good chunk of time this past spring, **DAVE MANCE III** was simply a father. One of the silver linings of the pandemic.

**DAVE MARTIN** raises sheep at Settlement Farm in Underhill, a typical old Vermont hill farm that supported many families over the years. It is no longer viable as a dairy farm, but his sheep keep the fields open.

A co-founder of the Vermont Center for Ecostudies, **KENT MC FARLAND** is a conservation biologist, photographer, writer, and naturalist. He's co-host of Outdoor Radio, a monthly natural history series on Vermont Public Radio.

**RACHEL SARGENT MIRUS** is a freelance teaching artist and science writer. She lives and works in the Green Mountains.

**LAURIE D. MORRISSEY** publishes poetry, essays, and articles in many magazines and literary journals. She is the author of a collection of haiku, *The Slant of April Snow* (Red Moon Press 2019).

**SUSAN C. MORSE**, the founder of Keeping Track, is on sabbatical this year. She's finishing up a book that will be published by Princeton University Press.

**AMANDA NAROWSKI** lives the good life in Bradford with her partner Ben. She enjoys woods walks, learning new skills, and seasons that allow for barefootedness.

Throughout his various careers as a Protestant minister, state senator, utility regulator, and energy policy consultant, **SCUDDER PARKER** has been writing poetry. His first book of poetry, *Safe as Lightning*, was published in June of 2020. scudderparker.net

**AMY PEBERDY** is content keeping her hands full in Corinth.

**NATHAN PERKINS**, 1749-1838, was a minister in Connecticut for 65 years. He took a two-month solo tour of Vermont in 1789 on horseback and was not often favorably impressed.

**DR. LEONARD PERRY** served as an Extension Specialist in horticulture with the University of Vermont for 35 years. Since retiring, Dr. Perry has continued teaching his online horticulture courses at UVM.

**BRYAN PFEIFFER** is a writer, educator, and consulting field naturalist specializing in birds and insects. He lives with his partner Ruth and their English shepherd Odin on a hillside in Montpelier. www.bryanpfeiffer.com.

**CARRIE PILL** is a skier, mountain biker, gardener, and nature enthusiast. Carrie graduated with a BFA from Green Mountain College and eventually landed in Rutland. carriepill.com

**VERANDAH PORCHE** is a cultural worker: poet, songwriter, mentor, scribe, and selectboard member, based in Guilford. Read her work on verandahporche.com or on Facebook.

**ALESSANDRA RELLINI** is a farmer, butcher, and psychology professor who was born and raised in Italy. She and her partner Stefano raise pigs, sheep, and chickens at Agricola Farm in Panton. agricolavermont.com

**MADELYN ROBILLARD** is a 7th-grade student at The Dorset School. She loves reading, writing, hiking, biking, skiing, and sailing.

**ARI ROCKLAND-MILLER** is co-founder of The Mushroom Forager (themushroomforager.com). He shares his passion for mushroom hunting through the written word, guided forays, presentations, and interactive workshops.

**AMANDA ST. PIERRE** is the executive director and a board member of Vermont Dairy Producers Alliance, a group that advocates on behalf of its members regarding policies and regulations that affect their livelihood. She is an 8th-generation Vermonter.

State Game Warden **MIKE SCOTT** has been a member of the Vermont Warden Service since 2014, currently providing Fish and Wildlife law enforcement services in eastern Orange County. In his off-duty time, he is an active sportsman and dabbles in maple sugaring and farming.

**BRETT SIMISON** is an editorial and documentary photographer and audio producer. The native of Citronelle, Alabam, now lives with his wife Amy, son Connor, and daughter Charlotte in Vergennes.

Born and raised in the Champlain Valley, **LEATH TONINO** is a freelance writer and the author of two essay collections from Trinity University Press: *The Animal One Thousand Miles Long* (about Vermont) and *The West Will Swallow You* (about everywhere else).

**BILL TORREY** is a woodsman, author, and storyteller who worked forty years slaying tall timber from the wooded ridges of Vermont where his family has lived since 1767.

**CATHERINE TUDISH** is the author of the novel *American Cream* and the story collection *Tenney's Landing*. She lives in Corinth

**ADELAIDE MURPHY TYROL** uses botanical, allegorical, and environmental themes in her fine art paintings. She lives in Marshfield.

**LAURA WATERMAN** writes on wilderness ethics and the importance of maintaining wildness in the Northeast Mountains. Her books include *The Green Guide to Low-Impact Hiking and Camping and Wilderness Ethics*. She lives in East Corinth.

**AMANDA WERNER** is a third-generation Christmas tree farmer. Her love of writing and the Vermont countryside came from her childhood exploring the farms and woods of central Vermont.

**ETHAN WEST** and his wife Annina Seiler run Republic of Vermont from their home in the hills of Goshen. They manage a treatment-free apiary with bees spread about the Champlain Valley along with a certified organic maple sugaring operation.

**PATRICK WHITE** is an editor at *Vermont Almanac* and runs Meadow Ridge Christmas Tree Farm in Middlesex with his wife, Tamara, and son, Aidan.

**CHUCK WOOSTER** owns and runs Sunrise Farm in White River Junction, where he lives with his wife, two dogs, and assorted sheep and chickens.

# PREAMBLE

This is the first edition of *Vermont Almanac*. When you build the first of anything, you're conjuring while you're constructing. And so for months now, we've found ourselves in the strange position of trying to explain to people what it was we were creating without knowing what the final product would look like.

We knew we wanted to make something that captured time – something that recorded what the weather was like and what people were talking about and dealing with in a given year. We'd start the year on October 1st, when things are at their peak in the natural world, and then detail the following seven months of decline and five months of renewal.

We knew we wanted to make something useful in the spirit of the old *Foxfire* books we loved growing up. Frost spoke of "the need of being versed in country things." You can read that as either a deep nod to an innate human craving for things that are real and of the earth, or as a simple, blunt reflection of rural reality: why live here if you don't want to put something in the ground?

We wanted to share our love of nature and wild things; we wanted to create a stage where rural voices could tell rural stories; we wanted to give readers a sense of how working farms and forests stay viable while celebrating the people who do the work.

And if we did all that, the hope was that we'd create something that would help people do right by the land. You can't love something unless you know it deeply. We wanted to create depth through which people could find or nurture a love of this place.

*The Editors, 10-27-20*

# OCTOBER

# October

O n calendars and on magazine covers, autumn is usually rendered glossy and exhilarating: the foliage always neon orange against azure skies, humans and their fall chores the cheerful equivalent of nut-foraging cartoon squirrels, busy-busy until winter tucks the earth in like a big fluffy quilt.

As for the dark days – days when a cold wind and driving rain wash the natural world gray – those days don't get much press. Those days we tend to take personally and keep to ourselves.

There's sadness in autumn's decay, in watching the weather take away the familiar. Of course the season is not literally sad. We can differentiate between symbolism and reality. We know, for instance, that the trees aren't really dying as they shake and fall apart before our very eyes. But it's impossible not to feel a kernel of loss as summer devolves, from green to red to shades of iron and slate.

Autumn is gorgeous and somber, somehow both at once. A glorious tragedy. We ponder passing patterns of geese, their mournful her-onking a dirge – the sad song of the evacuee. We turn animals into meat, that old regeneration-through-violence bit. Stuck hogs in a pile with skinned-over eyes, blood mixing with earth in spiritual symbiosis.

You could say that autumn is a melancholy season, but since that word's definition revolves exclusively around sadness and depression, it's not really the right word to use. Melancholy misses the joy in this seasonal sadness. It misses the fierce pride in a full freezer, even as we fondly recall chasing spring piglets. It misses the anticipation of winter, even as we pine nostalgically for the strawberry days of June.

Nostalgia is maybe a better word for the season, isn't it? You see ghosts in autumn. Blink your eyes at the river's edge and you're nightswimming again, her pale body emerging to glisten beneath some long-since-past summer moon. Pass a chunk of granite in the forest and you're deer hunting with your grandfather, him sitting motionless in red plaid, forever young . . . or young enough.

I saw an elderly couple the other day clutching freshly resurrected sweaters, just staring off at the turning hillsides. How many autumns did this make? I don't know what they were seeing out there, but their looks were a long, long way off.

My friend Lena lives in Portugal and she says they have a word in her country – saudade – that is untranslatable in English. She says saudade means nostalgia, melancholy, and joy all at the same time. You can feel saudade for a person, or a place, or an object. Essentially, the word declares: your absence has become the greatest presence in my life.

If you live your life through the seasons, I think this might be the right word to describe what you're feeling as you watch the leaves fall.

I clean-picked cucumbers from beneath frost-burned leaves last Monday, and afterwards I took a walk down to the lake for what may turn out to be the year's last swim. Crimson maple leaves floated in black water, cold water, water that prophesied the coming winter if you were in the right mind to listen. The earth smelt raw and sweet from decay. The wind carried curls of wood smoke from the season's first fires. Walking the tracks home, our glorious New England summer began to feel like a fish story; there was no going back now. Walking the tracks home, shivering against the cool evening breeze, I was thinking about my Grandpop and thinking about bow season coming up and stumbling through the Portuguese phrasebook that gathers dust in the back of my mind.

"Is it '*Tenho saudades*,' Lena? How do you say: I feel saudade?" —*Dave Mance III*

# Warm and Abnormally Wet

The perfect Trick-or-Treating costume in 2019 would have been something in the commercial fisherman genre: classic yellow rain slicker with the hood pulled up, galoshes buckled tight. Vermont racked up 3-5 inches of rain on October 31, thanks to a major storm that came across the Great Lakes and brought at least part of one along with it. With the water came wind gusts as high as 65 miles per hour. A bad day to be a broom-riding witch.

The event led to serious flooding, particularly along the Missisquoi, Lamoille, and Winooski Rivers. In fact, the Missisquoi set an all-time record level of 14.72 feet in North Troy. What might have been expected during spring snowmelt season was anything but at the end of October, and road crews were busy for days and weeks repairing washouts and other damage. About the only good news was that most of the storm was warm, with temps reaching the low 70s that day. The weather behind the front was cold, though, and the storm's last gasps left traces of snow in northern parts of the state.

The storm stripped any remaining leaves from the trees, though most were already on the ground courtesy of the Bomb Cyclone that struck southern New England on the 17th, spoiling what had been a good foliage season. That storm came with 40 mile-per-hour winds and heavy rain that left some 25,000 Vermonters without power. These storms were the headline events in a month that saw 15 days of measurable rain in Burlington and nearly double the total average October precipitation (8.50 versus 4.90 inches). In Burlington, the month went down as the wettest October in history; statewide, 2019 was the sixth-wettest October on record. Temperatures averaged between 1 and 3 degrees above "normal" in all of Vermont except the area around Burlington, which ran 3 to 5 degrees above the long-term average.

The month's deluge of rain is representative of the extreme weather that has become more commonplace in Vermont in the last decade. For those who make their living on the land, adapting to these events has become a critical undertaking. One of the biggest logistical challenges is figuring out how to do the mundane, process-driven tasks that used to be taken for granted, like driving a tractor on a field in October. An extra four inches of rain over 100 acres adds up to more than a million extra gallons of water, which left many fields saturated. In the "News from the Fields" section of Vern Grubinger's newsletter *Vermont Vegetable and Berry News*, one berry grower in Charlotte lamented how the October 2019 storms had left their fields too wet to get equipment into. Those who tried had to deal with rutted, compacted soil the following spring.

# NATURE NOTES

**TREE SEEDS WERE IN SHORT SUPPLY IN 2018** (with the exception of white ash), and so trees were ready for a mast year in 2019. The maples, yellow birch, hophornbeam, and white cedar all had notable seed crops. (Predictably, white ash took the year off.) There was a good beechnut crop in many places, and where the oaks grow the woods were full of acorns.

**BURDOCK SEEMED PROLIFIC,** too, but to dog owners, it always does. Try thin slicing the roots and soaking them in some ginger, garlic, soy sauce and apple cider vinegar. A culinary triumph, and fewer burs to untangle from the dog.

The timing of fall foliage was close to the long-term average in 2019. Red maple foliage peaked in Proctor Maple Research Center in Underhill, Vermont around October 9th – sugar maple peak was a few days later. And once things peaked, rain and wind brought the shot to a quick close. The length of the 2019 growing season was five days longer than the long term average.

Many foliage observers noted that the reds were especially vibrant this October, and the reason why is still somewhat of an open question. The yellow and orange colors you see on the hillsides are always there, under the green. When the trees sense the days are getting short, they curb the production of chlorophyll, and as it disappears, the underlying yellow and orange pigments in the leaf come out.

Reds, known as anthocyanins, are different in that they're produced by the tree each autumn, and in varying degrees. On overcast, rainy years, the reds often seem muted. And on clear, cool years, they seem to pop. One hypothesis is that these red-reflecting pigments are helping to protect the leaves from damage by sunlight, sort of like sunscreen. And so more sunscreen on sunny years makes sense. Cool weather might come into play because it's a stressor, which stimulates the tree to work faster to suck up all the nutrients it can, which stimulates the tree to produce more anthocyanins.

## STILL GREEN: EVERGREEN WOOD FERN, MARGINAL WOOD FERN, CHRISTMAS FERN

By late October you will see the fronds of three of the commonest ferns around here splayed out, flat on the ground. You might think that these formerly graceful, upright plants, caught off guard by wind and frost, have given up the ghost without bothering even to turn a respectful brown. Surprisingly, it's part of a plan for overwintering green. A short section of the leafstalk at the base of each frond in all these species weakens in autumn to create a hinge. The hinge is structured so that water from the plant's roots can still enter the leaf, and the frond can still ship out the sugars it makes.

These three ferns live in deep shade and because of being shade tolerant, they generally photosynthesize at a low rate. In late fall and early spring, the forest floor is flooded with light and the prostrate fronds can photosynthesize enough on warmish days to outweigh the cost of staying green. Below about 5 degrees C, however, photosynthesis comes to a halt.

All these ferns are on the large side and they grow in the shape of a vase. When they flatten in the fall, they make a big circle of green – a circle I'll try not to step on quite so often as I have done in the past. — *Virginia Barlow*

Wild mushrooms made unexpected late-season appearances this October, invigorated by a spell of wet, balmy weather. While hiking with my wife and daughter on the lower slopes of Camel's Hump on Halloween, we saw two gourmet species that I was shocked to see fruiting so late, especially at a higher elevation.

The first was a flush of mature hedgehog mushrooms, fresh and plump. I rarely see fresh hedgehogs later than early October, and it felt auspicious to see an old friend once more before winter.

It was even more startling to find a golden chanterelle – a heat-loving mushroom that thrives in July and August. This was not the chanterelle's cold hard relation the yellow-foot chanterelle, but a classic golden with rich orange autumnal coloring. Typically, even a heat-wave in October would not be enough to summon summer chanterelles. Temperature and rainfall are important variables, but so is the date.

My evidence may be too anecdotal to speculate that these late season finds were anything more than an aberration. That said, as mushroom hunters, part of the role we play is one of ecological awareness. With this awareness comes responsibility, and we can all contribute to citizen science by taking notes about the timing, patterns, and abundance of wild mushroom flushes in our favorite patches each year. —*Ari Rockland-Miller*

## AT HOME

### Filling the Larder

HARVEST IS UPON US.
HERE ARE SOME NOTES ON WHAT
TO DO WITH THE SURPLUS.

Complicated custom-made root cellars are all the rage these days. By all means build one if you have the means and time, but if not, a basement retrofit works, too. Richard Czaplinski, a sustainable living advocate from East Montpelier, has the following tips:

ONIONS AND GARLIC like cold and dry (55-60% humidity) conditions and will keep from 3 to 7 months. Unheated basements might be too moist, so you might be better off insulating an unheated space like a mudroom or closet to keep things cold but not freezing.

SQUASH AND PUMPKINS do best at around 55 degrees and in slightly dry (70-75% humidity) conditions. A cool spot in your house where the temperature does not fluctuate widely, such as an entryway or attic or cold pantry, may be ideal for keeping squash.

CABBAGE, CELERY, AND LEEKS, along with root vegetables such as carrots, beets, turnips, and potatoes store best at humid (90-95%) and near freezing conditions. Remember that potatoes must be kept in the dark or else they will become green, so use sacks or boxes. I put the other root crops in five gallon buckets between layers of slightly damp sawdust. Apples want a similar temperature and humidity level, but because they exude gases that affect vegetables, they should be kept separate, layered with newspapers in boxes that are relatively tight. An unheated basement is often ideal, especially near an outside door or window that can be used to allow cold night air to enter in the early season. A dirt floor in the basement is often sufficient to keep proper humidity levels. If you have a cement floor, you can water the floor periodically to keep things moist.

Another way to passively store CARROTS AND BEETS is to use the garden itself as a root cellar. If you just leave the crops in the ground, covered with heavy mulch or straw before or just as the ground begins to freeze, they can be dug throughout the winter. Of course you must protect them from deer and rodents or they will be gone before the snow flies.

LOUISE ROSSKAM

*Canning beans in Bristol in 1940.*

While canning is a noble art, it's also complicated and labor intensive. With the exception of pickles, everyone on staff has moved away from canning and uses a freezer instead. You don't have to worry about freezing a freezer, so having it live on an unheated porch or barn through the winter is no big deal, and in fact saves energy. As you prep food for the freezer, it's a good idea to blanch it. This will stop the enzyme action that degrades color, flavor, and texture. After you boil or steam, immediately cool in an ice water bath. Here's how we do it:

### WHOLE KERNEL CORN
*boil 4 minutes or steam 6 minutes*

### BROCCOLI FLORETS
*boil 3 minutes or steam 5 minutes*

### GREEN, WAX, SNAP BEANS
*boil 3 minutes or steam 5 minutes*

### PEAS
*boil 2 minutes or steam 4 minutes*

### TOMATOES
*technically you should boil for 30-60 seconds, chill, remove skins, freeze. But we often push the easy button and just freeze them whole. When you take the frozen tomatoes out and put them in a bowl of hot water, the skin will wrinkle right off and they'll be ready for coarse chopping almost immediately. Upside is you save time and bags, downside is they won't keep as long this way.*

### SEPTEMBER AT THE HOME

Her hands still farm the sheets.
When years outweigh the body, I perch
by her bed and whisper. *Speak to me.*
Chrome catches the diamond ring that

hangs from her finger as a good dress
would from the rack of her spine.
*By God* (she swears) *You'd better
believe.* We fill the larder, pare

core and quarter hours, scare up jars
of relishes and jams, mince, quince.
Lestoil douses cinnamon. We talk down
dim stairs where a new screw-in electric

bulb shaped like a summer squash sheds
light on all she's squared away. We slip
tomatoes from their skins easier than
children, shuck and strip cob's milk-

sweet, sticky silk. We tackle pickles:
bread and butters in pints, dills in brine
kept crisp with grape leaves, cool in the
crock held down by a plate and rock.

*You have no idea how much we had!*
she cries. Harvest holds
us in place. Our laps heap,
famous with all we have named.

*Verandah Porche*

# *I split my firewood in spring just like I was supposed to. So why is it still hissing in October?*

**TREES, LIKE MOST LIVING THINGS**, are full of water. You can imagine a piece of firewood as a mixed bundle of hollow and solid cardboard tubes. The hollow tubes are vessel cells that move water. The solid tubes are fibers that help make wood strong. When a tree is felled, water is trapped in the hollow cell cavities (called lumens), as well as in the cell walls. The amount of water per cell is miniscule, but multiply it by trillions and it really adds up. According to an extension service bulletin, one cord of red oak weighs 4,888 pounds when it's green and 3,528 pounds when it's dry. Divide the difference by 8.3 pounds – the weight of a gallon of water – and we learn that 164 gallons disappear, per cord, in the evaporation process.

So all this water has to migrate out of the wood before it will burn well. Water moves more easily with the wood's grain than across the grain, so the path of least resistance is out the ends of the wood. In other words, the shorter your pieces, the shorter the trip. Some will evaporate through the sides, so you can also speed up the process by splitting each chunk. Bark essentially exists to keep moisture in, so a piece with four cut faces will dry more quickly than a piece with the bark still on. And the smaller you split each piece, the easier it will be for the water to get out.

So why didn't the wood you split in spring dry right? Well, the drying process depends on three things: temperature, turbulence, and time.

Obviously, heat aids drying. The best place to put a wood pile is in the same full-sun location you'd put a vegetable garden. Stack the wood, don't leave it in a volcanic-looking heap, so the sun can touch each piece.

The importance of turbulence – i.e. airflow – is often overlooked. Best practice is to stack your firewood so that the prevailing wind is perpendicular and can blast the face of the entire row. A single long row is going to have better airflow than a block of stacked wood or a volcano. A tarp or some plastic on the top of a pile to keep rain off is alright, but do not wrap the pile; you want the wind to blow through and you want the moisture to be able to get out. If you build a woodshed, make the walls like a pallet so air can get through.

Unfortunately, as with all facets of life, the time part is the most difficult to reckon with. The reality is that most people rush their wood. Buying wood in the fall with the idea that you'll burn it that winter is a rookie move that won't end well – anyone with at least one year of wood burning experience knows this. But cutting, splitting, stacking in spring, the way so many of us do it, is still not optimal. In our experience, green hardwood that's been split and stacked for six months will still give you only mediocre fires. By about month nine the wood will be decent. By month 12 it'll finally be where you want it. All of which is to say that we should really be getting a full year ahead. The old timers with the neatly stacked piles that you never see go down because they sit the first winter are the ones who are doing it right.

ADELAIDE TYROL

# Know How Various Species Burn

When neatly stacked in a row, pieces of firewood look pretty uniform. All about the same size, shape, and color. But anyone who's ever worked up a mixed load of logs knows there's nothing uniform about it. When you're a 90-pound kid swinging an 8-pound splitting maul, landing it on top of a block of ash can make you feel like Superman. Come down on a piece of elm, though, and even a lumberjack can feel like a weakling. There's just as much variance in firewood when you try to light it up. Beech just wants to burn, cherry not so much.

But, at least from a heating standpoint, the biggest diversity in firewood comes in the number of BTUs contained by each species. (British Thermal Units represent the amount of heat required to raise the temperature of one pound of water by one degree Fahrenheit.) And because BTUs are what keep your family warm in the winter, they're pretty important.

Softwoods, burned mainly by those with outdoor wood boilers who don't have to worry about creosote build-up and chimney fires, almost uniformly have lower BTU ratings than hardwoods. (One interesting outlier is tamarack, which at 20.8 million BTUs per cord is better than soft maple or white birch, both of which are species you probably have in your firewood pile). But even within hardwoods, there is a wide range of BTUs present. You'd need to burn two cords of butternut to get the BTU equivalent of one cord of shagbark hickory.

Take a look at the chart (right) for specific BTU information on various hardwood species, and keep in mind that this data is for seasoned (dried down to 20 percent moisture) firewood. Burn it green and even the most energy-packed firewood will be using a lot of its energy trying to expel water.

## WOOD: MILLION BTUS/CORD

| | |
|---|---|
| Apple | 26.5 |
| Ash, White | 23.6 |
| Aspen | 14.7 |
| Basswood | 13.5 |
| Beech | 24 |
| Birch, Black | 26.8 |
| Birch, White | 20.3 |
| Birch, Yellow | 23.6 |
| Box Elder | 17.9 |
| Butternut | 14.5 |
| Cherry, Black | 19.9 |
| Cottonwood | 13.5 |
| Elm, American | 19.5 |
| Hickory, Shagbark | 28.5 |
| Hornbeam, Eastern | 27.3 |
| Locust, Black | 26.8 |
| Maple, Hard | 24 |
| Maple, Soft or Red | 18.7 |
| Oak, Red/Black | 24 |
| Oak, White/Bur | 25.7 |
| Sycamore | 20.7 |
| Walnut, Black | 25.3 |
| Willow | 14.5 |

# A LOOK BACK

## Plague Times

The story of the great October pigeon slaughter of 1760 actually begins with the story of the great army worm invasion that occurred that summer. A relentless phalanx of the crawling creatures made a gradual appearance in late July and grew in numbers and strength into September. *The Vermont Journal*, a newspaper from Windsor, Vermont, reported, "they marched with great speed and ate up everything green for the space of 100 miles in spite of rivers, ditches, fires, and the united efforts of 1,000 men." Some residents of the Upper Valley called them "The Northern Army," as they marched southward in an endless formation.

*Army worm*

When mature, the brown caterpillars with black and yellow stripes were the size of a man's finger and moved with great speed, stopping only to devour food – often crops. Grant Powers' *History of Coos County* (published in 1841) records their predations:

*They filled the houses of the inhabitants, and entered their kneading-troughs, as did the frogs in Egypt. They would go up the side of a house, and over it, in such a compact column, that nothing of boards or shingles could be seen. They did not take hold of the pumpkin-vine, peas, potatoes, or flax; but wheat and corn disappeared before as by magic. They would climb up the stalks of wheat, eat off the stalk just below the head, and almost as soon as the head had fallen upon the ground, it was devoured.*

In desperation, the settlers dug trenches one and a half feet deep around their fields, but the interminable column filled the ditches with their bodies, and those in the following ranks soon made passage on the backs of their predecessors. The farmers waged a constant vigil and were able, by their tenacity, to save at least seed corn for the following planting season. Finally, by September, the infestation began to wane. It is likely that the caterpillars had begun their metamorphosis into moths.

Powers noted:

> This visitation, which destroyed the principal grains of that year, was felt severely by all the new settlements; for it not only cut off their bread-stuffs, but it deprived them of the means of making their pork to a great degree, and reduced the quantity of fodder for their cattle.

> Jonathan Tyler, of Piermont, related to me, that the settlements in that town were left without the means of subsistence from their own farms. His father drew hay on a hand-sled upon the ice, from the great Ox Bow in Newbury, to support his cow the following winter. And had it not been for two sources opened for their support, they must have deserted the town.

The first source was the pumpkins that, by custom, had been sown between the corn rows. After the worms destroyed the corn, the pumpkins grew with a renewed vigor, and the harvest was so great that the farmers of Newbury gave pumpkins to neighboring towns in such numbers that people had to build rafts to carry them home on the river.

The second source was the immense flocks of passenger pigeons that migrated through the area that fall. Samuel Peters' 1781 *History of Connecticut* acknowledges this event:

> The inhabitants of Vermont would unavoidably have perished by famine in consequence of the devastation of these worms, had not a remarkable Providence filled the wilderness with wild pigeons which were killed by sticks as they sat on the branches of trees in such multitudes that 30,000 people lived on them for three weeks.

The Tylers of Piermont reportedly took 400 dozen in a matter of days.

> They carried them to Piermont, and made what is defined, in the Yankee vocabulary, "a bee," for picking pigeons; and two or three times a week the people of Haverhill were invited down to Mr. Tyler's to pick pigeons. Those who went had the meat of all they picked, and the Tylers had the feathers; and they made, says Jonathan Tyler, "four very decent beds of those feathers." The bodies of those pigeons, when dressed, dried, and preserved for the winter, were very palatable and nutritious, and proved a good substitute for other meats, of which the inhabitants had been despoiled by the Huns and Goths of the north.

Once so plentiful that they blackened the sky from one horizon to the other, wanton slaughter like this helped drive the passenger pigeon to extinction. The last bird died in captivity in 1914.

In the Upper Valley, the following spring, the famine was followed by flood, but nevertheless, the settlers persisted, despite many having their land buried under two to three feet of silt which made the acreage unusable for two or three years. The account in Hemenway's *Gazetteer* concludes, "This calamity, so soon succeeding that of the worms, was regarded by many a controversy of the Lord with his family."

Not surprisingly the tenacious spirit of the settlers in the Upper Valley was unbroken by famine and natural disaster and their progeny continue to prevail on the great river. While army worms have continued to threaten crops in other parts of the country, I can find no record of another outbreak of such proportion in northern New England. —*Paul Heller*

*Martha, the last passenger pigeon on record, in 1914.*

## INDUSTRY

# *Vermont's Evolving Apple Industry*

No. 44501.
"Jewell Red"
Mr. Dimock.
C. Corinth, Vt.

R. C. Steadman
11-23-'17
11-13-'17

USDA POMOLOGICAL WATERCOLOR COLLECTION

When one thinks of Vermont agriculture, dairy and maple are the first two things that come to mind. But apples have long held an important and iconic place, representing the third leg of Vermont's exportable farm products – those crops produced in far greater amounts than locals consume.

From settlement through the 1700s, apples were mostly produced from seedlings on diversified farmsteads throughout the state. The often-unrefined fruit grew on trees that would be considered huge today, reaching up to thirty feet in height and breadth. Most fruit was pressed and made into cider and brandy or fed to livestock.

Eating apples, or dessert apples as they were called then, were less common. If a family was lucky they might have one prized tree on the homestead for their own consumption. Because apples do not maintain their characteristics when grown from seed, grafting is required to maintain and propagate a specific variety. For centuries this was a pastime practiced on wealthy estates, less so on common farms.

In the 1800s, demand for dessert apples grew, and farmers began to try their hand at grafting and, subsequently, some experimented with commercial fruit growing. During this period hundreds of varieties were commonplace in America, and some, like Bethel, Magog Redstreak, and Northfield Beauty were selected and cloned on farms in Vermont.

By the turn of the twentieth century, railroads and, later, refrigeration, made it possible for farmers to ship fresh apples to urban markets. The advent of prohibition in the 1920s further pushed orchards away from cider production and more toward fresh dessert varieties, and farms became increasingly specialized. In order to meet the demand for consistency from packers, shippers, stores, and consumers, apple growers planted fewer varieties and focused on production practices to optimize quality for each one. Hard winters in 1917-18 and 1933-34 killed off many of the less-hardy varieties, which was a major driver in the adoption of the primary variety still grown today: McIntosh, Vermont's official state fruit.

By the 1950s, Vermont growers were producing over a million bushels of fruit annually that were sold to markets across the eastern US and in Europe. Orchards were located throughout Vermont, with important production centers in the Champlain Islands and Connecticut Valley, as well as Addison County, where about half of the state's apple crop was stored, packed, and shipped through the Shoreham Cooperative Apple Packers Association. During this commercial era, which ran from about 1910 through the 1990s, McIntosh and her daughters Empire, Cortland, and Paulared made up the vast majority of fruit grown and shipped. Growers were able to maintain a good standard of living with as few as 20 acres of fruit during this time, thanks to the co-op and other packing houses located around the state.

Also beginning around the 1950s, growers began to replant size-controlled rootstocks in their orchards. These were called dwarf trees, but that term has developed on a continuum such that a dwarf tree in 1960 would be a relative giant compared to one grown today. Changes in tree form and architecture made orchards more efficient, while also making some landscapes on hillier or rockier terrain less suitable for fruit cultivation.

The commercial landscape began to change in the waning days of the twentieth century. Modern orchard systems decreased costs of production, but also increased economies of scale. This allowed regions in western New York and Michigan to outcompete Vermont in producing McIntosh and similar apples suited to cool, humid northeastern growing conditions. Competition from west coast growers, especially in Washington, and from international producers in Chile, New Zealand, and other areas, put more strain on the wholesale apple industry in Vermont.

Today, Vermont has about 1,500 acres of commercial orchards, or about half that of its peak in the 1980s. McIntosh is still the top variety, representing about 45 percent of that acreage (down from over 65 percent in the 1950s). The majority of apple production is still shipped to wholesale accounts, but more fruit is being sold regionally or in-state. Of the roughly 50 commercial orchards remaining, six farms grow the bulk of the 600,000-800,000 bushels of apples that Vermont produces annually. However, with the decline in the wholesale apple industry, smaller orchards that market fruit directly to consumers have tried to cultivate a new niche. Pick-your-own sales have been increasingly important to orchards for the past several decades, and many orchards exclusively sell fruit at their farms to customers interested in supporting local food producers. Modern varieties like Honeycrisp and Ginger Gold provide new flavors to today's consumers. Orchards in Vermont contain a mix of older-style sprawling trees and modern dwarf trees that resemble woody tomato plants tied to tall, multi-wire trellis systems. With the expansion of the craft hard cider industry, everything old is new again – sales of apples to cideries now account for about 25 percent of the apple crop in the state, and large cideries now also need to use out-of-state apples to meet demand.

The farmhouse orchards of yesteryear are still a common sight, especially on hill farms and other areas where the modern commercial orchard systems didn't take hold. Many of those trees are near the end of their lifespans, having held on for a century or more. In those older orchards, heirloom varieties, often with names lost to history, can be found and enjoyed by local fruit foragers. Some cideries specialize in fruit from such trees. A few commercial orchards have merged old and new, and now grow antique apple varieties in more modern orchard systems for sale in local co-ops and specialty food stores.

I give a guest lecture on apple production in Vermont every year to our introductory agriculture class at UVM, where I outline everything it takes to grow a consistent, high-quality crop of fruit annually. At the end of my lecture, one student recently asked, "So if it takes that much work to grow apples in Vermont, why do we still have an industry here?" The simple answer is that apples want to grow here. While the days of commercial orchards in Highgate, Tunbridge, Clarendon, and other small towns all over the state are gone, it is clear from the feral trees that you see dropping fruit in every corner of the state each October that Vermont is perfectly suited to the apple.

*Terence Bradshaw, Ph.D.*
*Assistant Professor of Specialty Crops Production*
*University of Vermont Plant and Soil Science*

# Ten Thousand Thousand Fruit to Touch

**OCTOBER 1, 2019,** edging toward peak. 10:00 a.m., Clarence Elijah "Chief" Boston III, 68, spare and angular as the trees, strides through his orchard, surveying a bumper crop of premium fancy fruit. Up a dirt drive off Cowpath 40, Marlboro, Ames Hill Orchard spans two-and-a-half acres, 600 dwarf trees, deeply tended, strung on supports. "I'm in the business of growing apples, not wood," he laughs. Last week, Boston picked the Gravensteins, an early

*Clarence Elijah "Chief" Boston III*

tart-sweet variety with a short shelf life, but held off on the "money apples." While commercial growers pushed forward picking hard fruit with their crews, he took a week to watch and wait. Now ready, Chief Boston will tackle the challenge of harvesting 30 tons of perfect fruit, alone.

This abundance comes as no surprise. The good news is the bad news everyone knows. 2018 was a total loss. He realized what would follow. On the 20th of May, there was a "snowball bloom." "You walk through the orchard: the world is white. There's the delicate

COURTESY FORREST HOLZAPFEL, 2013

scent of blossoms, and all around, the hum of bees."

"Of course, with plenty to choose from, the brokers want you to sell cheap." His tone shifts from reverie to rant. "Nobody can wait for an apple to ripen in a commercial orchard. One bad apple tastes like any other. And the public has forgotten." He gazes at a Mac without plucking it. "The brokers want them magically to be red and hard. They pay for the color. But time and cold nights give you the color. They don't come early." He adds, "I believe brokers are partly responsible for the collapse of the apple economy. During my 40 years as a professional orchardist there have been three collapses or 'shakeouts,' when the crop isn't worth what it costs to grow it. Back in the 90s, the orchards only survived if they had real estate to sell."

Boston leases the land where his trees thrive. The stakes are always high. Though he grows twenty varieties, ending the season with Northern Spies and Lady apples, for wreaths, today his eyes are on the market classic McIntosh and Honeycrisp, the rising star.

Developed at the University of Minnesota, Honeycrisp was named the state fruit in 2009 for reviving Minnesota's apple-growing industry. This apple, their website boasts, is "explosively crisp & juicy," a fine keeper. "Think of it. You can have a great apple to pick and then store, sell or savor for more than half the year!" The piece concludes: "Make your world a better place. Try 'Honeycrisp' Apples."

Boston is unsentimental about heirloom apples with exotic names: Wolf River, Duchess of Oldenberg. Most disappeared for a reason: people voted with their teeth. Years ago, Boston embraced the cold-hardy, long-storing Honeycrisp. He payed the university a royalty of one dollar a tree, and set out to cultivate the best Honeycrisp in the East.

So, Boston walks down each row, and seeing red, bites, considers, spits. No one can consume eight or ten unripe apples a day, he explains. Biting and releasing "spitters" is perfectly polite in any orchard. "When you don't have to spit out what you sample, it's time to start picking."

Boston verifies the mouth-feel with "some hard numbers." He cuts an apple and dips it in iodine. The starch will stain purple if the sugar hasn't developed. He pours a little juice onto a portable refractometer, a device that looks like a little telescope. The BRIX number shows the sugar, indicating the degree of

*Honeycrisp apples*

maturity. He notes the days from full bloom. Time is genetically imprinted in the apple. Boston can taste and wait for the moment when his "apples ripen from the inside out."

Boston will pick alone. "Given the crop, the last thing I need is someone helping. *They* think the apples are beautiful, but they're not what I can sell: a 90 percent red apple: no marks. Zero tolerance for flaws. I have a specialty market: roughly three times the price for a Honeycrisp because of the quality."

He calculates, "I can pick 56 boxes a day, sorting on the tree. If it's not perfect, I don't touch it. No reason to put it in the picking bucket, in the box on the tractor, in the pick-up, and have to sort it out on the way to market." Mornings when he picks, Boston sleeps in. "I'm in no hurry. I lay out my boxes. My picking bucket, full, holds a bushel and weighs about 40 pounds. It's like you're pregnant with apples." He opens the straps, holding the skirt to let his apples gently down in the box. "You should never be able to hear the apples drop." He quotes a painter friend charged with training a crew: "You have to pick an apple like you're touching your lover's breast." Boston begs to differ, but offers no other metaphor. His life and business partner, Molly Welch, mastered the art of apple picking to his standard. A high school English teacher and rock musician, Welch handles the orchard's logistics in her spare time, reminds Chief to eat and sleep, and takes orders from no one.

"I knew I could only lose this crop through neglect or catastrophe." Luckily, there's been no disaster, and Ames Hill Orchard has never known neglect since Chief Boston pried the rocks out with a chisel plow and a stone boat twenty years ago.

. . .

Chief Boston inherited that commanding nickname from his grandfather, Editor-in-Chief of the *Winsocket Call*. His father, a venerable college football coach, returned to the military as a Colonel in the Joint Chiefs of Staff. His son could be known by no other name. All Chief Bostons lead by example. Brilliant, honest, they deplore hypocrisy. They never compromise or quit. Exasperated, with grudging pride, his father said, "Son, you don't take orders well."

Chief III turned 14, a prep school rebel at the top of his class; at 16, a page in United States House of Representatives, clean-cut, keenly observant. At 18, outraged at the bombing of Cambodia, Chief became "an anti-imperialist street fighter, like my ancestor the first Elijah Boston, in 1775, kicking out the Brits." His worried father flew him out of the country. In Ireland, sampling "The Troubles" he could not fix, Boston wandered into the countryside and listened to the farmers he met. Their rooted knowledge eased his restlessness. Back in the States, burnt out in New York City, Boston abandoned "The Big Apple" for his grandfather's farm in Western Massachusetts. He enrolled at UMASS, left History for Agriculture, and beat his sword into a plowshare.

Forty years followed: once a student of explosives, Boston mastered "the black art of spraying, Integrated Pest Management, more apples, less poison." He was much in demand. He designed orchards for wealthy clients, kept sheep and fended off predators, changed partners, had a son never called Chief, settled in a hill town, started his orchard. He ran for Constable fourteen years ago, and won. Had he come full circle from the rage-filled anarchist? Not really.

Mother Nature calls her shots; Chief Boston calls his. Breaking a "forever tradition," he decides to harvest Honeycrisps before Macs, "changing the play at the line of scrimmage. Everyone's been picking for three weeks. I held off. Now I'm going to pick. I'm out of step with the whole army. I can go into it with the energy which is harvest. You're lost. It's a beautiful thing, totally consuming. How often do you get to give more than you have?" —*Verandah Porche*

## THE UNSEEN

Jamaican workers have been a critical part of Vermont's orchard industry for generations, part of a migrant workforce that numbers in the thousands. In Jamaica, these men are farmers, truck drivers, chefs, construction workers, and policemen. But come the end of July, they travel to Vermont via the H-2A Temporary Agricultural Worker Program to help with the apple harvest.

I'm a professional photographer, and completed a set of portraits of some of these men in 2013, then put the project on the shelf for a few years. But I wanted to go back, revisit them and capture stories to accompany the original images. I tried to do this last fall, but things had changed. Whereas in 2013 they invited me into their lives warmly, in 2018 they had become furtive and hesitant to talk. The men just wanted to keep their heads down, not get noticed.

The image here was chosen for its ambiguity, a choice that speaks to this moment in time. It does not show a face or a specific orchard, so as not to put these workers at risk. I'd like to go back someday when the political climate has changed, but for now I'm giving them space. —*Brett Simison*

# *Value Added*

## BEYOND DESSERT APPLES AND CIDER

Apple Balsamic Vinegar of Vermont hit the shelves this month. Made by Side Hill Cider Mill in Vershire, it's a highly unusual product. Neil Hochstedler, the owner, has found only two other producers – one in Ireland and a small company in Massachusetts. He said his idea "seemed like a natural and logical" extension of his existing cider vinegar business.

Neil's been deep into apples since the 1970s, when he picked and pruned for a living. He brought his work home with him, grafting and pruning apples at his own place. Before long, he was producing more perishable apple juice than he could use, and he turned some into cider vinegar, which he has been selling for several years. Too much vinegar inspired him to diversify his offerings, so he created a balsamic line. With help from Sebastian and Sabra Ewing of neighboring Flag Hill Farm, they pretty much invented a commercial-scale production process and have gotten started on marketing.

Not unlike the more familiar balsamic vinegar made from red grapes, Neil's process begins with boiling apple juice to a sweet syrup, which is done in a small sugaring evaporator.

To make cider vinegar, the sugars in apple juice are first fermented to alcohol, and in a second fermentation step, acetic acid-forming bacteria that have survived the fermentation process are augmented with selected acetobacters which convert the alcohol to vinegar.

To make apple balsamic, the cider vinegar is mixed with the sweet apple syrup until the acid level is right. The mix is then aged in wooden barrels, with some oak chips thrown in. At every step, things can go awry. As Neil says, "There have been a lot of setbacks." But he finds the complicated relationships among the ingredients and conditions fascinating, and when the right apples, aeration, time, and temperature have been provided, the result makes it worth all the trials and errors.

Neil's other job is as a machinist, which has come in handy: he's converted a carpet steamer into a tool that shrinks the sleeves on the bottle caps and has modified aquarium pumps to aerate tanks of vinegar. The kind of electric mats made for starting seeds keep the tanks warm.

The label on the Apple Balsamic Vinegar of Vermont says that it's "Organic * Gourmet * Handmade * Subtle * Complex," and it's being sold at farm stands and co-ops at this point. Somewhat unexpectedly, Neil even likes the sales part, especially when he meets anyone interested in vinegar. It seems to have become an obsession. Now there's a storehouse of tanks, drums, and casks that should keep him obsessed for a long time. —*Virginia Barlow*

JOHN DOUGLAS / FLYING SQUIRREL

# *If You Want to Plant a Home Orchard...*

## HERE ARE SOME THINGS TO KEEP IN MIND.

**AN IDEAL SITE** will have well-drained soil and be located in an area that has some shelter from late frosts. Very low sites can be dangerous, since cold air pools. Very warm southern-facing sites can be dangerous if the microclimate leads to earlier-than-is-safe blossoms.

**THE IDEAL SOIL PH** for apple trees is between 6.0 and 6.5. Get your soil tested, and then adjust both acidity and nutrient levels. Since it takes lime a year to break down, it's best to amend your soil at least a year in advance if you need to raise pH. And don't overdo it with any inputs. Too much fertilizer is detrimental, especially in fall, when late applications of nitrogen can cause a late-season flush of growth that's then susceptible to winter damage.

**AS YOU CHOOSE YOUR TREES**, remember that apples are not self-fruitful: they require cross-pollination from another cultivar to set fruit. More trees + more complimentary varieties = more fruit. Most nursery catalogs provide information about which cultivars are good for pollinating each other. These catalogues will also give you a sense of cold tolerance and proper spacing, which will vary based on the rootstock.

**EARLY SPRING** is the best time to plant, as soon as the soil can be worked. When you plant, enclose the base of each trunk with a cylinder of quarter-inch-thick hardware cloth to discourage voles from chewing on the bark. It should be buried shallowly so as not to interfere

with the roots. If you're in an area with a lot of deer, you ought to make a plan for that, too, or your apple trees will soon become apple sticks.

**THE BASIC RULE OF THUMB** when planting a tree is to water it once a day for the first week, once a week for the first month, and then once a month for the first year.

**IT'S ALSO A GOOD IDEA** to start learning early about how and when to prune. This is an essential part of ensuring good apple production, and you're going to be setting the tree up for a lifetime of success or failure based on your inputs in the first five years. A good place to start your education is: www.uvm.edu/~fruit.

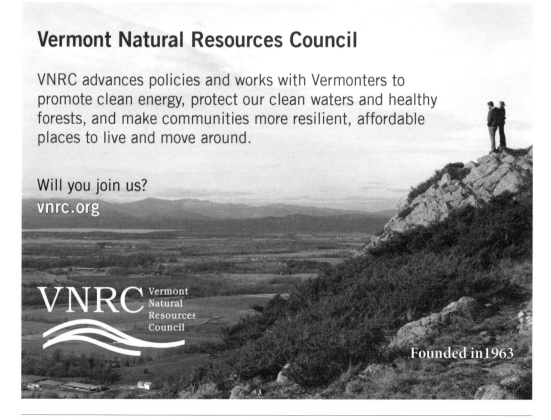

# NOVEMBER

# *November*

I used to think the best thing about November is that it's short.

By November, the garden was tucked in, the house battened down, and the arrival of rifle season gave me a good excuse to stay out of the woods. November was my chance to put a deep dent in the chair by the fire, and den up with a pile of books.

I love to read and to decode language for metaphor and meaning. In the opening of *Moby Dick*, when Ishmael describes his soul as "a damp, drizzly November," he's not just referring to the second to last month of the year with its dwindling daylight, but also to the spiritual condition of diminishing possibilities, of time running out.

The literature of English is only one language; the literature of nature is another. I've studied the pastoral language of agriculture with some success: growing fruits and vegetables, raising poultry and pork, keeping bees for sweetness and light. It took much longer to learn the language of the northern forest. For most of my life, I knew the forest only by hiking worn paths. Worse, when I tried to find my way off the blazed trail, I didn't just get lost – I panicked.

And then, on the verge of 60, I was called by an ancient, primordial voice that sounded like wisdom and changed the course of my life: *If you want to read the forest, you need to learn to hunt.*

I know people who can read the fine print of the forest without pursuing deer, but I need the deer to tutor me in the text and texture of the woods that make up 85 percent of Vermont's landscape. The deer teach me to decode the architecture of the forest as they inhabit it, sleeping in hemlock bedrooms, eating in bracken-filled kitchens, and traipsing between the two along hallways pounded by hooves.

November has never been the same.

I saw few deer until the tenth morning of my fourth season. The sun was up before I arrived at my hunting grounds, walking through mist that dissolved into golden light. Even the fallen leaves shimmered in a kaleidoscope of topaz hues. Despite my plan to hunt the ridge, the morning's beauty stunned me. I sat on a boulder above the ravine where I'd seen two doe the previous afternoon, the first deer I'd seen all season.

After a while, I continued slowly uphill. I saw two whitetails retreating into the hemlock and an unmistakable scrape, where a buck had pawed a shallow trench in which to leave his olfactory message – the woodland equivalent of an online dating profile.

I found a log beside a stump tall enough to hide my silhouette. As I surveyed the view before me, hoof beats approached. Four doe arrived from behind and screeched to a halt, like a cartoon. The lead deer, larger than the others, advanced toward me and stamped her forefoot. The three others did the same. I didn't crack a smile, but I wanted to grin.

The big girl stomped again. So did the other three. When I didn't move, she snorted; her followers snorted as well. It took effort not to laugh.

The face-off continued: the dominant doe stamping and huffing just feet from me. The others lost interest and pawed the leaf litter for acorns. The doe snorted one last time and ran back up the hill with her followers close behind.

I still didn't move.

It was my first-ever close encounter with charismatic megafauna in the wild. As far as I was concerned, I was done for the day, the way I feel when I finish reading a really good book, like Jane Austen's *Persuasion*. But I'd promised myself I'd hike to the top of the ridge, so I shouldered my daypack and rifle. The higher I climbed, the snowier the woods, the brighter the sun, the bluer the sky, the lighter my heart. Heart-shaped hoof prints pocked the snow, but I no longer cared about shooting a deer.

Now November is when I'm outdoors from sunrise to sunset, watching the light change, listening to the birds call, happily lost in woods I'm learning to read. —*Deborah Lee Luskin*

# Record-Breaking Cold

*November 21, 2019*

*Average Temperature Departure (˚F) November 2019*

The November temperature average for 2019 was sharply colder than normal by 6.6 degrees, making it the coldest November on record in much of the state. Interestingly, for two years in a row, temperatures in November were much colder than normal, due in part to a persistent weather pattern change associated with the loss of arctic sea ice. The lack of ice in the far north contributed to a displacement of colder arctic air being shoved south into the Great Lakes and northeastern US.

The early start to winter was hard on the heating bills. November 2019 heating degree days rose to a whopping 1,080 units – "normal" is 190 units. Overall, November was drier than normal, with 78 percent of normal total precipitation accrued. Still, there were nine days when measurable snow was measured at the E.F. Knapp Airport – the 7th, 8th, 11th, 12th, 14th, 15th, 20th, and 24th – and many other days when snowflakes were in the air.

It was cloudy 70 percent of the time, and this is standard issue for fall in Vermont. November, indeed, is the cloudiest month of the year, followed closely by December. Some would also say it's the ugliest month, due to the stark nature of stick season.

The warmest moment of the month was the first – it hit 67 degrees around midnight, when the calendar changed from October to November. Twenty-four hours later it was near freezing. In Burlington, a relative warm spot, it dipped below freezing on 23 nights in November. The coldest nighttime low – zero degrees on the 17th – set a new record for the date. It is unusual to see temperatures this cold this early, especially in recent decades as the climate warms. Yet, as we might expect, we were a notable outlier. Globally, November 2019 was one of the three warmest Novembers on record, differing only marginally from November 2015 and 2016. —*Roger Hill, Weathering Heights*

-7  -5  -3  -1  1  3  5  7

# NATURE NOTES

## A Closer Look at Antlers

The blast of a gunshot: a deep bass roar felt in his chest, followed by a treble ringing in his ears. The buck drops. The hunter remains in a crouch, watching the animal's last breaths through his scope. When the buck is still the hunter rises, trembling from the cold and the moment, and approaches.

He takes in the expanse of its body – a coiled spring in life that seems pretend somehow in repose. He's struck by the pure white hair on its belly, which seems unnaturally bright up close. His eyes follow the buck's swollen neck to the dark paired horns…er…antlers that are the same color as the tannin-stained water in the sphagnum bog from which the animal had just appeared. He smiles, imagining his grandfather bellowing, as he often did when his grandchildren misspoke: "They're not horns; they're antlers!" He was not a biologist, just a man who believed that words and details matter.

One crucial difference between a horn (cow) and an antler (deer) is that antlers are shed and regrow each year. In late winter this buck might have been mistaken for a doe. As the sap rose in the trees, his

antlers started to grow – at their peak of growth in summer they might have put on two inches a week. When they were growing, they had skin, arteries, nerves, and bone. And so you can imagine antlers as limbs that bucks regenerate each year, like the way a salamander can grow a new tail. Another way to make sense of things is to look at a growing antler like a tree. The velvet and skin on the surface is similar to bark; the bone beneath is similar to sapwood; and in between there's a thin layer of tissue, called the periosteum, that functions like cambium.

The hunter touches the coronets – the regally named flairs at the bottom of each antler. He touches the tip of each point. As he runs his hands along the beams he can feel the arteries that were beneath the velvet just a few months ago, etched into the bone like fossils. He touches the knobby pearlations at the base of the antler – they form where the periosteum merged with the connective tissue and skin on the outside of the antler. They're full of bark, as the buck used them to rasp trees throughout his range when they hardened. He smells the embedded wood shavings and determines it's spruce. The softwood pitch may account for the dark color of these antlers, or it could be that when the buck removed the velvet in September, the resulting blood stained the bone. Both theories attempt to explain the different shades of antlers; some dark like these, others lighter and wheat-colored, looking more like the antlers of the farm-country bucks seen in hunting magazines and the sun-bleached racks that adorn the barn's north wall.

They're big, he thinks, his hand circled around the antler just above the brow tine. He knows that if his middle finger can just touch the base of his thumb the antler is roughly three inches in diameter. He estimates the spread, the length of the beams, and the length of each point; does some quick math and decides it's a 140s-class buck. His best buck yet.

He dresses the deer, then flips it to drain. He attaches a rope to the antlers, then, leaving enough lead for leverage, attaches the other end to a stout pole. "It might outweigh me," he thinks as he leans into the drag. What a nice problem to have.

LOUIS MEGYESI / COURTESY VT ECOSTUDIES

## *The Butcher Bird Arrives*

N o, not the turkey on your platter. We're talking about northern shrikes, aka butcher bird – a predatory songbird that breeds in the far north and winters in southern Canada and the northern United States. Shrikes feed on small birds, mammals, and insects, and are known for impaling them on tree branches or barbed wire fences. Chris Rimmer and Chip Darmstadt discovered that northern shrikes can return winter after winter to the same territory. Using band recoveries, they found 12 cases in which shrikes were recaptured at or near the same winter location one to three years later. You can see if there are any reported near you on Vermont eBird, a project of the *Vermont Atlas of Life*. —*Kent McFarland, Vermont Center for Ecostudies*

**COLORFUL WINTERBERRIES** (*Ilex verticillata*) brightened Victory Bog in early November. The fruit remained untouched for months before being devoured in late winter. It may be that the toxicity of the berries is reduced with time.

**THIS ODD FROST FORMATION**, observed during rifle season, is an amalgam of frost and fungus. The fungus – *Exidiopsis effusa* – acts like hairspray and allows the distended ice strands to hold their long, thin shape. The strands of ice are 10,000 times longer than they are thick.

# Stump Sitters

When I was a child, I often accompanied my grandfather deep into the forest surrounding his farm to visit what he called "the old ones." Grand old hemlocks, white pines, and oaks towered above us. Though I couldn't appreciate exactly why at the time, I recognized that this forest was different. It was full of life at all levels – from the forest floor to the highest crowns of trees above us. We picnicked beside a huge hemlock that had long ago died and fallen. Within secret recesses we discovered fungi, liverworts, insects, spiders, other arthropods, eggs, pupae, and amphibians; the long-expired tree trunk was full of life. A tree this size could have been 300 or 400 years old, and its log will provide opportunities for biodiversity for as many centuries before it will completely decompose into a moldering pile of rich soil.

I am now my grandfather's age, and my childhood appreciation for the forest's nursery has deepened. Nurse logs, stumps, tip-up mounds, and other coarse woody debris are celebrated by ecologists as integral to a mature forest's dynamic, complex, and continuing process of life, disturbance, death, and regeneration.

Many hunters know this. We wait all year for the week we go afield and immerse ourselves in the forest as all hunters have done, human and beast alike, forever. During this cherished time of total quietude, the nagging clutter of modern society dissipates with the morning's mist at sunrise. We notice things – like the stump sitters pictured here. We may become stump sitters ourselves, elevated upon a cushioned stump to sit quietly for an hour or two and watch the run that tracks tell us the bucks are using. —*Susan C. Morse*

*Within the perched roots of this yellow birch is a disintegrating hemlock stump that provided the birch's seed with the supportive environment necessary for germination and growth. Yellow birch seeds are especially adapted to flourish in the moist moss and humus-rich substrate of decomposing deadwood structures. Nurse logs and stumps provide high-porosity seedbeds as well as an elevated growing environment that receives more sunlight. Plants growing on these structures experience less competition from other plants at ground level. In addition, new seedlings face fewer hazards from pathogens that are found in the soil beneath the stump or log.*

PHOTOS BY SUSAN C. MORSE

*Right: This rotting spruce stump is adorned with an exquisite garden. Lichens, mosses, two red spruces, and five balsam firs are surrounded by the trailing stems of creeping snowberry,* Gaultheria hispidula. *The small, egg-shaped white berries of creeping snowberry taste like wintergreen. Look for evidence of a stump-sitting red squirrel that was eating seeds from a spruce cone.*

*Below: Notice the pile of spruce cone scales and seeds on this red spruce's stilt-like root on the right. Red squirrels prefer to feed on elevated structures where they can better detect and avoid predators. The disappearing white pine stump within this spruce's roots was undoubtedly visited by generations of feeding red squirrels, one of which may have dispersed the seed that grew into this tree.*

*Bottom right: It is ironic, and at the same time reassuring, that we can find an ancient white cedar stump topped by a sturdy yellow birch tree, even within a forest that was recently clear cut. Trees know how to grow. But forests in today's world need our help nonetheless. New approaches in forest management that seek to emulate and increase old-growth attributes and structures, as well as to nurture mature forest ecosystems, are inspiring and promising. At the same time, ecologists and conservation planners are stressing the importance of permanently preserving expansive and connected late-successional forests.*

AT HOME

# Using More of a Deer

If you're a philosophical type, cutting up your own venison serves as closure – it's as integral a part of the hunting process as loading your gun and walking into the darkness on opening morning. If you're driven by practicality more than poetics, the act of cutting up your own meat saves you money and ensures the job is done to the highest possible standards.

As I've refined my techniques over the years, I've gotten better at using more of the deer. In the early days I took the four quarters, the backstraps, a neck roast, and the inner loins. The rest went to the coyotes. But I've learned that the shanks and ribs can be great with a little extra effort and a few cooking tricks. The bones can be boiled and the stock and loose meat turned into several meals worth of soup (though experts advise to keep the spinal cord out of the stock pot). The next frontier was the offal – "eating your gut pile," as one old Field and Stream story proclaimed. A properly prepared liver can feed a large family. Throw in the heart and kidneys and you have at least three additional meals per animal.

Recipes for these off-parts are just a Google search away. In this story, I thought I'd discuss some techniques and lessons I've learned in my related experiments.

### SHANKS

I think this word technically applies to just the forelegs, but I'm using it here to also refer to the thin part of the shoulder. You can bone these parts out and grind the meat, but if you haven't aged your deer, the meat will be tough and sinewy. I much prefer to keep the bone in and throw everything into a braising pot.

The first trick is to measure the bottom of your braising pot and cut your shanks accordingly. On most deer the full leg shank will be slightly too long for a 12-inch pot, and there's nothing more aggravating then gearing up to cook and realizing your meat's too big.

The braise itself is a relatively simple affair. Salt the shank, pat it dry, and brown it in a little bacon

grease or lard or oil. Then take the meat off and add some uniformly chopped onion, carrot, and celery to the pan; the French call this trinity mirepoix (pronounced meer-PWAH) – it's the foundation of pretty much every braise. As the onions sauté, they'll help deglaze the pan – add a splash of wine if you need more help. Then add whatever other ingredients you want to flavor the dish. Italians would choose garlic; Spaniards tomatoes; a Caribbean cook might add allspice and cinnamon; an Asian cook might opt for ginger, chilies, and scallions. I like to add woodsy accents to the braise – so Juniper berries, wild mushrooms, and whatever herbs I managed to dry in the fall, but especially rosemary and thyme. Then add liquid. Red wine and beef or venison stock are the traditions – two cups of wine plus two cups of stock will get you close. You need enough but not too much liquid, which is to say don't drown the meat. It should cover about a quarter or a third of the shanks. When everything is ready to go, seal the lid of the braising pot with parchment paper or foil and then put it in a 300-degree oven and cook for three hours or so. You want the meat to be falling – not fallen – off the bone.

## RIBS

The rib cage can seem intimidating, but the bones are light and easy to cut. As the carcass hangs, I make one cut midway through the rib-cage, then another at the connection with the spine. I then use my butcher knife to process the ribs into freezer-bag-friendly rectangles.

I've made and enjoyed venison ribs traditionally, which is to say bone-on, in the spirit of pork ribs. Old, long, lean, deer ribs will never be young, fat, succulent pork ribs, though, so you want to cook them with slow, moist, moderate heat (a season, wrap in foil, add liquid type of technique). Once they're cooked, you can add a glaze and finish them on the high heat of a grill, or under your broiler, just to give them a sweet crust. A glaze I especially like involves rosemary-infused maple syrup (just add rosemary sprigs to the syrup, heat to almost boil, and then let cool) and horseradish. I'm pretty sure I learned this in a Molly Stevens cookbook but I can't find it to confirm.

## LIVER

The secret to organ meat is to get it on ice quickly – it doesn't hold up particularly well to heat and age. We keep a small styrofoam cooler in camp for this purpose.

The other secret is a good soak before you cook it. Cut the liver into inch-thick pieces, then soak them

in a light brine (two tablespoons kosher salt and two tablespoons maple syrup per quart of water should do the trick) for a few days. You can also use milk, which is what the old-timers did. Or both. Change the liquid at the end of each day. What you're doing is drawing out the blood. Each time you change the water it'll be pungent and a bit off-putting. But if you do this right, none of that smell or flavor transfers to the finished dish.

Once the liver has been prepped this way, fry it up with some bacon, onions, and scallions or chives to add a little green. And be brave and eat it medium-rare.

## HEART

Cooking has an element of fashion to it, and just like any fashion, things go in and out of style. If my grandfather ate his venison heart he likely stuffed it and baked it, which was the rage for a while. These days it's more en vogue to grill it lightly and eat it pink.

The first step to cooking a heart like a steak is to turn it into tiny steaks. Trim the visible fat, and then lop the top, messy part off. You'll see the four chambers inside – use them as a guide and cut each chamber free until the meat lies flat. Trim the spider-webby stuff that's on the inside, and trim the outside in the same manner you would the silverskin on the backstrap. When done you'll have four or six little steaks. Soak them in your favorite venison marinade, or invent one especially for this cut. Then grill it to medium-rare just like you'd cook a regular venison steak. If you've never had heart before, you'll be surprised by how tender it is – it'll rival a good inner loin. And it tastes more like steak than organ meat.

### KIDNEYS

I should have photographed the kidneys as they appeared in the viscera, as they're covered in fat so they don't stand out. You'll have to feel around for the two kidney-shaped lumps, then pop them out of the membrane. When you get home, split them in half lengthwise and remove the white gunk in the middle. Then soak them as you would a liver for a couple days, changing out the bloody milk or brine as need be. At this point you might follow an Irish or British recipe for lamb kidney – the Grand Isle being synonymous in my mind with this particular cut of meat. The breakfast in the accompanying photo was prepared by dicing the kidney, sauteeing it in butter, then adding a mustard/cayenne/Worcestershire/lemon juice/tomato paste mixture at the end. Slather onto an English muffin and dust with Maldon salt and parsley for the finish.

### CAUL FAT

The caul fat, sometimes called lace fat, surrounds and insulates the deer's stomach. In cooking, it insulates your meat, providing a nice moisture and fat seal that bastes the lean meat as it cooks. It also holds any goodies you want to add to the package, looks stunning, and adds a pleasant, crisp crunch to the finished entrée.

The historical western use for this item is in making crépinettes – a French term for small, flattened sausages wrapped in caul. It's also a great touch on venison burgers. As you gut the deer, set the fat aside. When you get home, wash it, then cut it into meal-sized pieces. (There are either three or four burgers in a pound of ground meat, so put your fat up accordingly.) When you're ready to cook, soak it in either water or brine to make it flexible. Then prepare your burgers however you'd like, and when you're done, wrap them in caul fat and bake them. You're not going to want to use a grill, since the open flame will likely ignite the fat. —*Dave Mance III*

## VERMONT'S 2019 DEER SEASON BY THE NUMBERS

Reported deer kill:
16,550

Previous year's
reported deer kill:
19,011

Average of the three previous
years' deer kill:
17,072

Number of antlered bucks
reported in 2019:
10,058

Number of adult does:
5,457

Number of fawns:
1,035

Percentage of the harvest that
occurred during bow season:
23

Percentage of the harvest that
occurred on youth weekend:
10

Percentage of the harvest that
occurred during muzzleloader season:
22

Percentage of the harvest that
occurred during rifle season:
45

Percentage of rifle season harvest that
occurred on the first weekend of the season:
46

Number of replies to the state's
annual hunter effort survey:
1,754

Average number of hours these
hunters spent afield:
36

Average number of deer sightings
per 10 hours of hunting:
2.3

Average number of hours spent hunting
before seeing a buck:
29 HOURS

Number of towns that had deer
harvest totals among their 10 best:
59

Number of towns that had deer
harvest totals among their 10 worst:
28

Number of reported deer
exceeding 200 pounds:
88

Heaviest deer weighed on a
certified scale (in pounds):
248

Number of licensed hunters:
77,289

Estimated number of active hunters:
66,000

Number of individual successful hunters:
13,687

Number of hunters who killed
more than one deer:
2,479

Approximate number of venison
servings generated by the harvest:
3.3 MILLION

# A LOOK BACK

## *Sooty-faced Colliers*

It's easy to look back on the early days of European settlement in Vermont as a wasteful and environmentally unenlightened time. It was. But judgement on the wisdom and ethics of those days aside, there was a sound, circular logic to the state's deforestation. The people who settled this region were farmers who thought that cultivating the land was its highest and best use. If you were going to cultivate, you needed to clear trees. And if you were going to go through the effort of clearing the trees, you needed to capitalize on all that effort somehow. Some of the wood was used to build the homestead, some to fuel it. And the excess, in the really early days, was burned and turned into potash and pearl ash (potassium carbonate), which was used to make soap and primitive baking soda.

As the settlers established their neo-European version of America, European-style industrialization followed. To be modern, you need metal. To run a foundry, you need heat. And to make heat at that

time, you needed charcoal, which burns hotter and more evenly than air-dried wood or bituminous coal. Foundries sprouted in every part of the state, and it seemed like there was endless forest with which to fuel them. In Europe, it was common practice to use prisoners to cut the wood and make the charcoal that fueled the foundries. In the south, slaves provided the labor. But in Vermont, for a while anyway, this was a circular part of the farm economy, too. In the winter, a farmer could harvest wood on his own land, which was turned into charcoal to fuel the same local forge where he bought plow points and cut nails and horseshoes and cauldrons and stoves and all the other iron implements that he relied on. (While the iron industry took most of the charcoal, in some pockets of the state it also fueled copper, brass, and glass industries.)

At some point, though, the agrarian landscape became mostly established, and the supply of excess wood from farmers dropped off. So iron companies bought up large tracts of wooded acreage to fuel their foundries – this in the face of Thomas Jefferson's early admonition that "the small landholders are the most precious part of a state." The iron barons scaled up, to use today's parlance, making the railroad tracks that connected Vermont's resources to urban markets and their appetites for both iron and wood products. Fortunes were made, but the circular system, and huge swaths of forest, were lost in the process.

The men who made charcoal were called colliers, and it was hard, dirty work. Woodchoppers would work all winter clearing the forest and cutting the wood into four-foot bolts, and then the colliers would work from the end of one winter to the start of the next making charcoal. They'd make 30- to 40-foot-diameter mounds from this wood – about 30 cords per mound. Then they'd cover it, vent it appropriately, and tend it while it burned. As the mound contracted, they'd walk the top and repair the earthen cover: take a second to imagine the heat, the soot and smoke, not to mention the danger, as one gust of wind could turn the whole mound into a flare. It took about a week to make the product, and the typical collier was burning a number of mounds simultaneously. If a pile burned too hot, he had to pay the company for the lost wood. When the charring was complete, he raked the piles to cool them, and helped the teamsters load the charcoal into carts to take to the foundry. He often lived alone on the mountainside in a hut beside his mounds.

As the industry developed, the mounds were replaced with kilns. Early kilns were made of stone. Later ones of brick. Some were rectangular but most were circular, typically around 30 feet in diameter at the base and up to 16 feet high in the center. Fancy ones had rows of iron vents, simpler ones just had gaps that could be unplugged and plugged with bricks. It took four or five men to load the 40 or 50 cords of wood per charge and about 10 or 12 days until the charcoal was ready. If you could get 50 bushels of charcoal per cord of wood, you had an efficient kiln and a good collier working it.

A typical blast furnace making six tons of iron a day might consume 270,000 bushels of charcoal annually, which at moderate efficiency would equal around 7,000 cords of wood. You can picture that as a 230-acre clearcut. If it takes 30 years to make an 8-inch-diameter hardwood log, to make a sustainable business of this, you'd need almost 7,000 acres to rotate on a 30-year cycle for that one furnace. But it's probably safe to say that no foundry had this much land or that much organization. Like so many early industries, most were speculative, bootleg operations that would rise, gobble up the low-hanging resource, and then go under. In Vermont there were more than 500 charcoal furnaces in the 1860s; around 250 by the 1880s; fewer than 100 in the 1890s; not even 50 after 1900.

By the turn of the century, Vermont had lost about 75 percent of its forested land, so the lack of raw material was the biggest driver in the industry's decline. But nationwide, the iron industry had also begun to favor charcoal made from coal, called coked coal, over that made from wood. Iron forged from wood charcoal made the train parts and rails that connected New England with Appalachia, but the train cars came back loaded with coke, a new product that rendered the old system obsolete.

All of the statistics in this piece were taken from Victor R. Rolando's exhaustively researched book on the iron and charcoal industry in *Vermont: 200 Years of Soot and Sweat*. It's a must-read for history buffs.

*Kiln remains in Woodford.*

I N D U S T R Y

# The Great
# Vermont Hemp Boom

Industrial hemp was an important crop in early America, but after getting swept up in Prohibition-era policies that lumped it in with its mind-altering cousin marijuana, it was effectively banned for close to a century. This all changed in 2013, when the federal farm bill allowed states that had legalized the production of industrial hemp to develop pilot research and development programs – work that was carried out by UVM Extension. In December 2018, a new federal farm bill basically legalized hemp as a farm crop, allowing anyone to grow it, as long as they followed the rules. That's what led to the Hemp Boom of 2019.

Hemp can be grown for many end uses, including fiber and fuel, paper and biodegradable plastic. But the part of the plant that really got everyone's attention and drove the dramatic increase in production was the cannabinoids that are in the flower buds, used to produce essential oils such as CBD (cannabidiol). Growing a hemp plant for its flower buds is really no different than growing marijuana for its flower buds; the only difference is that hemp plants don't contain high levels of THC, the chemical that gets people high. (Regulations require that industrial hemp have THC levels of 0.03 percent or less.) Practically speaking, this means that in Vermont, hemp is more of a horticultural crop than a typical agricultural crop.

The reason that hemp production in Vermont in 2019 was so nuts is because the price that was being paid for the cannabinoid was nuts. People were paying more for it than they were for marijuana. The return was about $40,000 per acre – that's the return! There was no other crop in Vermont, or anywhere, that could compete with that. So people just went bonkers. They started doing the math: $40,000 times 5 acres, times 10 acres, times 50 acres. The promise of a pot of gold at the end of the rainbow just made everyone jump in full-force with both feet, whether they were farmers or processors or just newspaper readers.

But, as most people know, it's easier to create a business plan than it is to see things through from start to finish. And like everything else, the rules of supply and demand apply. By summer of 2019, the number of acres of hemp in the ground had already exceeded the demand for CBD. So we were over-supplying before we really even got started. That caused the market to completely plummet, and the results were pretty ugly. People were left holding the bag on lots of hemp all around the country, and it was no different here. Most people started growing without having a market lined up; they assumed that the demand was so high and it was selling for so much money that it was worth the risk. And then there were CBD companies that entered into contracts with farmers and didn't make good on them.

The surge in demand created problems right from the beginning of the season. There wasn't enough seed or plants, and that led people to sell and buy poor-quality seed, seed that was "hot" (over the limit on allowable THC), or seed that wasn't feminized – meaning growers were paying lots of money for plants that were supposed to be female but weren't. So a lot of growers were doomed right from the start. All along the way there were issues that stem from trying to scale up quickly to grow a crop that hasn't been grown anywhere in the world, really, for more than 100 years. And many of the people planting hemp were non-farmers. How did anyone expect that it would all work out in the end?

To make matters worse, the spring of 2019 was cold and wet, which delayed the entire planting season. Most growers ordered their plants for delivery by late May, but didn't get them planted until July. And things got worse at the end of the season, when harvesting and drying the crop became major issues for most growers. We had grown hemp on the UVM research farm for three years prior to that, so we had an idea how labor-intensive harvesting is. I kept warning farmers that they'd never be able to harvest everything they were growing – it's just not possible to harvest a large acreage of hemp without having a lot of people working around the clock.

It's also a challenge to dry. The plan that many had for drying their hemp was to bring it inside and hang it. But these plants are essentially small Christmas trees – about five feet tall and five or six feet wide – and you need a lot of room to hang thousands of Christmas trees with some air space. There wasn't enough storage capacity in the entire state of Vermont for the acreage that was put in the ground. What's really effective is commercial dryers, but there wasn't nearly enough dryer capacity either.

So between the demand tanking and the lack of labor available to harvest, a lot of things went wrong in 2019. We just couldn't get to the finish line. Some growers were able to use machines called buckers which strip the buds and leaves off the stems to speed up the harvest, but having leaves and some stems in the mix really does dilute the product. In some cases, the crop remained in the field.

There were some success stories, and for those growers who stayed in the game, 2020 was a much better year weather-wise. And a smaller number of growers on a smaller number of acres, with some lessons learned, has resulted in a much smoother process for most. In 2019, there were more than 9,000 acres of hemp registered in Vermont's hemp program. In 2020, there were about 1,500. Which is still a lot, if you think about it, especially for a brand new crop. Especially a specialty row crop.

The growers left in the game continue to focus on the flower bud itself. In fact, some are selling smokable hemp buds which are selling for anywhere from $200-$800 a pound.

I think that hemp definitely has a future in Vermont, but it will be in value-added approaches like this. Because hemp can be grown almost anywhere, the demand for large-scale production can be met by large farms in large states. I see us excelling in the high-value, high-quality, specialty markets. There are growers in Vermont who are in it for the long haul, and despite the growing pains we've had with the crop, I don't see hemp going away.

*Heather Darby, Ph.D.,*
*Professor and Agronomy Specialist*
*UVM Extension*

# A Roller-Coaster Ride

## NORTHEAST KINGDOM HEMP IS THREE YEARS INTO GROWING A NEW BUSINESS IN A NEW INDUSTRY.

Cam Devereux grew up on a dairy farm in Barton – back when there were 11 other farms just on that same road. There are none now, a sign of what's happened to the dairy industry over the past three or four decades. Like many, Devereaux looked for other ways to make a living; for him, that meant a 30-year career as a welder and heavy-equipment mechanic on big construction jobs – almost all of them out of state. "So he was always gone in the summer," said his wife, Karen Devereux. "And we have two kids, so the boys and I were here."

Karen works as a school teacher, and when she came home from school one day back in 2017, Cam asked her, "Did you know that you can grow hemp in Vermont, and it's legal? And that they're finding out that it's really healthy for people?" "OK, but how does that apply to us?" Karen replied. Little did she know at the time that hemp would take the family on what

she calls "a roller-coaster ride" for the next three years.

For Cam, hemp farming was an opportunity to be able to get off the road and spend more time at home. He also saw it as a way to be able to devote more attention to the blacksmithing work he did on the side – farm in the summer, hammer in the winter.

That inspiration struck in February, so the next couple of months were spent frantically researching hemp: learning what it took to grow the crop, where to get high-quality seeds. "My husband is the kind of person that, if he's going to do something, he goes full speed ahead," she said. What they found was that those already growing hemp were pretty tight-lipped. "We weren't businesspeople, so we didn't really understand anything about competition," says Karen. Part of their research also involved her mother trying CBD oil to help treat arthritis, and it did yield some benefits.

Initially, the couple planned to clear a little land

around their house to grow the hemp, but they soon realized that ground was too wet in the spring. So they approached a neighboring farm about leasing an acre of land to get started. "And that's where we've grown ever since – it's just a beautiful field," says Karen.

## SMALL SCALE, BIG LEARNING CURVE

That first year – 2017 – they put 1,000 plants in the ground. In part, they realized they were completely new to this and wanted to start at a manageable scale; in part, they decided that they wanted to really be able to focus on quality and be able to care for their crop. "If you only grow 1,000 plants, you can tend them pretty carefully," says Karen.

Their intention that first year was simply to grow the hemp and then sell it to a dispensary in the state, which had told them it would buy everything they grow, and pay $200 to $400 a pound for high-quality product. So again, the Devereuxs focused on quality, even investing in a vacuum sealing system to preserve the freshness of the crop once it was harvested. "But when it came time to sell it that year, they said, 'Oh, there was a lot more hemp grown in Vermont than we thought there was going to be, so we're not going to buy any from you,'" she recalls. "So, there we were sitting on a ton of hemp, and we had nothing to do with it."

Everyone growing hemp in Vermont at the time was learning, and the lessons the Devereuxs learned weren't only agronomic: they learned that they really couldn't bank on a third party to buy their product. The experience caused many to give up on hemp farming, but the Devereuxs were not so easily dissuaded. "I tell people, there's a fine line between being stubborn and being persistent, and I think maybe we were stubborn," says Karen. "But we thought, if we turn the hemp into something – an actual product – then maybe we could sell it. It seemed like there was a market for oil."

So in early 2018, with their crop vacuum-sealed, the couple went back to the drawing board. They found a couple of different labs that extracted the oil for them, a little bit at a time. They then bottled the oil and began looking for a market. "We started out basically by giving it to any store that would take it on consignment, and saying, 'Hey, if you sell it, great; if you don't, we'll take it back'. So there was no risk involved for them." They also entered into a contract – written, this time – with another dispensary whereby

the dispensary would process 500 pounds of their crop over 10 months and split the oil produced with them. That's an approach that many Vermont hemp farmers have used in order to avoid the investment – in time and money – of buying their own extraction equipment and doing their own processing.

Again, though, things didn't work out as planned. After six months, the dispensary had only processed 50 of the 500 pounds. So in early 2019, the Devereuxs went back into research mode and started looking into getting their own extraction equipment. They took trips to Oregon and Washington, where the hemp industry has been around longer and is more advanced. There, they found farmers willing to share information. More research was done back home and they finally settled on a $CO_2$-based extraction system made by a company called Green Mill in Pennsylvania.

With that, Northeast Kingdom Hemp was truly born. They converted Cam's welding shop (he hasn't had time to touch a blacksmithing tool since they began farming hemp, says Karen) into a fully equipped extraction lab. And they kept pounding the pavement looking for outlets to sell their products.

They also realized that they needed to make some bigger-picture plans for their operation. With Karen still a little way away from being able to retire from her teaching job, and Cam overloaded trying to keep up with both the hemp farming and the oil production, they needed some extra hands. Their older son, Camden, had been away at UVM but decided to move home and focus his work on running the extraction lab and overseeing post-processing. And younger son, Joel, just graduated from high school in 2020 and now also works on the farm full-time. Karen moved to .6 FTE this year at school, so she's home and in the office working on selling by about 1 p.m. each day, and more able to help with planting and harvesting.

## FINDING THEIR NICHE

Northeast Kingdom Hemp already had a couple of years under its belt before the hemp industry truly exploded in 2019. Karen says they watched as investors tried to make big bucks by planting big acreage, without knowing how to grow the plant or having a way to harvest it or to sell it. They got lots of calls from perspective growers and, remembering their own start in the business, tried to be helpful. But many went full steam ahead only to end up failing. "It was sad," she says. "Cam said from the first day, this will become just like dairy farming if we're not careful. He said that Vermont couldn't compete with the big farms in other parts of the country in dairy, and we're not going to be able to do that with hemp farming either."

Instead, the Devereuxs made a conscious decision from the beginning of their enterprise to stay small and create a niche with quality. "Sort of like the craft breweries in Vermont have done," says Karen. "They just do their own thing." Northeast Kingdom Hemp planted three acres last year, but has since scaled back to about one acre. That's a scale they can manage themselves and keep control over all aspects of their operation.

Even at a relatively small scale, there's a lot of work involved. Northeast Kingdom Hemp bought seeds its first year. During that growing season, the family all walked around the field picking the premiere plants in order to clone them for seed production. The harvested seeds are started in the family's basement in March before being moved to six-inch pots in a greenhouse once the outside temperatures warm up. By the time they're planted, they're each about a foot tall with an extensive root system.

There's plenty of mowing and grass-trimming in the summer, as well as tending to the plants themselves. "Then the harvest is intense," says Karen. They learned that quickly during their first harvest in 2017, when some friends came to help and they figured they'd make a fun weekend of it. The first day they worked nine hours and managed to harvest only 82 of the more than 1,000 plants. "I said, 'Oh, this is gonna take more than a weekend,'" she recalls. "Yeah, we really had no idea what we were getting into."

Harvest entails cutting the plants – you might call them shrubs; they're about the size of a small Christmas tree – and bringing them into the barn, and the greenhouse, and anywhere else they can find to hang them to cure. "Then, as they cure, we have to take each one of those plants or branches down," Karen explains. It is then bagged to preserve just the right amount of moisture and then processed further, depending on whether it is hand-trimmed to be sold as a smokeable flower, or ground and processed in the extraction lab. Cam monitors each step in the process carefully. "I feel like it's the Vermont farmer in him that he handles it so many times," jokes Karen. Really, though, she says it's the ability to control little details that sets the finished product apart. "What we produce is better quality because we didn't destroy all

the terpenes (aromatic compounds) and goodness of the plant."

In November 2019, no one could have imagined the pandemic that was about to come. Wholesale orders would drop tremendously in 2020, though the fact that Northeast Kingdom Hemp already had an ecommerce website allowed it to keep some retail sales going. A silver lining in 2020 would be the planting and harvesting season, which would be less hectic because business was slow and more manageable because everyone was around to work together. And that togetherness, really, was the entire point of founding the business. Karen says that Cam put it well: "You know, if it all goes belly-up tomorrow, we've had a bunch of fun. We've had our kids working with us out in the field and they weren't on their cell phones. I wasn't living in a hotel room somewhere. We've been able to make a living with all of us working at home here." —*Patrick White*

**Join us and make a real contribution to wildlife conservation.**

- Vermont Loon Conservation Project
- Vernal Pool Monitoring
- Mountain Birdwatch

- iNaturalist Vermont
- Vermont eBird
- eButterfly
- …and more!

VERMONT CENTER FOR ECOSTUDIES
Uniting People and Science for Conservation

Learn more at vtecostudies.org

PO Box 420 Norwich, VT 05055 | (802) 649-1431 | info@vtecostudies.org

© Barb Wood

**spc**
**PRINT.**
INTEGRATED.
A VERMONT FAMILY RUN BUSINESS
FOCUSED ON SERVING VERMONT CLIENTS

SPC wishes the best to the
Vermont Almanac

## Northeast Organic Farming Association of Vermont
# NOFA·VT

We believe that a food and farming system that supports a robust economy and healthy communities where all are fed is possible. Join our movement.

At NOFA-VT, we promote organic practices to build an economically viable, ecologically sound, and socially just Vermont agricultural system that benefits all living things. We all have a role to play in creating a more equitable and resilient food system, with joyful and vibrant agricultural communities at its heart.

We build programs to serve as bridges from the world we have now towards the world we need. We provide technical assistance and education, raise awareness for eaters and community members about how to access and grow good food, advocate on the state and national levels for small and medium scale farmers' and farmworkers voices to be heard and supported, offer programs to ensure that limited-income people in Vermont can access organic food, travel the state with our mobile pizza oven to build community and share meals, and more. We hope you'll join us in this work!

Get involved at **NOFAVT.ORG**

*I support NOFA-VT not only because the mobile pizza oven rocks as it brings together farmers and their communities, but also because the dedicated, rockstar staff of NOFA continues to carry out the many-faceted mission. NOFA-VT works for organic and sustainable farming practices for the health of farmers, eaters, and the environment in Vermont and beyond.* — ANDREW KNAFEL, CLEAR BROOK FARM

# DECEMBER

# December

A large basswood tree grew at the edge of the woods in our backyard. As it gained age and height, it leaned progressively away from the shade cast by taller trees behind it, toward the lawn and sun. It went from vertical to a 45 degree angle, then the leaning became too severe and the trunk fractured at the base. But the tree did not snap, only sagged more; it remained suspended in a near-horizontal position for many years.

I contemplated cutting it down, as it posed a danger as we skied or walked the trail under it. But it was a beautiful tree that had shared our lives for 40 years, and it had figured in many of my wife's nature notes and watercolor sketches. So we left it to the dignity and timing of its own demise.

A smaller, neighboring hophornbeam, whose branches had grown long reaching for the light, seemed to catch the basswood as it reached the horizontal, then cradle it. The hophornbeam kept bending under the basswood's descent, its branches like arms lowering the tree gently, until the basswood crown finally touched ground. The hophornbeam, released of its burden, let go and slowly returned to its former erect position, its branches poised protectively above the tree which once overshadowed it. Still, the basswood did not give up, but formed a low arch over the trail, an unsteady gateway buttressed on either end by its faulty base and the splayed branches of its crown.

For two more years its buds broke in the spring, new leaves unfurling. It refused to die completely. We continued to use the trail, having to crouch under or veer widely around it. Then, one day, my wife came in to tell me the tree had rolled over and was lying on the ground. We looked at each other, no words. Its time had finally come.

There it will remain, untouched, uncut, as it settles into soil. It has earned our respect and forbearance. We will step or ski over it, for as long as we must. When we pass, we will sometimes stop to sit on its bole, in momentary connection or remembrance.

Rest in peace, old basswood.

· · ·

High up on another tree further along that trail, a large broken branch hung precariously, seemingly detached from the tree, ready to fall at any moment. I kept thinking, indeed hoping, for safety's sake, that the next wind or snowfall would knock it down. But it persisted for months, years, withstanding the strongest gales, the heaviest snows, and thick coatings of ice.

The branch came down eventually, when it was ready, on its own schedule. It was I who had to adjust, detour, postpone wishes, change expectations. That branch taught me a thing or two about accepting the way things are.

· · ·

My friend was frozen in his worries and wanted to talk. So we went to a cafe, found a quiet corner where the sun was flooding in. He did not say anything at first, but turned his face to the warmth, and closed his eyes. A thin, pained smile formed on his lips. Soon, his face relaxed and the words began to come.

This December, an early morning, I bundle up, go to my car with a scraper and hack away at the accumulated ice on the windshield. Frustrating work, in the dark, in the stiff cold. But I could just as well have waited and let the sun do its work, and in a while the ice would have softened into little cakes, then melted, and slid away. —*Charles W. Johnson*

# Wild Oscillations

The first week of December 2019 was colder than normal, carrying over from the deep freeze of November, but considerable change came in the form of both warm and rainy conditions, followed by arctic outbreaks.

Overall, temperatures were about average, with 1,283 heating degree days compared to a normal of 1,301. This helped, since heating bills coming out of November's deep freeze were up, and wood piles were considerably dented.

During the first eight days of December, the warmest reading at the Barre/Montpelier airport was just barely above freezing, at 33 degrees – this came on December 5th. But when the moderating temperatures came, thermometers reached into the upper 40s and low 50s on December 9th and 10th. Temperatures then cooled some for the middle of the month as an Arctic chill settled in for what turned out to be the coldest period of the month, roughly from the 16th through the 21st.

Unfortunately, a warm oscillation developed again prior to the Christmas holiday. We reached an unseasonably warm high of 52 degrees on the 23rd, and natural snow depths were reduced to about half of what they normally are at ski areas. Of course snowmaking held its own with the preceding period of arctic air, and low dew points and cold dry conditions, negating

snow loss at the bigger ski resorts. For cross-country skiers and snowshoers, though, it was an inauspicious start to winter. And the opening of Vermont's snowmobile trails, scheduled for December 16th, was put off due to the lack of snow.

The oscillations in temperatures meant that what was on the ground was frequently ice, thanks to the thaw-refreezing cycle and occasional rain and mixed precipitation. All of this made for super-slick road conditions even though not much snow actually accrued. —*Roger Hill, Weathering Heights*

CHRISTMAS TREES OF VERMONT / L.H. STOWELL & SON

*What a difference a week makes. Above: December 8 at Christmas Trees of Vermont in Springfield – the kind of weather that tree-sellers dream of: just the right amount of snow and sunny skies. Not so much the following weekend, when rain fell. Left: December 14 at L.H. Stowell & Son in Brookfield: a cold, wet, long day.*

# NATURE NOTES

**THE DECEMBER FULL MOON** was at its fullest on December 12 at 12:12 a.m. eastern time, according to NASA. It was the last full moon of the year and the last full moon of the decade.

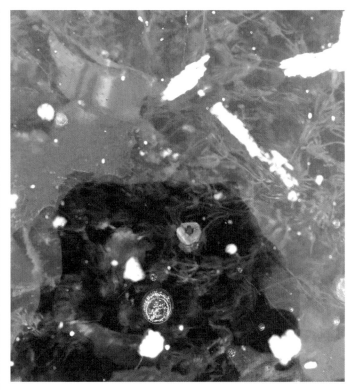

December's cold, dry weather created the perfect conditions for black ice, which in turn provided a window into subaquatic life on a miniature scale. Dragonflies, mayflies, caddisflies, stoneflies, and other insects overwinter as nymphs, floating along or crawling on rocks. (If you look closely, you'll see a caddisfly nymph in this picture.) Whirligig beetles swim slowly or crawl on the underside of the ice. There are gazillions of tiny crustaceans such as fairy shrimp, freshwater shrimp, water fleas, cyclops, and copepods, which feed on dying algae and plant matter. —*Laurie D. Morrissey*

**THIS BEAVER BEETLE** *(Platypsyllus castoris)* was observed and photographed by a trapper in the Northeast Kingdom. These sightless, wingless bugs spend almost their whole lives in a beaver's fur, eating dead skin cells and fat secretions. The only time they leave the host is when they lay their eggs in the beaver's lodge.

# Ursine Robbery

In good nut years like this one, black bears – especially males – are in no hurry to hibernate. This photograph shows where a bear discovered (with its nose) and then tried to raid an underground storage chamber full of acorns cached by an eastern chipmunk. A bear's sense of smell is extremely good – it is estimated to be about seven times better than a bloodhound's.

Chipmunks store up to half a bushel of nuts and seeds in chambers that are 1.5 to 3 feet underground. They semi-hibernate, and wake up on a roughly bi-weekly schedule to consume the food. How do we know this is a chipmunk rather than a squirrel larder? Because gray squirrels engage in scatter hoarding, burying nuts individually about an inch below the surface of the ground, while red squirrels store their winter food supply (typically cones of hemlock, fir, spruce, and pine trees) in a single stash or pile referred to as a midden, usually located above ground.

Thanks to Ashley Wolff, who discovered and photographed the scene of the attempted ursine robbery, and to Forrest Hammond, Vermont Fish & Wildlife bear biologist, for sharing his expertise. —*Mary Holland*

AT HOME

## How to Get a Pig Down a Set of Stairs

This is the last week the pigs stay outside, and some of the small ones have already started to come back to the barn. Among them is a rambunctious group of 12 that learned to run through the electric wire as fast as they could so as not to feel the electric shock. And so it was no surprise when these same piglets, once inside the barn, decided to explore the hay loft. One of them holds the distinction of becoming the first pig in the history of pigs to go up a staircase of 12 or more steps.

Have you ever looked at the anatomy of a pig? Pigs are not made for stairs. They hate stairs. How did it get up into the loft? I have no idea. How did I figure out a pig was up there? I heard weird noises from above. At first I thought of a mountain lion (I always think the worst). Then I counted the piglets...but no, it couldn't be. It was dark already, so I called my partner, Stefano, and the two of us slowly climbed the stairs. Sure enough, there was a piglet, running laps around the 20x50-foot empty hay loft. She saw us and came over, wagging her tail, and then looked at the stairs and looked at us – it was clear from her look that she had no idea either how she got up there.

Lessons about pig management you will never learn from any course on pig and pork production: how to get a pig down a set of stairs. If you look at their back legs, they do not bend like ours, so their back legs are useless in this regard. So... fold the back legs under the pig and let her use her front legs to get down the steps. From a human point of view, it looks like a sort of pig-sled. But it worked. My fear is that the little piglet taught it to everyone else, so tonight when I come home, I'll see a bunch of pigs pig-sledding down the stairs like kids in a Christmas movie. —*Alessandra Rellini*

ANNE HUNTER

## Winter Teas

Foraging green things is almost half a year away, but there are plenty of woodland teas you can make in the meantime to get you through the cold, dark days of winter. For those who enjoy wintergreen flavor, black birch *(Betula lenta)* should be a staple. Brewing is as simple as filling a stock pot with a handful of small twigs and simmering on a cookstove. The simmer part is key – boiling water vaporizes the volatile chemicals that impart the characteristic odor and flavor. And you'll need to simmer for a long time; we keep a pot on the stove that gets good after a 24 hour steep; even better after 48.

To make white pine tea *(Pinus strobus),* you'll want to strip the needles from the twigs. The piney flavor is strong – our friend Ben Lord, a prolific forager who writes the Foraging Family blog – recommends steeping only a teaspoon or two of fresh needles in about a pint of water. Unlike with the birches, use boiling water, and steep for only about two to three minutes before removing the needles.

Chaga mushroom, also called the clinker polypore or birch conk, is a popular tea medium – not for its appealing taste, but for the supposed medicinal value. Wild food proponents (and not a few venture capitalists) claim it cures everything from the common cold to cancer, and there is some scientific evidence that compounds in chaga can kill cancer cells selectively and stimulate the immune system. The flip side of this is that it might interact with drugs; it's high in oxalates, and it's never been scrupulously tested as a regular medicine, so don't go overboard. We can say that it tastes like the earth, and if flavored with a little syrup or honey and ginger, makes a nice winter drink if you feel a cold coming on. Our go-to technique is to use a hatchet to smash the conk into cube-shaped pieces, steep it on a warm wood stove all day, then drink before a hot bath in the evening.

### LEEKS

The leaves become their
stockings underground.
By fall the stems are layers
of thin socks tugged up on
each other – no feet at all.

I plant early, deep;
slim threads with catfish
mouth for roots. Green
stretching up, white
knitting itself south.

So little drama:
no flowers or raucous vines.
I mound handfuls
of soil to hide stalks
deeper in the ground.

I loosen with a fork,
coax the long stem up;
strip outer leaf down
to a black fish of soil –
expose the pearly sheaf.

Stacked in my basket,
like a wagon of small
lumbered trees – I will
have thick soup before
December's iron freeze.

*Scudder Parker*
*from* Safe as Lightning,
*Rootstock Publishing 2020*

# How to Make a Classic Balsam Wreath

Whether hung indoors or outside, a classic balsam wreath brings the unmistakable scent of Christmas. While there are several types of machines used to speed up commercial production of wreaths, a basic hand-wired wreath is a fun project that you can easily make yourself or with your children.

This tutorial is for a balsam wreath, but get creative and use what you have available. The process is the same with other types of greens, and pine, cedar, spruce, juniper, and other types of evergreens all will work. —*Amanda Werner*

### STEP 1: GATHER YOUR TOOLS
You will need:
- 3–4 pounds of balsam branches
- A 12-inch wire wreath frame (or larger if you're feeling ambitious)
- Hand pruners
- Floral wire on a spool
- Wire cutters (if your pruners don't have a wire cutting notch)

### STEP 2: ATTACH WIRE TO THE WREATH FRAME by wrapping it a few times around the frame.

### STEP 3: CUT THE BRANCHES INTO TIPS
that are 8-12 inches long. Make a small bundle of tips. For a standard door-sized wreath, the balsam tips should extend a few inches past your fingertips when held against your hand. The balsam tips I'm using here are very full, so I only need 3–4 tips per bundle. With flatter tips (such as cedar) you may want to use 7–8.

### STEP 4: SET THE BUNDLE ON THE WREATH FRAME where you attached the wire. The bundle should have at least 4 inches of stem sticking past the wire attachment so you can wrap the wire three times around the stems, moving ½ inch to 1 inch around the frame with each wrap.

**STEP 5: CONTINUE MAKING BUNDLES.**
When attaching each, overlap the previous bundle so the green tips cover the branch ends that you're wrapping the wire around. Continue adding bundles until the wreath is almost completely encircled.

**STEP 6: WHEN YOU GET THE FINAL BUNDLE,** you'll need to tuck the branch ends underneath the green tips of the first bundle. Hold the first bundle back with one hand, and slide the branch ends of the last bundle underneath them. Wrap with wire until they are snug against your original wire attachment.

**STEP 7: FLIP YOUR WREATH OVER.** Cut the wire, leaving an extra 12-16 inches. Secure the extra wire by looping it a few times around the wreath frame. Then use the excess to make a hanging loop by twisting the wire around itself.

**STEP 8: ONCE YOUR WREATH IS COMPLETE,** check for any gaps and adjust as needed: You can gently comb the branches with your fingers, or trim long ends that stick out. Display your finished wreath with pride!

---

### A FEW WREATHMAKING TIPS

- It may help to make your bundles ahead of time, so you can make sure they are all similar sizes and weights. Try to space them evenly around your ring.

- Pay attention to covering the branch ends; you want a lush, full wreath with no bare patches.

- You can easily combine different types of greens for a different look. I make mixed-green wreaths by putting one piece of pine and one piece of cedar on top of my balsam bundle. This evenly distributes the mixed greens around the wreath.

- If you end up with a bare spot, put a bow or some pinecones over it. Nobody will ever know that the bare spot was there.

- To make a wreath last longer indoors, hang in a cool spot away from direct sunlight.

---

A  LOOK  BACK

*Christmas trees delivered and set out for sale in New York City, circa 1903.*

# Christmases Past

According to the latest USDA Census of Agriculture figures, Vermont ranks 19th among all states in Christmas tree production. Pretty impressive for a small state with limited acreage, but a far cry from what once was. The stats from 2017 show that there are roughly 3,650 acres of cultivated Christmas trees growing in Vermont. Figure an average of about 889 trees per acre at 7x7-foot spacing and that's 3.24 million trees in the ground. (To be honest, this figure seems high, but let's go with it.) At an average rotation of 10 years, that would mean about 324,000 trees are harvested in the state each year. Keep in mind that these are cultivated Christmas trees. Back before there was such a thing – when dairy and livestock farmers simply cut and bundled the scrawny volunteers growing in their abandoned fields and shipped them off to the big cities – the number of Christmas trees coming out of

Vermont was simply astounding.

"In Vermont, where Christmas trees grow to the brightest emerald and to the best shape, two factions have developed," reported Fred O. Copeland in the December 21, 1919, issue of *The New York Times*. "One, with a foresight of the forests the young spruce trees will make, and the paper they may some day furnish, bewails the cutting for Christmas trees. The opposing school urges the Christmas tree for the reason that it clears the land for the farmer and at the same time allows more cheap feed for the young beef stock, which is allowed to run wild during the summer months. But, whether or no, 5,000,000 Christmas trees are being shipped out of Vermont this year."

Copeland noted that there was no shortage of abandoned farms in the state at that time, "especially in the Green Mountains, where more than forty years ago thirty actively worked farms existed and where there are now but two families living. These sections lie in the high valleys in the foothills of the Green Mountains. Land that was once under the plow is coming back into forest." This "fern-choked" former farmland was the perfect place to grow trees for holiday harvest, he wrote: "Young spruces come up and in the open sunshine take on a vivid green, and – more than that – the branches are a lively green clear to the ground. Christmas trees cannot be cut in areas of spruce forest, because when they grow in dense clusters the under branches die for lack of light."

Copeland followed as one "gang of twenty choppers began cutting and bundling with twine bunches of from one to six young spruces." That part of the harvest began in October and was arduous, but, as he noted, perhaps the easiest part of getting the product to market. After cutting and bundling, a Herculean effort began to get *millions* of trees from the mountains of Vermont to urban areas in a short window of time with limited transportation options. "The trees must be hauled for miles to the railroad and at this time of the year the mountain roads are frozen ruts and water holes." At the railroad stations, in town after town, he described seeing mountains of 8,000 trees each waiting to be loaded onto flatbed cars. "As the great piles of trees are mined and packed...the fragrance the sun has distilled from the emerald cones fills the air and it is a most delightful place to be."

*From time to time, some overzealous moralist decides that we are depleting our forests by cutting millions of young Christmas trees every year for a momentary pleasure, thus robbing ourselves of tens of millions of feet of lumber. But out of every ten young trees in the forest, nine are destined to lose out and die. No harm but only good can follow from the proper cutting of young Christmas trees. And the destiny of Balsam, loveliest of them all, would otherwise too often be excelsior, or boards for packing cases, or newsprint*

*bringing horror on its face into your home. Far better that the little tree should arrive, like a shining child at your door, breathing of all out of doors and cupping healthy North Woods cold between its boughs, to bring delight to human children. —Donald Culross Peattie,* A Natural History of Trees of Eastern and Central North America, *1948*

INDUSTRY

# Christmas Tree Industry Overview

It is said that money does not grow on trees, but that is not entirely correct. Money can grow on trees – Christmas trees to be precise. But like every other agricultural enterprise, there is no certainty of success. And unlike most crops, Christmas trees take many years of care after planting before they can be sold. Still, Christmas tree farming can be profitable, with effort and the right ingredients (land, equipment, labor, capital, and the cooperation of an independent and sometimes troublesome Mother Nature) in the mix.

Exact figures on the number of Christmas tree growers in Vermont are tough to come by, but more than 100 farms in Vermont belong to the New Hampshire-Vermont Christmas Tree Association, which was founded in 1965. The organization holds three meetings and publishes three newsletters each year to exchange information and learn – those thinking of getting in Christmas tree farming will find a group eager to share what they know. Members include large wholesale growers selling several thousand trees annually, as well as small choose-and-cut farms selling just 100 or 200. Some farms have a mix of markets, selling from their farm as well as to wholesale buyers and/or at their own off-site retail Christmas tree lots. Some even offer online mail-order services, shipping boxed Vermont Christmas trees and wreaths to customers all around the country. Many Vermont families prefer to visit the farm to pick out their tree, an experience that may include a wagon ride, complementary mulled cider or hot chocolate, and a gift shop. Member farms are geographically scattered throughout the region, so they are close by for anyone who wants a farm-fresh tree.

Balsam fir is native to Vermont, and it continues to be the primary species grown on farms here. But weather and soils in much of the state have proven to be favorable to Fraser fir and Canaan fir, and there has been diversification. Genetically speaking, both of these species are "cousins" to the balsam fir.

Frasers are native to the mountains of western North Carolina; Canaans are native to a small area in the Pennsylvania, Ohio, and West Virginia triangle. All are in high market demand, either because of fragrance or superior needle retention. Each species has advantages and disadvantages, and from a farming perspective, care must be exercised to match the species with the soil characteristics of the site. Fraser firs prefer well-drained sites, while Canaan firs can tolerate wetter conditions. Fraser are somewhat slower growing than the others. Depending on species, properly sited and managed seedlings can be expected to reach an acceptable market height and quality in 6-8 years. Not that long ago, that time period would have been 8-10 years, but the time required to grow a marketable tree has been shortened through better site selection, soils testing and fertilization, improved genetics, minimization of competition from a variety of weeds, and the management needed to dovetail all of these factors. Spruce and pine are sometimes grown for Christmas trees, as are several exotic species not native to the area, but all in limited numbers in Vermont.

Throughout the Northeast, 2019 was a good sales year for the Christmas tree industry. Supply and demand were pretty much in balance, and prices were good for growers. That has not always been the case: our industry, like others in agriculture, periodically goes through cycles where overproduction can stunt prices. There has also been competition from the artificial tree industry, and in previous years market share of real trees has declined. But the artificial tree competition has recently stabilized, and even declined. There is increased interest in fresh, local produce and farmers markets, and there is increased interest in a real tree rather than a fake plastic one. The choose-and-cut segment of the industry, in particular, has seen growth in each of the last several years, and that growth is expected to continue as families prioritize the experience of visiting a farm. Nationally, the Christmas tree industry has created a "check-off program" – similar to those in other ag industries such as dairy and beef – whereby farmers are required by the USDA to contribute a certain amount for each tree sold to the national "It's Christmas – Keep it Real" marketing campaign.

At the time of this writing, we are approaching the 2020 sales season, which should be another good one for the Northeast Christmas tree industry. While lack of adequate rain early in spring and early summer this year was a problem for some new plantings, late-season rains were more plentiful, and this year's crop looks good. Wholesale orders have been strong, and pricing remains favorable for farmers. Most choose-and-cut farms have been selling out in recent years, a trend which is expected to continue.

Now we have to hope for good weather during the harvest season – for wholesale growers, wet or snowy weather in November can seriously complicate the job of getting thousands of trees cut, wrapped, trailered out of the field, and loaded onto semi-trucks. Even a few inches of rain or wet, heavy snow makes the whole process take much longer, and if temperatures are warm enough to get things muddy, there's a risk of damaging fields when tractors, trucks, and trailers are brought in. For choose-and-cut farms, a little snow on the ground in December adds to the experience for families arriving to select their perfect tree, but too much snow makes access difficult and makes it tough to tell one tree from another. For Christmas tree farmers, weather is important throughout the year, but it's especially critical at sales time – we have only a few weeks to sell products that we've spent a decade or more growing.

One additional hurdle this year will be selling in the midst of Covid. Christmas tree growers have spent the summer watching and learning from the protocols put in place by farmers' markets, CSAs, and pick-your-own fruit and vegetable farms and have put plans in place to make sure the Christmas tree season will be a safe and enjoyable one.

*Jim Horst, Executive Director*
*New Hampshire-Vermont Christmas*
*Tree Association*

*Trees large and small:
Amanda Werner and cousin
Heather Layn pull a 15-foot
balsam fir out for a customer;
Natalie Layn (also a cousin)
helps harvest tabletop trees in
the Werner's off-site field
in Lincoln.*

# A Family Affair

For the Werner family in Middlebury, Christmas trees have been the gift that keeps on giving. Literally. Back in 1980, David Werner's father gave David and his wife Cheryl about 15 Scotch pine seedlings to plant on their farm; as those trees grew, the couple decided to keep planting more. Today, Werner Tree Farm in Middlebury has 25,000 trees in the ground at two different sites, and children Amanda, William, Jessie, and Crescent Remaniak all play a role on the farm.

While Scotch pine was a common Christmas tree species back when the Werner's started, most growers in Vermont have moved on to other species. The Werners, for example, now grow mainly balsam and Canaan fir. They have a few Fraser fir and Fraser-balsam hybrids. And somewhat recently they even put back in a few Scotch pine. "We have people who missed them, and they handle heavy clay soil in some heavy parts of our field," explains Amanda Werner, who fills the role of marketing guru for the whole operation. "And we've tried a lot of different exotics, too – some things that have worked and some that haven't." A cross between Korean fir and balsam fir is one example that's shown promise, she adds. "We like to just keep experimenting and see if there's going to be something that's nicer."

## PLANTING AND SHEARING

During busy times of the year – planting, shearing, and sales seasons – the family's labor is supplemented by high-schoolers, many of whom stay on through their college years. But this year, planting season came during the confusing early days of Covid, so it was only family on the job. The Werners put in about 2,000 transplants each year on average, hand-digging the holes with shovels. More problematic than Covid was the dry weather that followed; like many Christmas tree growers in the state, the drought-like conditions of summer 2020 led to high levels of loss among the newly planted trees. "On our mountain fields, the trees did okay, but on the main farm fields, it was brutal," says Amanda. Fortunately, the larger trees, which have well-developed root systems, were able to better weather the weather.

Amanda says the most time-consuming part of Christmas tree farming is the annual shearing – a sentiment many other growers would echo. Once trees reach about knee-high, they have to be sheared every year. The Werners do the work themselves with shearing knives – think machete, but with a blade that is long, thin, and razor sharp. High-schoolers help out with safer tasks like hand-clipping the tops and basal-pruning (trimming off the very bottom branches so there's bare trunk to slide into a tree stand).

They start by shearing pines first, because the new growth comes earliest on those trees. The next job is to do the few spruce trees they have because that new growth gets woody quickly. Then much of

*David Werner tags a balsam fir.*

the summer and early fall is spent working through the balsam and Canaan fields. One of the nice things about growing Christmas trees, as opposed to, say, dairy farming, is that there's usually some flexibility built in; the trees don't need to be milked every morning at 4:30, they just have to be sheared before customers arrive in late November. For a family in which everyone also has a job off the farm (Cheryl just retired as a teacher of plant and animal science at the local career center), this sort of farming is ideal. But it also means a lot of evenings and weekends are spent working in the fields.

*The Werners sell their trees and wreaths – as well as their own maple and honey and other Vermont products – out of a Christmas shop that's open daily in December.*

## FRESH FROM THE FARM
Some of that flexibility is lost during the busy selling season. The Werners sell all of their trees from their farm. Predominantly, that's to customers who want to cut their own, but they also bring in pre-cut trees that they grow on leased land in Lincoln to customers who prefer that option. And everything is run out of an inviting gift shop (one that's heated by a woodstove and that doubles as David's woodworking shop the rest of the year); the shop's open every day except Monday. Inside, customers can see the Werners hand-making wreaths, and also pick from a selection of the family's other agricultural offerings. In addition to Christmas trees, they produce maple syrup and honey. There's free hot chocolate and cookies and a G-scale model train that makes the rounds, as well as a selection of other offerings made by local artisans.

That holiday season gift shop is the main avenue the family uses to sell its maple and honey products. Amanda says that customers appreciate being able to cut their own fresh tree and also pick up these other items that are made right on the farm – it makes a real connection for people. "I think it adds a lot of value to people when they can see how things are happening," Amanda says. The family recently constructed a new sugarhouse next to the Christmas shop, so customers can see where their syrup comes from.

## KEEP ON INNOVATING
Another recent addition to the Werner farm has been a small flock of Shropshire sheep. The hope is that they might replace glyphosate as weed control in rows of Christmas trees, while also reducing the need to mow between the rows. "We came across an article about a Christmas tree farm in England that was using Shropshire sheep to eat the grass and weeds that compete with the young trees," Amanda says. "We read more and more about it. And they're one of the pickiest eaters among sheep breeds. If they have other options, they won't eat the Christmas trees."

The experiment is still in the early stages. "This is our second summer with them. We didn't want to buy a whole flock and have them eat everything in sight, so we have four of them right now," Amanda says. So far only one tree has been damaged and the sheep have taken care of some weeds that are difficult to remove even with herbicides. "We had a fair number of horsetails in sections of our farm and the sheep love them; where the sheep have been pastured,

*David Werner, Cheryl Werner, Amanda Werner, William Werner,*
*Crescent Remaniak, and Jessie Werner. Front row: Annie.*

horsetail is basically gone." She's not sure the sheep can completely replace other methods of weed and grass control in the trees, but thinks they might be part of the solution.

While the sheep leave the trees alone, Werner's Tree Farm does occasionally suffer damage from deer. About five years ago, a large local deer population, combined with a particularly hard winter, created a perfect storm and there was significant damage done to many trees. The deer didn't just eat the buds off the tips of the branches, but in many cases browsed the branches off completely.

Christmas tree farming – if you're in it for the long haul – is by its nature a sustainable enterprise. For every tree cut and sold, another is planted. And because it can take 8-10 years from the time of planting until sale, decisions have to be made well in advance. While the Werners currently buy their transplants from other nurseries, they've recently started their own seedbed operation. Amanda says it can sometimes be difficult to find the exact tree varieties they want and to arrange to get them at precisely the right time for

planting; it'll be extra work to plant the seed and grow the trees from scratch, but growing their own planting stock will give them greater control over these critical factors. "Vertical integration," she points out. What started out as a gift of just a handful of seedlings has become a family enterprise. *—Patrick White*

*The Shropshire sheep at the end of a day of weed and grass control in a field of Canaan fir.*

# On Faith

Why is religion such a big part of rural life? An author I read once decided it was because there are more poor people in rural places, and poverty fosters the idea that there's a better home a-waiting in the sky, Lord, in the sky. Another thought involved the idea that rural places are homogenous, and it's hard for people to go against the intellectual grain of everyone around them.

I don't find much truth in either of these theories – come to town meeting in my town and you'll find that most people make it a point to go against the intellectual grain of everyone around them on principle. And so I'm more inclined to think it has something to do with the fact that urban places are testaments to human beings, with all the self-interested baggage that entails, while rural life involves a closer communion with nature. There's something very temporal about asphalt and steel towers and municipal services. There's something very eternal about the wind through the tree branches.

I was raised Catholic and have a fondness for that church (especially our Pope), but like a lot of people my adult spiritual life is less denominational. It's a kind of magpie faith – little snippets of this and that brought back to build the nest. Or maybe mockingbird faith, where I gather sermons that resonate and sing them back: "Science without religion is lame; religion without science is blind." "You can't approach the subject of God without metaphor... literalism, like legalism, is an attempt to shrink God to recreate him in our own image." "One of the moral diseases we communicate to one another in society comes from huddling together in the pale light of an insufficient answer to a question we were afraid to ask." (Those snippets from Albert Einstein, Paul Hewson, Thomas Merton.)

Sometimes in the midst of autumn's hunting and slaughter seasons I dream of being a prey animal, but it's not a nightmare. There's a peace in it – in the idea that this ritual is circular in nature; in the idea that the cards get shuffled and it repeats. The idea of reincarnation was taught to me as a Buddhist philosophy, but you see it often in the faiths of traditional hunting cultures around the world. The Inuit thought that the soul is reborn over and over again, and they pointed seal skulls towards the new hunting grounds so the animal souls would know where to go. "That's how we kill the same seal over and over," one explained. (That from a book by Gretel Ehrlich.)

The whole life and death exchange would be impossibly cruel if you didn't allow yourself to feel some sort of divine or mystic logic. The same thing applies to felling a tree. Hugging a centenarian and then cutting it. Feeling its fall in your chest. You might have a

*East Orange, Vermont*

western religious take, where your faith is guiding you to own this under threat of punishment, or an eastern one, where you're an expression of God and it's implied that you'd better act accordingly. But you've got to feel something. You're not feeling basal area as you fire up the chainsaw.

(There's a self-interested expression of faith here too, of course. The sign of the cross before a power that could crush you – that might someday crush you.)

I see religious mystery in silence – those still, bone-cold winter mornings. I see it when nature reminds me of how much I don't know, like when people ask me how the oaks know to mast together and I say they talk to each other somehow. There's plenty that's not mysterious, too. The exquisite architecture of an open grown maple tree. The vertical pupil in a cat's eye.

It's hard to pull together the month of December without thinking of Christmas specifically, and so I'd like to wish all our Christian readers a Merry Christmas. My favorite detail of the Christmas story is that God – this incomprehensible power – chose to express itself not as a king, not in a golden tower, but as a child born in a pile of straw in a barn out in the country. —*Dave Mance III*

# JANUARY

# *January*

Suddenly, in January, I'm aware of how much time I spend filling things. Each trip to the kitchen, I check the woodstove and firewood rack to see if they need more logs. Each time I walk past my cello, I strum it – a nervous habit; A-D, D-G, G-C – to see if it's in tune, if its pegs have slipped from the dryness and I need to refill the humidifier. Each time I look outside, I check the birdfeeders and suet holders to make sure they're not getting low. With the holidays over – houseguests gone, boisterous meals and music-making finished – you would think all I do with my time is go between the house and the woodshed, the house and the birdfeeders, the humidifier and the kitchen sink, carrying things, pouring things. Yet I get annoyed if Craig fills the feeders before I've gotten to them; I've made it clear that hauling wood and messing with the suet are my jobs.

There is satisfaction in filling things: keeping our house warm, providing sustenance for the birds, keeping my cello happy. There is pleasure in going outside so often: a glance at the sky, the wind in my face, the brief shelter of the woodshed, my hands on the icy feeders. There is information to be gained: the frequency of trips to the woodshed, the speed with which the birds are chowing down, the effort it takes to keep the humidity at 40 percent.

These tasks are my way of keeping tabs, and in January, I need to keep tabs. It's the one winter month in which weather is everything. There are no distractions. And for someone like me, who thrives in the cold, for whom memories of Januarys past contain so much snow you could (I'm not making this up) *take it for granted*, the stakes are high. If winter is going to happen – I mean *really* happen – then it needs to happen now. January is winter in Vermont under severe performance pressure, its every move under watch.

And so: the cold, the dryness, the activity of the birds. By filling things I stay alert to the merest hint of winter. Nothing, not a precious bit of it, will be squandered. We've kept the side porch filled with our skis since the season's first snowfall in November. They've been there through the multiple freezes and thaws that then followed, and they are there on the January day it hits 59 degrees and pours. But they are also there, six days later, when it's minus one, there's half a foot of snow in the Champlain Valley and even more in the mountains, and we grab them, *fast*.

Filling things is an act of faith. I fill the firewood rack because I have faith it will continue to be cold; I fill the birdfeeders because I have faith the birds will continue to come; we keep our skis on the porch because we have faith it will snow again.

But there's more here than an act of faith. Somewhere along the way these tasks turned ritualistic. They became acts of agency. I fill the firewood rack so that it will continue to be cold. I fill the humidifier so that it will continue to be dry. We keep our skis on the side porch so that it will snow again. Back in December, we lit candles and made music to ensure the return of the sun. Well, in January, I carry firewood, seed, and water to ensure winter, to ensure the continuation of even just some of what January was once able to ensure on her own.

A-D, D-G, G-C.

The sound of the cello's fifths in tune reassures me. It means there's sufficient humidity in the air to keep the pegs from slipping. It means I've been diligent in keeping the humidifier filled, that I'm keeping up my part in this.

A-D, D-G, G-C.

Call it a nervous habit. Call it a ritual. Call it a prayer. —*Judy Chaves*

# Record-Breaking Warmth

The year 2020 got off to an abnormally warm start. January's average temperature was about 6 degrees above normal for the month. This warmth saved the wood pile and heating bills, but kept snow conditions for skiing, snowmobiling, and other outdoor recreational opportunities only so-so. Heating degree days were lower than normal: 1,305 versus 1,500, a significant difference during this, our coldest month of the year. As the temperatures oscillated upward on January 11, a new record high temperature for the day was set at 60 degrees at the Barre-Montpelier Airport. Of course, less than a week later saw the coldest two days of the month, on January 17 and 18.

While generally on the warm side, January 2020 was an active month. Temperatures oscillated frequently with alternating storm systems bringing warm temperatures and colder conditions. There were approximately five warm-fronts/cold-fronts that tracked through the region. The freeze-thaw cycles they generated were coupled with many precipitation

*January 16 saw 5-8 inches of snow blanket the state: The view that day from Newmont Farm in Bradford.*

types, including rain that got into the many cracks on asphalt roads at this time of year, contributing to even bumpier than usual driving conditions. January 2020 was more like that of March, which typically produces the worst frost heaves.

Getting around the dooryard wasn't much easier, as we saw multiple precipitation types, including rain that joined forces with melting snow to accumulate and then freeze to ice.

Overall, it was a below-average month for snow. Just 22.5 inches fell at the Barre-Montpelier airport (1,165 feet in elevation). But just a bit of elevation change can make a big difference, especially in warmer winter months. Worcester, just 10 miles away and at 1,375 feet elevation, recorded 32.9 inches of snow. As is always the case, the higher the elevation, the more pristine the snow.

On average, the coldest day of the year in Vermont comes around January 22. In decades past, a spike in temperature – known as the January Thaw – would typically occur around the time of the coldest readings. But as 2020 exemplified, the January thaw is becoming much harder to identify as temperatures are routinely spiking up and down due to more frequent warm oscillations. —*Roger Hill, Weathering Heights*

# NATURE NOTES

**MALE KINGFISHERS** will be flying, fishing, and rattling where there is open water, even in Vermont. They conserve energy by roosting in burrows at night. Female kingfishers winter farther south. It may be that the males are keeping dibs on next spring's nesting sites.

**THIS IMAGE OF BLOOD** in coyote urine was taken on January 23. It's a sign that the female is in proestrus, and that the endometrial lining in her uterus is starting to develop. Writer Natalie Angier once wrote lyrically that "the uterus is like a deciduous tree, and the endometrium acts like the leaves." A tree pumps water and nutrients to its leaves, which are both metabolically expensive and generative in that they provide the tree with the means of nourishing embryonic seeds. The coyote's body pumps blood to her endometrium, which she uses to nourish her embryos. Trees shed their leaves once a season; humans shed roughly once a month; coyotes do not shed – their uterine lining is reorganized for the next breeding season. Unlike domestic dogs, which typically have two estrous cycles a year, coyotes have only one, generally in February.

MARY HOLLAND

Sulphur
Cinquefoil

Mullein

St. John's
Wort

Black-eyed
Susan

Evening
Primrose

Queen
Anne's Lace

Yarrow

Goldenrod

# Wild Bird Seed

Humans have a long history of feeding birds. As early as 1500 BC Hindus provided birds (as well as dogs, insects, "wandering outcasts," and "beings of invisible worlds") with rice cakes. In 1825, one of the first bird feeders was constructed out of a modified cattle trough. Bird feeding grew in popularity in the 1900s, and by 2019, roughly 60 million people in the US were feeding birds and spending more than $4 billion annually to do it. Bird feeding has become such a common practice that many people wonder how seed-eating birds survived long, cold winters before humans fed them.

In fact, birds do very well without a helping hand from humans. A large number of winter bird species in the Northeast, especially sparrows and finches, are granivorous (seedeaters), and there are many wild sources of food for these birds, often found along roadsides and in fields. These plants, called weeds by some, are known for the copious seeds they produce. Ragweed, pigweed, bindweed, thistle, and smartweed are some of the plants that are popular with seed-eating birds. Some of the more familiar flowering plants such as sulphur (or rough-fruited) cinquefoil, mullein, St. John's wort, black-eyed Susan, evening primrose, Queen Anne's lace, yarrow, and goldenrod also feed a host of birds with their bounteous seed crops. Something to think about next autumn as you consider whether or not to brushhog the fallow field. —*Mary Holland*

**WE CAME ACROSS** this oddly beautiful chunk of cherry gum while bucking up firewood. The gum is produced in response to an injury, and is common in black cherry and other members of the Rosaceae family.

AT HOME

## Sheepskin Care Guide

Getting our sheepskins from animal phase to fluffy fiber product phase is a labor of love. We work with a USDA-inspected slaughterhouse to get hides back as intact as possible. We bring them back to the farm as soon as possible, and the Farm Kid starts the cleaning and salting process. He trims and cleans off any meat or fat with a sharp ulu. Then, he carefully applies a thick layer of salt to every inch of each hide. Each day the skins are checked, and more salt is applied as needed. After several weeks, the

skins are sent to the tannery.

When we get them back, they're lush and soft enough to lay a baby on. Our customers buy them in this condition, but as with any garment, you need to maintain a sheepskin over time. Here are a few simple rules on caring for a finished sheepskin.

Don't ever dry-clean a naturally tanned skin. It will be off-gassing the crud used in the cleaning process, and you really do not want that on your skin, or in the air you breathe.

Your sheepskin will change in appearance over time. That's ok! Sometimes the leather will slightly yellow with age, or the hair fibers will get matted. To freshen your sheepskin, roll it up and take it outside. Shake it out and get a two-minute upper body workout. I wouldn't recommend the rug-beater attachment on a vacuum. Try a sticky-roller to get off any pet hair.

You can use a comb or pet brush to fluff up the fibers. If you do this and it's not the look you wanted, just run a very lightly dampened washcloth over it, moving from neck to tail. The moisture helps it get back its original crimp.

Someone spill on it? Spot-clean without getting the leather side wet, if possible. Use a microfiber or cotton cloth that's damp, and move the fibers in one direction. Don't scrub back and forth. If you must use a detergent, use one that's mild, like Dr. Bronners or Eucalan. Let it air dry and then brush.

After a few years I do wash mine. Leather and water aren't a great combo, though, so I'd only recommend doing it when absolutely necessary. It will change the appearance of your sheepskin, but done right, it won't ruin it. I use my front-loader (but you can also use a bathtub) with a wool wash or very gentle detergent set on the delicate cycle, but skip the spin cycle. Just know that to make felt, one agitates or wiggles wool back and forth. Once you take it out of the washer, roll it up and shake it outdoors. In summer I hang mine to dry in the shade outside, but in January, a drying rack set in the bathtub works too.

Never dry your sheepskin on metal or stained wood as it could change the leather's color.

If you have a wet sheepskin to dry, remember to give it the occasional shake and roll/unroll it so that the leather stays pliable. When it's dry, work the wool in small sections with a wide-tooth comb to make it fluffy again. —*Kate Bowen*

# *Successful Softwood Pruning*

For many forest landowners, cutting mature crop trees and getting them to market is either technically or logistically impossible. But there's other woods work to be done that can generate value on your woodlot, including pruning forest trees in order to produce knot-free wood. A study by researchers at the Yale School of Forestry found that the cost of pruning white pine could yield a compound interest return of as much as 13 percent, even when the trees were not harvested until 30 years after pruning.

Good white pine, if you have it, is the best place to invest your pruning hours. The first step is to choose the right trees. Prune only the healthiest, most vigorous, straightest trees that will make good sawtimber. You'll want to prune between 35 and 60 trees per acre. This corresponds to a spacing of 27 to 35 feet between pruned trees. A good time to prune is after the first thinning, when the trees are about 6 inches in diameter – doing it this way means you don't have to worry about logging damage to recently pruned trees. You can do it earlier.

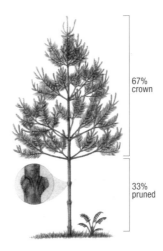

67% crown

33% pruned

Trees can be pruned any time of year, but late in the dormant season is best. This allows the burst of spring growth to be directed toward growing over the injury. As you prune, be careful not to damage the branch collar, which is the source of the defensive chemicals that the tree will use to wall off decay. This advice applies even when you're cutting dead branches. Remove all the dead branches, and leave one-third to one-half of the tree's height in live branches when you're done. Applying a wound dressing does not do any good. One other tip: if your forest ends at a road or field,

leave the outside trees untouched. This keeps the sun and hot drying wind from penetrating the stand.

If possible, prune as high as 17 feet above ground level in order to have a standard, 16-foot log on a one-foot stump. However, pruning to any height over 9 feet will result in a knot-free merchantable log. Even though you'll have to wait 25 to 50 years to recoup your 10- or 15-minute-per-tree investment, your grandkids will thank you. And sometimes having an excuse to showshoe into the woods on a sunny winter day with a pruning saw can yield a pretty good return immediately. —*Virginia Barlow*

## *Keep Sharp*

I learned how to operate a chainsaw before I learned how to operate a file. Oh, I thought I knew how to sharpen a saw. I was 16, and when you're 16 you figure you know everything. I'd sit alongside the saw and scratch at it and it would cut a bit better and sometimes in a straight line. I even purchased a file holder that shows you the proper 25-degree angle. But it was still a long shot with a limb in the way to get my saw cutting like it should.

When I was 19, I lucked into a job cutting for a life-long logger. When ol' Glenn saw me swiping at my chainsaw with a file he asked, "What ya' doing young feller?"

I replied, "I'm sharpening my saw."

"I don't think so," he said with a chuckle.

"Can you teach me how to file?"

And he did. He set my chainsaw on a stump and put my work gloves on top of it. "First thing you have

KATHLEEN KOLB

to do is get your ass behind ya. Get above the bar and look at both sets of cutting teeth in the same way so you're able to compare them to each other and file two-handed." He had me kneel down behind the throttle handle and lean forward and put my chest on top of the saw to hold it steady, using my gloves for padding and the bar pointing straight away from me. This was probably the smartest thing I ever did to file a saw. It gave me a consistent platform to work from. And that is what a filer needs: consistency. What is done to one tooth must be done to all. Glenn taught me the basics but said it was up to me to practice and learn by doing.

Since that day on the mountain where Glenn gave me my lesson I figure I've sharpened a chainsaw over 15,000 times. That's a lot of practice and doing. I'll share with you some nuggets of wisdom that I've learned while I honed my skill.

Having the saw held steady is key. Whether you rest on it like I described, or lock it in a vice, or use a pounded-in little clamp on a stump, get the saw to stay still whilst you sharpen it. I always do my filing on a log or stump, sometimes a tailgate. I keep my files wrapped in a small towel that I use to wipe the sweat off my brow and add it to my gloves for padding. Keep your files clean and free from rolling around and rubbing together, as this wears them out. And don't use a file until it feels like a nail. You want to file the tooth, not polish it. Files are cheap compared to a visit to the E.R., as pushing on a dull saw is dangerous and tiresome to boot.

Before you begin, make sure the chain is snug, without any slack. Look the chain over to see how dull it is. It might be only dull from cutting wood and need just a couple strokes per tooth to get it back cutting like a bandit. But maybe you nicked a rock or the logs you were cutting were dirty. That might call for seven or eight swipes with the file to get a good edge back. Mark the chain where you're starting so you'll know when you've come around. I file a mark on top of a chain link that I reference for the life of the chain.

On most chains there is a witness mark scored on the back end of each tooth at the proper angle to file. Do your work as far out on the bar as is comfortable. Use two hands, one on the file handle and one on the end, pushing and pulling the file through the tooth and keeping the file level in relation to the bar. Be an equal opportunity filer. If you give seven strokes to the left side teeth, dole out seven to the right side. Even if they don't look like they need it. You might hit something that damages one side of the teeth more than the other, but all the teeth must have equal wear to have the saw cut straight. Don't use much downward pressure, as this will put too much hook in the tooth and cause the chain to grab.

Pressure should be consistent with each stroke, backward and a touch upward. Only sharpen two to four teeth before moving the chain forward to the next candidates. This keeps you consistent in your perspective and technique. There is no need to twist the file on the stroke, and don't back drag it through the tooth as this wears out the file. Tap the file every so often on the bar to remove debris. Glenn would file all the teeth on one side and then do the other side, comparing as he went. I do them all as I go, back and forth, swapping the file from hand to hand in a neat rhythm that came with practice. As the teeth get filed down, eventually the rakers have to be filed down too. These are in front of the tooth and determine how big a bite the tooth takes. Some people use a depth gauge that sits on top of the tooth and file off what sticks out with a flat file. I just take a couple swipes on them every fourth or fifth time I sharpen my chain. Don't take too much off – if you do the chain will grab and tend to kick back on bore cuts.

As I've gotten older, curiosity has overcome vanity. I now wrap a pair of reading glasses in the towel with my files. My dad taught me to make things easier in life: don't swing harder, sharpen your ax. And there's a nugget that will serve for chainsaws as well. —*Bill Torrey*

# A  L O O K  B A C K

# *Starting the New Year with* Walton's Register

Well before the *Vermont Almanac*, there was *Walton's Vermont Register and Farmer's Almanac*, published continuously for over 190 years. The book was a standard reference for the inhabitants of Vermont's cities and towns and a must-have each January. With a string looped through a small hole punched through the upper left corner, the handy compilation of facts and forecasts could be hung from a nail near the kitchen window and consulted for myriad purposes. A farmer could sow his crops in consort with the phases of the moon, or plan a fishing trip during the most propitious times for angling success.

There were countless versions of these "farmer's almanacs," and most resembled the pocket-sized, yellow tome that is still ubiquitous in New England. An important feature was the calendar of celestial events, such as the rising and setting times for the sun and moon, eclipses, and other astronomical occurrences. Essential to all such predictions are basic mathematical calculations, and for *Walton's Register,* the mathematical reckonings were formulated by Vermont's preeminent practitioner of natural science, Zadock Thompson, who prepared his celestial calendar "calculated for the meridian of Montpelier."

The publication's founder, E.P. Walton, was born in Canterbury, New Hampshire, in 1789, and moved with his family to Peacham, Vermont, while still a boy. In Peacham he was apprenticed to Samuel Goss, who printed a local newspaper, *The Green Mountain Patriot*. When Goss came to Montpelier in 1807 to purchase the *Vermont Precursor*, E.P. Walton came with him. They changed the name of the newspaper to the Vermont Watchman, and in six years' time, Walton bought a 50 percent interest in the enterprise. A few years later he became the sole proprietor. Concurrent with his business interests, he also served in the Vermont Militia, ultimately attaining the rank of major general.

The *Watchman* served a wide readership, and Gen.

Walton, an innate entrepreneur, built a successful paper-making mill on the Berlin side of the Winooski River. Eventually the printing plant of the *Watchman* filled a space now occupied by Montpelier's City Hall. His printing business flourished, and he became the official printer for the State of Vermont, adding that imprint to all official publications of the Vermont state government. He first published *Walton's Register* in 1817, and it was continually printed in Montpelier until 1868 when production was moved to Claremont, New Hampshire.

An essential feature of Walton's Register, along with approximate weather prognostications, was the inclusion of the signs of the zodiac, "names and characters of the aspects," and "chronological cycles." It was believed that these astrological phases could help determine the best times to plant crops, breed cattle, and make fodder for livestock. Robb Sagendorph's *America and Her Almanacs* delineates the primitive conviction that,

> *All vegetables and flowers, the blossoms of fruits of which are to appear above the ground, should be planted in the light of the moon and those from which the harvest is made below the ground (such as beets or potatoes) are to be planted in the dark of the moon.*

Other superstitions concern the most advantageous of times for cutting brush, trees, or fence posts – even weaning calves.

Regardless of publisher, an almanac's astronomical information was essential to rural Vermonters who planned their seasonal chores and recreations in accordance with the availability of daylight or lunar illumination. One famous illustration that shows just how reliant people were on almanacs involves Abraham Lincoln and his use of the reference tool in the defense of a man accused of murder. As recounted in many biographies of the 16th president, the young lawyer demonstrated that the prosecution was in error when it claimed that his client was seen murdering James Metzger by the light of the moon on August 29, 1859. Brandishing a copy of the *Old Farmer's Almanac*, Lincoln proved that the moon was only in its first quarter that night and was also riding low on the horizon, thus discrediting the testimony of the prosecution's eyewitness. Lincoln argued that the witness did not have enough light to make a decisive identification, and the jury agreed, rendering a not-guilty verdict.

*Walton's Register* may or may not have ever been cited in court, but it was relied upon daily by citizens of the state as a useful source for health, veterinary advice, and household tips. One graphic example in the 1828 edition involves a remedy for bloat in cattle:

*When an animal has too much green herbage it ferments in the stomach and produces carbonic acid gas, which occasions bloating. To destroy the gas, make the animal swallow a spoonful of ammoniac mixed with a glass of water. Perhaps a dose of lye would do as well.*

Sound, seasonal advice – albeit a bit general – was also proffered in the monthly calendar section. For November 1828:

*Continue your preparations for winter, and keep pace with your business, and then the cold and storm will not come too soon for you. See that your ploughs, harrows, carts, and your farming utensils are all carefully and neatly laid up under shelter.*

The overwhelming preponderance of the volume was given to general reference information regarding national, state and local government – information that would otherwise be difficult for a rural resident to find. Officials in state and local government are delineated in detail and, as the annual editions evolved, a plethora of commercial and professional information was also included.

As the contents of *Walton's Register* and competing almanacs became more detailed, charges of inaccuracy were leveled by rivals of the Montpelier company. In the 1860s, with the appearance of several competing almanacs, the Montpelier publisher launched its own attacks against the veracity of its competitors.

With the appearance of *Atwater's Vermont Directory* in November of 1866, the editor of *Walton's Register*

took it to task in the pages of several Vermont newspapers, noting in a variety of important areas, "Atwater is imperfect." Specifically, it was pointed out that "the grand list for 1866 is not yet completed, the last corrections for County Officers have not been made, in town returns, a number of towns are missing, we notice an imperfect list of stamp duties, no table of population, governors and elections in the several states...."

In response, the editors of *Atwater's Vermont Directory* published a counter-attack, citing a *"spirit of low jealousy on the part of Walton's Register. If the waning fortunes of his pet register are at so low an ebb as to render it necessary to disparage its rivals in order to keep his own alive, the sooner he throws the old fogy concern overboard, the better for all concerned."*

It is possible that the *Vermont Directory* hit the mark with its criticism, for the following year (1868) *Walton's Register* was sold to the Claremont Manufacturing Company of Claremont, New Hampshire, which published the almanac until 1881. It then returned to Vermont, moving to White River Junction, St. Albans, and then to Rutland, where it was published by the venerable Vermont house of Charles E. Tuttle. In 1930 *Walton's Register* became the *Vermont Yearbook*, publishing continually until the first decade of the new millennium.

Today, it might seem quaint and old-fashioned to consult a printed reference book for technical data which, by its very nature, was out-of-date the moment it was printed. But in the days before the Internet, the local almanacs were the standard for weather and directory information, and some Vermonters still lament their passing. —*Paul Heller*

# INDUSTRY

## *A Changing Forest Industry*

Forest products have been a part of Vermont's history since even before the state's founding. Over the centuries, there has been a constant evolution in the ways that Vermont's wood has been used. And these changes continue today.

Currently, less wood is being harvested in Vermont than there was just a few decades ago. The number of high-value sawlogs coming out of our forests has declined significantly, largely as a result of changes in demand for hardwood lumber in the US. The US furniture industry was a major market for domestic hardwood lumber in the 80s and early 90s. But as wood products producers found themselves in competition with imported goods from China, many moved their production facilities overseas to take advantage of more favorable operating costs. The result was a decrease in demand for the North American lumber; between 1997 and 2019 US hardwood lumber production dropped 22 percent.

In some ways, changes in the low-grade wood markets have been an even bigger story. Pulpwood (poor-quality wood that's used in paper production) harvest in 1998 was over 400,000 cords, but by 2018 that number had dropped to just over 160,000 cords as pulp mills in the region closed and were dismantled.

The lack of low-grade markets is a worrisome

trend. If there's no market for bad wood, then only the nicest trees in a forest are harvested. Imagine a farm where the most vigorous cows are sent to slaughter and the runts kept for breeding stock – that's what we're up against here.

Vermont households burn about 400,000 cords of firewood annually, making residential firewood the state's single largest market for low-grade wood. And anecdotal reports from firewood dealers indicate that demand is, and will continue to be, strong. During 2020, Covid has heightened the desire to be as self-sufficient as possible, and heating with wood is one popular way to do that. Roughly a third of all woodburning households in Vermont cut their own wood.

Other major consumers of low-grade wood are the state's wood-fired electrical generating stations. Vermont is home to two wood-fired power plants, and there are many more scattered around the region. These plants primarily use sawmill residues or whole-tree chips produced from treetops and poorly formed stems. The relatively low cost of fossil fuels, particularly natural gas, continues to challenge the profitability of wood-fired generation in the region due to the abundance of natural gas fired generation and the resulting low wholesale power prices in the New England market. A number of wood-fired plants have recently closed in New Hampshire, but the Vermont plants remain an important outlet.

Roughly one-fourth of our annual low-grade harvest has to leave the state to find a market. That includes all of Vermont's pulpwood, which must be trucked to mills in Maine, New York, or Quebec. Paper markets, and ultimately the demand for pulpwood, have fluctuated in the past few years, but overall the market for pulpwood has shrunk considerably over time. Electronic communications have greatly reduced the demand for printed materials, and markets for newsprint and papers used in magazines have shrunk significantly as a result. The Covid pandemic has further reduced demand for printing and writing papers. With offices, schools, and colleges shut down and people working from home, paper use has declined even more, leading to an oversupply of finished product and the need for mills to throttle back production.

It is difficult to make sweeping generalizations about forest product pricing because markets can change direction in a heartbeat. That said, as I write

this, producers in the hardwood industry are expecting reduced demand for lumber and corresponding price reductions. One outlier seems to be producers of tool handles, which have seen a marked increase in demand since Covid stay-at-home orders were instituted and interest in gardening boomed. Likewise, white pine producers are seeing increased demand for lumber, which appears to correspond to stay-at-home orders and the resulting increase in home improvement activity. That demand has continued as people have begun going back to work and construction activity has restarted. An increase in housing starts combined with sawmill curtailments in the West and South has recently led to steep increases in the price of softwood framing lumber. The increases may not be long-lived, but they are currently a bright spot for Vermont's forest products producers.

*Paul Frederick*
*Wood Utilization & Wood Energy Program Manager,*
*Vermont Department of Forests, Parks & Recreation*

# Cherry-Picking Logs

I n Paul Frederick's essay on the forest products industry in Vermont he writes:

*It is very difficult to make sweeping generalizations about forest product pricing because markets can change direction in a heartbeat.* Here's an example borne out in dollar figures.

We conducted a harvest in spring 2020 and sold some reasonably nice cherry. You know, American mahogany; that gorgeous burnt-sienna-colored species that has traditionally been among the most valuable trees on a Vermont woodlot. Fifteen years ago, #1 logs – that is to say logs of average quality – were bringing between $700-800/MBF. Ten years ago, the same #1 logs had lost roughly half their value in the face of the recession at the time. Markets clawed their way back; in fact, we did a harvest in 2018 and were paid $750/MBF. But then this spring, the price, from the same mill we'd sold to in 2018, was $500/MBF. I asked Dan Wood, who works for Allard Lumber, what explained the drop and he said that the Chinese market didn't want it anymore. He said that tariffs have made the Chinese choosier, and they're focusing their cherry buying in the Allegheny region where the wood doesn't have pitch pockets like Vermont cherry does.

Because things are so lean, having a good logger who knows how to maximize the value in each log is crucial. If you have a 20-foot cherry log, with one defect at 9 feet and the other at

11 feet, and you cut the thing right in the middle to make two 10 foot logs, then you've got two logs that will sell for $500/MBF. But if you cut out the middle four feet and get rid of the blemishes, thus producing a clear 8-foot butt log and a clear 8-foot second log, the logs could get bumped up to the "choice" [C] grade that brings $1,000/MBF. You can see here that one choice cherry log from our harvest sold for almost 20 percent of the combined value of 13 #1 logs.

Forward-thinking forest landowners in southern Vermont should probably be watching black birch prices, as on many woodlots that seems to be the future. Deer don't eat the saplings, so where there's a lot of deer pressure, the understory skews to black birch and beech (another species deer don't like). I've heard foresters poo-poo both species, and because beech gets diseased that makes sense. But I don't see why black birch couldn't make gains as a crop tree. It has interesting grain and density that compares to yellow birch. Mature trees don't have the girth of yellow birch, but it grows like a weed. If some entrepreneurial forest business owner could cultivate a black birch specialty market, my guess is that they'd have an ample supply in Bennington and Windham counties. I know that forest landowners would appreciate the market.

Report Date: 04/29/2020  
Report Time: 11:50:25  
ALLARD LUMBER CO.  
PAWLET LOG YARD  
Page:  1 of 2

LOG SCALE PRICE TICKET  
INTERNATIONAL 1/4" LOG RULE

Scale Ticket # :  413938    Scaled: 04/29/2020 10:16:51  
Seller1: HUNTER EXCAVATING INC  
Seller2:

SCALE SLIP TOTALS

| Spc | Grd | Description | Numb | Gross | Def | Net | % | Price | Value |
|-----|-----|-------------|------|-------|-----|-----|---|-------|-------|
| AS | 1 | Ash #1 | 3 | 245 | 0 | 245 | 3.4 | 575.00 | 140.87 |
| AS | 1L | AS 1L | 1 | 160 | 0 | 160 | 2.2 | 625.00 | 100.00 |
| AS | 2 | Ash #2 | 4 | 255 | 0 | 255 | 3.6 | 475.00 | 121.12 |
| AS | 3 | Ash #3 | 3 | 225 | 0 | 225 | 3.2 | 375.00 | 84.37 |
|  |  | AS Totals: | 11 | 885 | 0 | 885 | 12.4 | 504.37 | 446.37 |
| BB | 1 | Black Birch #1 | 1 | 95 | 0 | 95 | 1.3 | 500.00 | 47.50 |
| BB | 2 | Black Birch #2 | 1 | 50 | 0 | 50 | .7 | 400.00 | 20.00 |
| BB | D | BLACK BIRCH D | 1 | 45 | 0 | 45 | .6 | 500.00 | 22.50 |
|  |  | BB Totals: | 3 | 190 | 0 | 190 | 2.7 | 473.68 | 90.00 |
| CH | 1 | Cherry #1 | 13 | 1600 | 0 | 1600 | 22.4 | 500.00 | 800.00 |
| CH | 2 | Cherry #2 | 7 | 500 | 0 | 500 | 7.0 | 300.00 | 150.00 |
| CH | 3 | Cherry #3 | 4 | 260 | 0 | 260 | 3.6 | 200.00 | 52.00 |
| CH | C | Cherry C | 1 | 140 | 0 | 140 | 2.0 | 1000.00 | 140.00 |
| CH | T | CHERRY T | 4 | 290 | 0 | 290 | 4.1 | 275.00 | 79.75 |
|  |  | CH Totals: | 29 | 2790 | 0 | 2790 | 39.1 | 437.90 | 1,221.75 |
| HM | 2 | Hard Maple #2 | 1 | 65 | 0 | 65 | .9 | 625.00 | 40.62 |
| HM | T | HARD MAPLE TIE | 1 | 80 | 0 | 80 | 1.1 | 275.00 | 22.00 |
|  |  | HM Totals: | 2 | 145 | 0 | 145 | 2.0 | 431.89 | 62.62 |
| PO | 2 | POPLAR 2 | 1 | 65 | 0 | 65 | .9 | 150.00 | 9.75 |
| PO | 3 | POPLAR 3 | 8 | 550 | 0 | 550 | 7.7 | 100.00 | 55.00 |
|  |  | PO Totals: | 9 | 615 | 0 | 615 | 8.6 | 105.28 | 64.75 |
| SM | 1 | Soft Maple #1 | 10 | 1170 | 0 | 1170 | 16.4 | 525.00 | 614.25 |
| SM | 2 | Soft Maple #2 | 7 | 635 | 0 | 635 | 8.9 | 375.00 | 238.12 |
| SM | 3 | Soft Maple #3 | 3 | 200 | 0 | 200 | 2.8 | 250.00 | 50.00 |
| SM | T | SOFT MAPLE TIE | 7 | 510 | 0 | 510 | 7.1 | 275.00 | 140.25 |
|  |  | SM Totals: | 27 | 2515 | 0 | 2515 | 35.2 | 414.56 | 1,042.62 |

2,455 BF < $325 = 2.455 MBF @ $30 = $73.65  
4,685 BF > $325 = $2,369.36 × 50% = $1,184.68  
$1258.33

Probably someone's flipping the page and thinking: why didn't they just leave the cherry standing, and come back in five years? It's a good question without a satisfying answer. If we'd had a large cherry component in the stand, we would have postponed the sale. But most of this harvest was mature pine. The plan going in was to cut heavily to regenerate pine, but in patches – we wanted to leave some of the stand intact for the animals that like mature forest and as a hedge against warmer winters. We've noticed that deer, especially, congregate there on hot winter days to stay cool. These uncut areas might also act as mycorrhizal reservoirs, where the beneficial fungi that have symbiotic relationships with the trees can be retained. The point, where the cherry is concerned, is that we weren't looking at the standing trees thinking: how are we going to wring every dollar of timber value out of the existing trees; we were looking at the forest and seeing the harvest as the first step toward creating another nice pine stand in 75 years.

Even if timber value were the driving factor, there's no guarantee we would have been able to get the wood out in the future. If we'd changed plans on the fly and left the smattering of cherry, there would likely not have been enough volume to entice the mechanized loggers we worked with to come back and cut them selectively in five years if the price did go up. Looking at the numbers on a scale slip can lull you into forgetting what an enormous task it is to get a two-and-a-half-ton tree out of

the woods and to market; if a logger can't make money doing it, it won't get done. In this scenario, a small-scale logger with low overhead could likely cherry-pick profitably, but in pockets of Vermont, this work force is threatened.

In Frederick's essay he points out that a healthy forest economy needs diverse markets for all different kinds of wood – from low grade to veneer. This same kind of diversity is also important in a logging workforce. In a perfect world you'd have big mechanized crews capable of cutting for volume, small outfits with small equipment for low-impact work, and everything in between. It's hard to get an accurate bead on how the small guys are doing because they're shapeshifters by necessity – log prices go up and they coax the 1970 Timberjack to life and log; prices go down, they hire on as a dirtworker. But we do know it's an aging workforce. And the flickery nature of it makes it awfully hard to plan ahead.

Maybe we should have left the cherry uncut forever; I could make an argument for that. Forestry is a mix of art and science, and there are often multiple solutions to the same problem. If you own a chunk of woods and want to manage it – that could mean harvesting timber or it could mean encouraging wildlife or maximizing carbon sequestration, or all of the above – finding a good forester to work with is a good first step. There's a county forester in each county in Vermont; he or she can give you a list of consulting foresters in your area. —*Dave Mance III*

## COUNTY FORESTERS

**ADDISON COUNTY**
Chris Olson
802-388-4969 X333
chris.olson@vermont.gov

**BENNINGTON COUNTY**
Cory Creagan
802-505-0068
cory.creagan@vermont.gov

**CALEDONIA/ESSEX COUNTY**
Matt Langlais
802-751-0111
matt.langlais@vermont.gov

**CHITTENDEN COUNTY**
Ethan Tapper
802-585-9099
ethan.tapper@vermont.gov

**FRANKLIN/GRAND ISLE COUNTY**
Nancy Patch
802-524-6501
nancy.patch@vermont.gov

**LAMOILLE COUNTY**
Emily Potter
802-888-5733 X406
emily.potter@vermont.gov

**ORANGE COUNTY**
Dave Paganelli
802-461-5304
david.paganelli@vermont.gov

**ORANGE/WINDSOR COUNTY**
A.J. Follensbee
802-595-2429
allen.follensbee@vermont.gov

**ORLEANS COUNTY**
Jared Nunery
802-595-5754
jared.nunery@vermont.gov

**RUTLAND COUNTY**
Kyle Mason
802-595-9736
kyle.mason@vermont.gov

**SO. WINDSOR COUNTY**
Hannah Dallas
802-622-4169
hannah.dallas@vermont.gov

**WASHINGTON COUNTY**
Dan Singleton
802-476-0172
dan.singleton@vermont.gov

**WINDHAM COUNTY**
Sam Schneski
802-257-7967 EXT. 305
sam.schneski@vermont.gov

**MAN & MACHINE:** Greg Haskins, seen in action on page 92, tells us a little about running a feller-buncher.

*When you get up to the tree, your instinct is to grab the trunk with the clam, but if you're holding it, the saw will bind.*
*You've got to cut the tree and then close the clam almost simultaneously. If you're off, the tree can fall back and land on*
*the machine. Once the tree is cut and you've got hold of it, you need to move it to where you want it to lie.*
*Remember in Little League when they showed you how to balance the bat in your hand? (He demonstrates.)*
*You need to find the balance point of the tree. It takes a while to get the hang of it. It takes more brains than balls....*

When Copeland Furniture began in 1975, our goal was to make products from locally sourced hardwood. Initially we built cider presses, then butcher-block kitchen furniture and Adirondack chairs, items that were functional and affordable for baby-boomers as they furnished their first homes.

What started as a one-man operation in an old garage in East Corinth has grown into a state-of-the-art company on the banks of the Connecticut river in Bradford. Today, Copeland offers a line of quality hardwood furniture. Using a combination of leading-edge technology and craft technique, we create pieces that feature classic proportion and modern simplicity.

We still make our furniture out of hardwoods from the Northern Forest. And our facility is setting a gold standard for sustainable manufacturing. Making furniture is energy intensive. And with much of the furniture industry having opted to manufacture overseas, ocean transport of both raw materials and finished products exacerbates the already intensive energy consumption. Our furniture is made in America with American wood. In 2016, we built a 626 kWh solar array that now produces electricity equal to 64% of what we use; by the end of 2021, we'll have increased that to almost 100% with an additional solar array. Sixty-five percent of our heat is provided by our own wood waste; by the end of 2021, an additional biomass boiler will have us up to 90%, and we'll be displacing over 30,000 gallons of #2 oil per year.

We're proud to be building award-winning, heirloom-quality furniture in a virtually energy independent factory. And just as proud that this now 45-year-old Vermont company is embedded in the community and providing fulfilling careers for the men and women who come to work here every day.

copeland
FURNITURE

**Copeland Furniture Factory Outlet** 241 Waits River Rd., Bradford, VT 05033

**copelandfurniture.com**

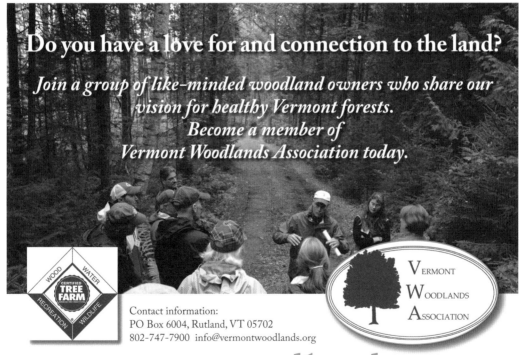

# FEBRUARY

# *February*

We were on the road before dawn, C and I, steaming coffee against the greenish light of the dashboard, the truck cab sauna-hot. Some gravel-voiced country singer on the radio lamenting that he was "too drunk to dream." Winter music – right? – a soundtrack for those pre-dawn hours when the world's shrunk to a circle of headlights and introspection seems easy. Above us, distant stars suggested a break in the weather, but the roads still bore the mark of recent heavy snows.

We traveled from pavement to gravel, the houses along the route mostly dark but for a few dim lights. Early risers in contemplation over coffee or day-sleepers shutting down with the waning moon. The faint blue glow of a television, here and there, telling stories about warmer places, different lives. A high-definition window into the future – showing rural people where the world's going.

The gravel road thinned to a trail. The road sand stopped. The path ahead lay white and shining, packed powder wheel ruts outlining a canvas full of boulder tops and undercarriage drags. We accelerated over the unimproved road which scabbed the mountain for a quarter mile or so before turning sharply and climbing towards the sky.

The road sunk into the earth through this first cut, banks on either side worn skyward by hooves then feet then wagon wheels then the lumber rigs. Just an old sunken road showing rural people where the world has been. A corduroy trail where men drove fir poles into the mud, then a Lombard run where those great iron beasts hauled tandem log loads into the valleys, chugging, screaming, belching steam and smoke and fire. Now just a Jeep path and us over old tire tracks: what do you think, last night? Maybe Friday.

As the truck climbed into the mountain the forest seemed to crowd in above us, snow coating each tree branch until they drooped to ground, the trees white now and spectral through the dark, the glowing limb-wood like bleached bones. Brake lights now, a blood-red glow.

"Cat?" C asks, throwing the truck into park. We get out. A straight track through twin circles of light. Though the Jeep trail had been packed to ice, the storm's last gasps lay like gauze upon the road; cold snow, the kind where you can count snowflakes, every two-hundredth one upturned at an angle, catching the light and refracting like crystal. The fresh bobcat track upon this quilt. Circular, almost dainty. No claws.

We turn back to the truck, open the door to heat, music, light, rumble on towards the dawn.

The road crests and carries true across a mountain plateau. Dark structures emerge from the gloaming, rusted-out trailers and tar-paper shacks and a stick frame in the foreground, red paint peeling, choker chains hanging from 4x4 porch posts, log-length firewood in haphazard patterns around the structure.

Boys in camp there, a thin scarf of blue smoke rising from a rusty tin straightpipe. Pick-ups scattered randomly like matchbox cars between trees. Kennels in the truck beds. Men and dogs in dreams of the hunt, of white rabbits who circle through fir glens. Old men on aged mattresses with heads full of white rabbits circling through spruce and balsam fir. Old bay dogs who twitch before the woodstove and dream of circling white rabbits across boreal summits.

The pond lay just over the next hill, on that wood road – there – off to the left. Yes there's a road there buried beneath that fresh snow.

"Could this be what Robert Frost meant?" C deadpans as he noses the truck up to the road's shoulder. He revs the engine then goes for broke: a violent carom over hard, dirty snow and then held breath and silence as the truck pushes smoothly through virgin powder, that odd feeling of weightlessness, a feeling like gliding in a catamaran over calm seas. —*Dave Mance III*

# A Somewhat Normal Month

February temperatures were only slightly (1.3 degrees) above normal for the month, but this does not tell the whole story. While daytime highs were generally typical, nightly lows on at least three occasions neared record cold in Central Vermont. These occurred on February 9 (minus 16 degrees), February 15 (minus 20 degrees), and on February 21, which tied a record low at minus 15 degrees.

While many people associate the effects of climate change with warmer and rainer weather, highly variable conditions are also a symptom. And to this point, the winter weather has been highly variable. Studies have shown that as the Arctic warms more rapidly, the loss of sea ice, due to warmer ocean temperatures, affects the weather. This is known as arctic amplification.

There's evidence that arctic amplification has contributed to a change in prevailing weather patterns by weakening the jet stream. Strong jet streams bring consistent weather; weak ones bring wobbly weather that can be abnormally warm or abnormally cold.

After an unprecedented cold November, and a wobbly December and January full of freeze/thaw events, there were notably few big roller coaster oscillations in temperature during February 2020. This was mainly a function of a colder air mass being held in place. Instead of having storms track across portions of New England as in prior months, storms during February tended to track just to our south, which helped to preserve our existing snowpack. There were only two days on which sleet/freezing rain fell.

That's a good thing, because just 29.6 inches of new snow was reported at the Barre-Montpelier airport during the month. The snow depth at Mount Mansfield's fabled stake maxed out unusually early for the season, with 83 inches recorded on February 27. On average, the accrued snow depth reading at the stake reaches its highest level around March 24.
—*Roger Hill, Weathering Heights*

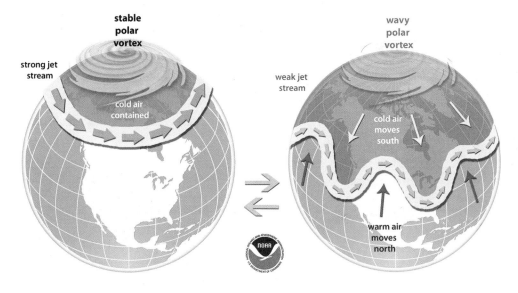

*Air pressure and winds around the Arctic switch between these
two phases (arctic oscillation) and contribute to winter weather patterns.*

# N A T U R E   N O T E S

## *A Feathered Visitor*

For the past six winters, a barred owl has been a daily visitor at my house. For most of these years, he roosted all day every day from December through February on a white birch tree just outside my door. Although I usually try not to interfere with the natural rhythm of things, one year when the snow was exceptionally deep, making hunting quite challenging, I decided to offer the owl a daily treat – one small rodent. Enough to entice him but not to satiate him or make him dependent upon this source of food. (I once opened up the gizzard of a road-killed barred owl and discovered five small rodents – about the average number they consume each day.) Thanks to the listserv in my town, I could appeal to neighbors for small rodents (trapped, not poisoned), which they generously deposited in a specially marked box outside the Town Hall, freshly frozen.

Every afternoon like clockwork the barred owl would become alert and open its eyes. If it had left its perch during the day, it would return at dusk, precisely at 4:30 p.m. The timing appeared to be in sync with the amount of daylight, as it arrived a bit later as the days lengthened. Most mornings I would take a mouse from the freezer and let it thaw. (When I forgot, the microwave came in handy.) I would take the mouse outside, dangle it by its tail to alert the observing owl, and place it on the railing of my porch. Practically before my hand released the mouse the

MARY HOLLAND

owl would fly in, grasp the mouse on the fly in its talons and disappear into the woods. More than once I felt the tips of his wings brush against me.

Six years, 60 days a year, comes to 360 days…this owl has spent nearly a year, one-tenth of its life, outside my door. I came upon the remains of a barred owl not even a quarter of a mile from my house this week. I can only hope it wasn't my friend. —*Mary Holland*

**THESE FISHER TRACKS** in the sugarbush ran from tree to tree, just like the human tracks left by tree tappers. It was likely a male looking for a receptive female. Female fishers give birth in later winter, and around two weeks after giving birth, they mate again.

**THE MICROBES IN A DEER'S RUMEN** change with the seasons, as the rich summer diet full of greenery shifts to a fatty, nut-based diet in fall and then to a nutrient-poor, highly woody diet in the winter. Mushrooms are an important part of a deer's diet year-round, and in our observations, the choice of fungus reflects the state of the deer's stomach. In summer, we've noted browsing sign on many soft species, including those in the poisonous-to-humans amanita family. In winter, they seem especially fond of woody polypores.

## AT HOME

❧

# *What Medium-Sized Mammal Made That Track?*

There are a wealth of good tracking books out there; the problem if you're just learning to track, though, is that it's easy to get overwhelmed by the minutia therein. In the spirit of simplification, we present the following six photographs that show the foot detail of six, similarly-sized mesopredators you'll find in Vermont. As our friend Susan Morse is fond of pointing out, feet make tracks, so instead of illustrations we went with photos of the real thing. By all means, consult the tracking books for information on pattern and gait and fine-tuned details. If you've got a good print, though, just match it to one of these feet.

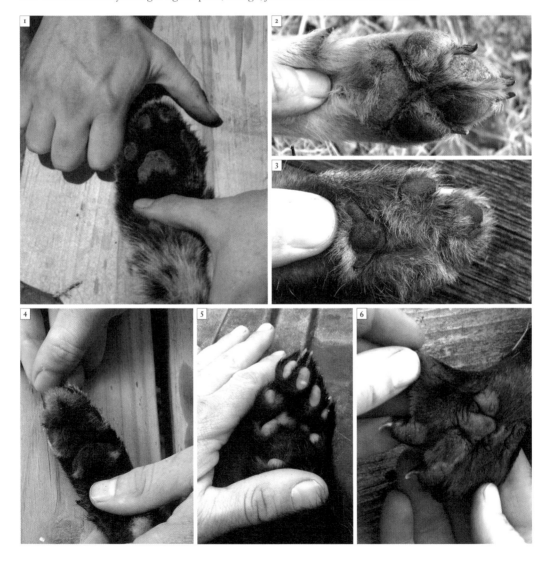

**BOBCAT** [1]

Feline toe pads are not symmetrical or paired. They're more like the fingertips on your hand in that none quite line up.

**COYOTE** [2]

Overall track size is key, as is the size and clarity of the individual pads. Note how big, prominent, and symmetrical the paired pads are – two toe pads in the front, two toe pads in the back.

**GRAY FOX** [3]

Gray foxes have less hair than reds, so their paired front and back toe pads are usually visible. Their tracks are generally rounder than those of a red fox. Their nails leave tiny, pin-sized impressions.

**RED FOX** [4]

Red foxes have furry feet in the winter, which can make it very hard to find a toe pad print in the track. The negative space between the toes is exaggerated by the fur.

**FISHER** [5]

Fishers have bizarre-looking asymmetrical feet. In good conditions you can clearly see five toes in the track.

**OTTER** [6]

Otters have partially webbed feet, which may or may not register in the track. They have five toes. If you're unclear if it's otter or fisher, just follow it a ways and see if the animal slides. Otters slide, fishers don't.

**WANT TO LEARN MORE ABOUT TRACKS AND TRACKING?**
These three books are among our favorites:
*Wildlife and Habits* by Susan C. Morse (available through keepingtrack.org.)
*Tracking and the Art of Seeing* by Paul Rezendes
*Mammal Tracks and Sign* by Mark Elbroch

# Tree Tapping Tips

The first step to properly tapping a tree is to identify any old tap holes so you can avoid them. Some sugarmakers paint the holes as they pull taps, which makes them easier to see the following spring. Others tap formulaically, using a regular spiral pattern, or clock-face pattern, which lends some uniformity to the search. Ideally, you want to keep at least 4 inches of space horizontally and six inches vertically away from a previous season's taphole; if you tap in that dead-wood zone your yield will suffer dramatically.

Once you've selected a place to tap, brace yourself properly against the tree. Sloppy drill control leads to oval-shaped holes that can leak. Drill at full speed, making one in-and-out motion. It should take about 2 or 3 seconds.

Tim Perkins, at the Proctor Maple Research Center in Underhill, Vermont, recommends a taphole depth of about 2 inches, including the bark, for maximum sap flow with the least amount of staining. Wrapping a piece of tape around your drill bit at this depth gives you a quick guide when drilling.

Tap the tree with a proper tapping mallet – not a household hammer that will likely overdrive the spout – and use your ears; the mallet will make a distinctive change in pitch after two or three artful taps, letting you know your job is done.

## WINTER STAY
## IN A PEAT BOG

*Leland Kinsey (1950-2016),*
*from* Galvanized.
*Published with permission*
*of Green Writers Press.*
*We just couldn't publish*
*a book about rural life*
*in Vermont and not include*
*one of Leland's poems.*

Cold runs downhill
and in this great bowl
collects like a physical thing.
At 40° below zero
I can hear the air sizzle
as moisture turns to ice,
and now and then a tree will ring
like a bell as it splits
its length. I can believe
I'm gaining knowledge
of how a friend in northern Labrador lives,
and when I fall on my skis
and tumble down a pitch,
I think of him falling down a slope
with too great a load of caribou
frozen to the shape of his back
but unyieldingly heavy,
how hard it was to rise.
I'm camping here for several days,
could die I suppose,
but not brave
or in much danger, just cold.
At night I listen to coyotes bark
on the trail. I'm glad I'm sleeping,
but I walk the trail each night
as Orion swings his sword
between the walls of trees.
Waking in deep woods in deep winter
is like rising in mid-spring at home,
a thin but solid wall of bird song.
The birds gather where I urinate,
they eat the mineral stained snow.
One day I found tracks across fresh snow,
feet and tail tracks as if all in a flurry,
but all on the surface
like some Jesus lizard of snow had passed
and crossed the bog
where even now the rot below
sends mists up through snow vents.
Then I see rags of birch bark,
loose pages of the world's manuscript,
that the wind has stripped from the trees
and walked through the snow,
how light and soon passing their passage.
Behind me
is my whole trail to this point.

SUSAN C. MORSE

A  L O O K  B A C K

# *The Cat in Black Comes Back*

Bill Walsh lives in East Barre. When we had lunch at a downtown restaurant a while back, he handed me a picture of a fisher that he had photographed through his living room window. The black, furry creature, walking through Bill's backyard, seemingly indifferent to the surrounding civilization, its eyes closed to the bright sun, as if savoring the warmth.

I have seen a variety of wild creatures during my lifetime in the Green Mountains, but Bill's photo provided my first glimpse of a fisher in the wild. I've heard plenty about them, though. Folklore has it that fishers have a propensity for eating house cats and a ferocity seldom matched by other denizens of the woods. In Vermont, they're often called fisher-cats, though they don't fish and aren't cats – perhaps explaining why that nomenclature is seldom used elsewhere.

Moreover, the belief that the fisher finds the domestic tabby a near-irresistible delicacy is unfounded.

In reality, the fisher is a member of the weasel family, albeit one of prodigious size. In 1842, Zadock Thompson's *Natural History* cited the following dimensions. "Length from the nose to the insertion of the tail, 23 inches; tail, including the fur, 16 inches." Thompson elucidated further:

> *The name is badly chosen as it is calculated*
> *to deceive those unacquainted with the animal*
> *with regard to its nature and habits.*
> *From its name, the inexperienced would conclude*
> *that it led an aquatic mode of life, and that*
> *like the otter, it subsisted principally upon fishes.*
> *But this is by no means true; and they, who have*
> *had an opportunity to observe its habits,*
> *aver that it manifests as much repugnance*
> *to water as the domestic cat.*

Thompson noted that the animal is much valued in the fur exchange, and its pelts would fetch from one to two dollars from a trader in hides. (Editor's note: The fur market is in crisis in 2020, so it's hard to speculate about today's value; prices averaged around $30 for well-handled pelts last year.) Indeed, the fact that fishers were prized for their pelts and trapped was one of the major factors – the other loss of habitat as Vermont was largely deforested – that led to their extinction in the state by about 1900. In the 1950s, though, the Vermont Department of Forests and Parks reintroduced them with the hope that the effort would help to control the population of porcupines, which had been wreaking havoc on the state's forests since the time that fishers disappeared.

Vermont naturalist Ron Rood recounts one logger's description of the fisher's work in the north woods.

> *When I nudged that porcupine with my foot*
> *I got a big surprise. He'd been sliced*
> *down the middle almost as if with a knife.*
> *Then he was hollowed out from the underside*
> *the way you'd scoop out a muskmelon.*

In 1959, foresters released a dozen fishers in the Appalachian Gap area. Each fisher requires at least one square mile of territory in which to live its solitary life. An article in the *Burlington Free Press* soon after noted that,

> *The animals released in Vermont by the state*
> *were trapped in Maine, where they are currently*
> *flourishing. The fisher, and the state's poison apple*
> *system of controlling porcupines in their dens*
> *in the winter time, has superseded the bounty*
> *hunter who received a fee for turning in a pair of*
> *porcupine ears at a town clerk's office.*

In 1962, state forester Arthur Gottlieb reported that from three to ten fishers had been released in each of seven Vermont counties. Gottlied explained at the time that, "ranging almost continually over a large circular

route, the fisher may cover up to 75 miles in a week. It stops to kill and devour every porcupine it encounters."

Now, Kim Royar, a wildlife biologist for the State of Vermont, says that the reintroduction of the fisher to the state half-a-century ago has been an important part of restoring a natural equilibrium to Vermont's forests. "It was the maturity of the second growth forest that made this possible. It restored habitat for the fisher and, therefore, allowed a natural check on the porcupine population." —*Paul Heller*

*Old barn in Fairfield, 1941.*

# Dairy by the Numbers

Where it comes to agriculture in Vermont, dairy is king. According to the Vermont Agriculture and Food System Plan, released in January 2020, it's an industry that has an economic impact of $2.2 billion annually and adds nearly $3 million in circulating cash to our state daily. Eighty percent of all open land is managed by dairy farmers.

But it's a feeble king, a mere shell of its former self. The number of dairy farmers in the state shrank from 19,000 in the 1950s, to less than 3,000 by the late 1980s, to only about 650 today. The price of fluid milk has been below the cost of production for five years running. As the phosphorus levels in Lake Champlain and associated blue-green algae blooms grow worse, the industry also finds itself in something of a PR crisis for its role in the problem.

So what can be done? There was a lot of talk this year about establishing some sort of program where farmers can be paid for the ecosystem services they provide. The idea is that instead of subsidies, the state could create a system where farmers were paid for the carbon they sequestered and the stormwater they managed by virtue of their farming practices and commitment to open land.

Some small- and medium-sized farms that couldn't compete in the commodity milk market have found success going organic. According to the Food System plan, sales of grass-fed organic dairy products grew 56 percent in 2018 alone. The 200 or so dairies selling organic milk were averaging around $35 per hundredweight in early 2020, as opposed to the $15 their conventional counterparts received. While the cost of production goes up and milk production goes down when you transition to organic, there's still, on paper, a margin that can put a farm in the black.

Some who can't go organic are finding solvency by adding value to their own milk or producing milk for a specialty processor, such as those that avoid fermented feeds. Market research shows that cheese remains an economically viable option, particularly in the specialty marketplace into which most of Vermont's small-scale processors fit. Since 2010, Vermont has seen a 130 percent increase in the number of dairy processing plants, many of them on-farm cheese makers.

The dairy industry's struggles are not new. In George Belleroses great book on the industry, *Forty-six Years of Pretty Straight Going*, he notes the following excerpts from a Dairyman's Association convention in 1920:

*It is impossible for the farmer, who is obliged to rely on his farm receipts for the maintenance of himself and family, to compete with prices paid at manufacturing centers . . . We hear constantly about the appointment of this or that commission to investigate the farmers' price of milk . . . have any one of you known a committee appointed with the idea of reducing those things the farmer is obliged to buy?*

*The West with its cheaper feeds is going to constantly threaten your market. The West already dominates your butter and cheese market, and you must keep your price to the consumer down or it will dominate your milk market.*

*Why is it that so many [successful business] men go out and buy farms . . . without knowing the first thing about farming? Such people are going to apply business principles to farming, but I have never known such a one to make the farm pay for the labor. There are reasons for that, and one is because such a man can't compete with the farmer and his wife who have been working for nothing in many cases.*

But the word crisis that's being thrown around these days does not seem hyperbolic. We've lost 350 farms in Vermont over the past 10 years. At that rate, there will be none left in 20 years. In response to the crisis, the State has initiated a Northern Tier Dairy Summit; Dairy and Water Quality Collaborative; Future of Agriculture working group; Working Lands Enterprise Initiative dairy-focused funds; Vermont Milk Commission; legislative dairy farm tours; Secretary's Dairy Advisory Committee; USDA Dairy Innovation Initiative; Payment for Ecosystem Services working group; a positive dairy messaging campaign; a dairy market assessment; and the aforementioned Food System Plan, which can be read at agriculture.vermont.gov. We hope to be able to report a real-world example of how an ecosystem services scheme worked in next year's *Almanac*.

CAROL HIGHSMITH

*Modern barn in Richmond, 2017.*

# Dairy 2020

Vermont dairy farmers have always been resilient – they have continued their work, day after day, through the Great Depression, two World Wars, and decades of civil unrest, not to mention long periods of drought and heavy rains that resulted in poor crop years and precarious finances. There have been countless market challenges along the way.

Even with all that said, 2020 really stood out. It will be remembered as one of the most challenging years in at least the last quarter-century. Four years ago, we began a typical financial-cycle downturn. It normally would've been a three-year cycle, but it lasted longer due to volatile markets around the world, financial stress, lack of farm transitions to new generations, and loss of our fluid milk markets to alternative beverages. Still, we ended 2019 seeing markets finally begin to trend upward, and we were poised for the upswing.

Then Covid hit, and its effects on dairy farming were nothing that any of us could have expected. Markets basically shut down, milk was dumped, vendors could not get paid, and farmers were doing everything they could to provide for their farms and employees while dealing with social distancing, masks, quarantines, and children sent home from school. Vermont's two dairy cooperatives, Dairy Farmers of America and Agrimark, implemented market stabilization plans to reduce the amount of milk, requiring farmers to produce less or take a financial reduction on over-production. Dairy farmers are still learning how to manage that mandate while trying to make ends meet with prices in the $11 per hundredweight range.

One report by Vermont Dairy Producers Alliance estimated that Vermont dairy farmers saw $42 million in lost revenue over the three month period after Covid struck. And financial uncertainty has continued, with prices substantially lower than typical at this point in the economic cycle. Government subsidies were often spent before they arrived, often going to vendors so that crops could be planted in the spring. The result of this turmoil was that we lost farms and they will not return.

Farms that market their own products saw additional challenges. Some opened stop-and-shop sites where consumers could pick up their own milk and

*During the pandemic, sisters Hannah, Bresee, and Maddie (riding on back) Gladstone use their lunch break from online school to water the calves at Newmont Farm.*

other dairy products directly from the farm, and others began offering delivery options for consumers who did not want to leave their homes due to the risk of Covid.

The effects of the pandemic were compounded by a summer of hot, dry weather. With the arrival of fall, many of us were getting ready for harvest only to see crops damaged by summer drought. This added to the urgency of cutting costs, working to manage milk production, researching new insurance options to establish price floors, booking commodities, and managing debt. Not surprisingly, farmers (deemed essential workers during this crisis) saw an increase in stress-related health problems, including strained mental health.

And dairy farmers already had plenty on their plates, notably ongoing work to become more environmentally sustainable. We understood that if we were going to farm into the future, we had to do it in a way that was smarter and more cost-effective than ever. The Vermont Dairy Producers Alliance partnered with University of Vermont Extension Services to study and monitor phosphorus while instituting new farming practices and investing millions of dollars in infrastructure to become national leaders in phosphorus mitigation efforts. That work helped to create new partnerships and studies around the issue of carbon offsets, exploring how markets could be developed to increase dividends to farmers who manage their lands with that goal in mind.

Despite all of the challenges, a new hope has emerged: the realization that we can get through this. We are essential. We are doing good work and our results are showing across the board. There was a new appreciation for farms as low food inventories around the country made people question where their food would come from if things shut down again. There has also been a renewed emphasis on foods that are natural, healthy, and filled with vitamins and minerals.

Being out on our farms, surrounded by our beautiful Green Mountains, is not a bad way to do our part for our country. And having made it this far, I feel that a new determination has been born. I am a seventh-generation Vermonter, and farming is my family's heritage. We have seen a lot of developments since 1986, when my husband and I began our own personal journey in dairy farming. The way we farm today is significantly different in every area. Our adult children remain hopeful for the future and grateful for the opportunities dairy farming has blessed us with. I think that most farmers today would say the same. It may look radically different, and at times the growth has been painful, but we are confident the dairy industry will come out the other end better than when we entered 2020.

*Amanda St. Pierre*
*Executive Director*
*Vermont Dairy Producers Alliance*

*A cold morning and warm breath at the farm in Bradford.*

APRIL SCOTT

# A Real Cowman

Gabriel says that the way to help cows not be scared of you is to touch them. Lay a hand, be gentle – it cuts down on their stress. You don't want cows stressed because then they give less milk and have more difficulty conceiving. Since cows learn to recognize people by their smell, not by their looks, the more often they smell you and the kinder you are, the more they trust you. Contrary to what many people think, cows are curious, intelligent creatures. Gabriel's current favorite is a Brown Swiss named Charlotte, Charlo for short, because, among a herd of Holsteins, she's unica, unique. Other than that he can't really explain why – nor can one of the dairy owners, when I ask her if she knows. Just as with people or dogs, you like some better than others. I ask Gabriel if the Holsteins ostracize the few Jerseys and Brown Swiss among them, and he smiles at this ridiculous notion.

Twelve hours a day, six days a week, Gabriel checks up on a herd of 1,500 heifers, locating the ones who are in heat and ready to be bred. All the heifers wear in their ears a computer chip that communicates, among other things, how much the heifers are moving around. When they're "running around like crazy," chances are good they're in heat. And when he first checks on the heifers in the morning, Gabriel carries a can of pink paint that he sprays on the rump of cows not already painted. Then he notes which cows have lost most of the paint they wore before. This occurs because other heifers, aware that another is in heat, are inspired to impersonate bulls and mount her. They rub against the paint and the paint comes off. I can't help but wonder who thought of this – shall we say – interesting method. For those of us who grew up thinking that to milk cows you brought them in from the field, filled a bucket with milk, and dumped it into a bulk tank – not to mention persuaded a sometimes recalcitrant bull to fulfill his fatherly duty – this is a futuristic world.

Like all the larger dairy farms in the state, in order to survive this one has to work the economies of scale. With about 1,500 milkers, despite the sophistication of their own systems (the quantity of milk each cow gives is measured daily by computer), the owners still don't know from month to month how much money they'll be able to count on. Trying to comprehend the complex regulations governing the milk industry is more mind-warping than trying to make sense of the I.R.S. tax instructions. Says one of the owners, "There are only two people in the country who understand milk pricing, and one of them just died." To be able to make a profit, the farms have to milk the cows three times each on a 24-hour cycle, so a lot of help is needed.

Modest, unassuming, completely reliable, with a gently wry outlook on the world, Gabriel is a trusted and valued employee, one of a dozen or so migrant workers on this farm, and one of the between twelve and fifteen hundred in the state. Without them, the dairy industry, which has steadily declined since its high point in the 1920s when there were almost 30,000 dairy farms, would collapse. In Vermont there are now around 650 dairy farms, large and small. As one of the owners says, there are not enough people locally who want to do this work: the long hours for the kind of pay that the industry can afford. The situation is manageable for these workers, as most of them are provided housing as well as a paycheck, much of which they send back home. (There are a few workers in Vermont from places like Honduras and Guatemala, but the great majority are from Mexico.) Few of the workers at Gabriel's farm have cars, so once a week a farm van drives them to a local grocery store. Some favorite foods that they can't buy there – certain kinds of chiles, for example, or canned cactus – are supplied by someone who travels around peddling to farm workers. It used to be you could tell when the local workers had been to the grocery store because all the corn tortillas would be gone, but somewhere along the line the management has seen fit to order a lot more.

When Gabriel first came to this farm, he milked and cleaned the barns for three years. Says one of the owners, "He's very talented. It's like being an artist: either you have a feel for it or you don't. Gabriel is a real cowman." The owners have a vested interest in keeping Gabriel learning and stimulated, so he was sent to "breeding school," where besides learning how to inseminate the heifers he learned how to give shots and check their feet to see if they need their hooves trimmed. He inseminates between five and ten heifers a day, and on Fridays forty or more. On that day he has help, because it's hard, tiring work. But it's critical work. Cows who don't get pregnant end up on the beef truck.

Gabriel has been in the US now for 14 years. The first two he spent in North Carolina, working in construction, which he liked, but during the recession of 2008 the work was cut back to two or three days a week and an uncle who worked in Vermont told him about a job opening here. Besides being good at his job, he likes cows – and he likes the state. Just like Guerrero, the state in Mexico where he's from, Vermont is mountainous and still part wild. There are many of the same animals in Guerrero: deer, raccoons, skunks, squirrels – although no chipmunks or wild turkeys. And there, he tells me, there's a kind of mosquito that makes honey. When Gabriel was young he and his friends would look for their nests on trees to collect the sweet treat. "Are they really mosquitoes?" I ask, making a buzzing noise. We have that kind too, he says, but these are different. "Not wasps? *Avispas?*" "No, we call them mosquitoes," he says. Sensing my skepticism, he had a friend at home take a video to show me: the mosquito crouched on a tree and, nestled in the bark beside it, its tiny golden-colored nest which it closes up at night.

When I asked him once how he learned so much about the natural world, he said, "Los abuelos." All the grandparents in town. Town is a village of 20 to 25 houses. Gabriel's daughter, who is 15, lives there with Gabriel's mother. Her own mother is in another town, because that's where she can make a living. There's little work for anyone there. To keep in touch, Gabriel and his daughter talk by phone or video-chat a couple of times a week. She's in school and is interested in computers but just as in many remote locations in Vermont the internet there is unreliable. Gabriel currently has no plans to go back, though he says he supposes he will one day.

He would like to have a farm of his own, but he owns no land and the land in Guerrero is very expensive. Many of the men who have returned from the US farm corn, but it's subsistence living. Here, Gabriel likes the work, though the winters can be difficult, when so many things are frozen. He doesn't complain about his circumstances – about feeling *encerrado* (literally, encircled), unable to move around safely outside of the farm. Like Gabriel, most of the workers are here without their families and haven't seen spouses and children for many years. And rarely are they able to get to know people off the farms or meet a spouse, if they haven't one. If the immigration laws were to change, Gabriel would like to stay and bring his daughter to live here. So would many of the other workers. In a state that urgently needs more young people to start and nurture families here, one would think that providing these essential workers with visas, if not citizenship, and welcoming them into aging communities would make sense. Yet, despite Vermont's having been in the vanguard of a number of political and social advances over its history, immigration laws are under federal purview, so it's not up to us. —*Kathyrn Kramer*

# Goodbye to a Local Legend

On September 10, Thomas Dairy – which had operated in Rutland for 99 years – announced that it would be going out of business. Milk cost 11 cents a gallon when the company began delivering it in 1921. Over nearly a century, the dairy had weathered its fair share of hard times, but the impact of the 2020 pandemic was too much to absorb. "With gratitude, pride and heavy hearts, we have made the difficult but necessary decision to close Thomas Dairy at the end of the month," the family-owned business stated. "The decrease in business from colleges, restaurants, and tourism during the Covid shutdown has hit us hard, and the future remains uncertain."

News reports noted that thousands of Vermonters had grown up drinking Thomas Dairy milk at school, and not surprisingly, thousands took to social media to express their sorrow at the loss of the iconic company. Carrie Pill took things a step further, sharing her feelings with art.

"Today was going to be another series painting, but I needed to pay homage to a local legend and acknowledge the emotions that have sprung from yesterday's news," she posted, along with an oil painting of a Thomas Dairy milk container from her refrigerator. "Our community is shook. There's a feeling of helplessness and loss. My husband said 'but I don't want to buy (insert faraway mega company) milk.' I know we're not alone in feeling this way. Keep showing up for your local businesses and farms, my friends. They are your friends, family, neighbors; they are your community. Buy their products, be their ambassadors. These are the hardest of times on them, and they will need your continued support."

CARRIE PILL

Tapping in 1947
Inset: Tapping the same tree in 2014

Here's to family breakfasts.
Here's to food that tastes like the place it came from.
Here's to craft that's passed down through the generations.
Here's to local products made by local people.
Here's to the resilience that keeps rural industries afloat.
Here's to the hope, and ambition, and hard work
behind new endeavors.

MANCE FAMILY TREE FARM
is proud to support the *Vermont Almanac.*

MANCE FAMILY
TREE FARM

*We Ship! Order today at* MANCEMAPLE.COM

**Prospect**

SKI

**Prospect Mountain Nordic Ski Center** sits on the spine of the southern Green Mountains in Woodford. It features 30 kilometers of groomed trails and a rustic lodge that has been a gathering place for skiers since the 1940s. It's a fixture of the community here; in fact, the community owns it. Faced with the prospect of closure or sale to a private party in 2018, local skiers took it upon themselves to raise money and purchase the beloved institution. Major funding came from Williams College alumni and the Vermont Housing & Conservation Board, but the rest came from local people and businesses who found a way to articulate their love of this land.

The mountain will be fully open for Nordic skiing and snowshoeing as soon as conditions allow it, and with a base lodge at an elevation of 2,160 feet, the snow usually comes early and stays late. There will be some indoor facility restrictions during the 2020-2021 season due to the Covid virus. Check **www.prospectmountain.com** for more information. Season passes, multi-day passes, day passes, and ski and snowshoe rentals are available online or on the mountain.

Our best wishes to *Vermont Almanac* on their inaugural edition – another great example of Vermonters articulating their love of the land.

# MARCH

# *March*

The sun shone brightly. The temperatures tipped the scale at 34 degrees F. The wind ceased its assault, and for a moment it felt warm. I hung my sheets to dry. The change isn't here yet. But soon. Very soon the wind will shift and bring the warmer air. Some brave birds have taken up their chorus of welcome.

I head to the local market. It's still fairly new, and I marvel at how quickly I can get there. I drop the girls off at the middle school, and head over to the store. I think of the years this building was the shop for the lumber mill. I can still see all the activity. We would head over there for sawdust for the farm. I move through the aisles to gather my few items. Potatoes for a shared meal in the evening. Fruit and bread for the house. I notice the local chocolate shop has a display. I love the idea of supporting our local businesses.

Small town living.

My thoughts are interrupted. A woman introduces herself. She recognizes me. I recognize her name. She lives in this small town and has followed our farm's story. We chat there in the store. Strangers becoming friends. She, a military mom. We find other connections. My heart is warmed by this exchange.

I continue on with my shopping and see another dear woman in the faith. One I highly admire and look up to. We chat briefly. Both of us with much to do. I head home to make a potato salad and get ready for the afternoon performance at the middle school. I am still carrying this sense of community as I watch, for the second time, these young people perform. At the end of the performance the eighth-graders stand up and pay tribute to the drama directors. It is a beautiful thing.

I head home to prepare for a gathering at a neighbor's. Neighbors meeting together a few times a year. We catch up on life. We talk of winter's grip and the spring. A meal is shared.

It wasn't a particularly spectacular day. It was just little moments here and there. Life in a small town.

*I wrote that piece on March 24, 2018. Two years later, in March 2020, I'm missing these gatherings and sense of community. Yet, there is something else happening. I hope we all notice and take note. We're being creative. There's a sense of slowness. Neighbors helping neighbors. A little more outward perspective is happening. I don't want to miss the lessons we need to learn in this time.* —Tammy Davis

# *Well Above Normal*

In March of 2020, the temperature was well above normal, by a departure of 4.0 degrees. In southern Vermont in the early part of the month, sugarmakers were battling highs in the 50s and 60s and nighttime lows in the 40s for extended stretches. On the 20th, it hit 64 degrees in Barre.

Temperatures in March oscillated, with a total of 6 warmups and 5 cooldowns keeping conditions frequently changeable. On the 3rd, Barre tied a high temperature record of 52 degrees. On the very next day, the high temperature was 21. Temperatures in Barre reached above 60 degrees on the 9th and the 20th. On the flip side, temperatures dropped below 10 degrees on the first and the 16th of the month, owing to setups with clearing skies and the nighttime drop due to radiational cooling. Across many of the deeper valleys, nightly lows frequently dip 5 to 10 degrees more than on the adjacent hillsides.

There were more clouds than sunshine during most days in March, owing to a flow of air frequently arriving from north of the Great Lakes. March can also yield big snowfalls, and indeed a solid 9 inches fell on the 23rd. Outside of this snowfall, there were few other snow days. Though rare this early in the year, a thunderstorm rattled through on the 29th.

The windiest day was March 13, when a strong cold front produced wind gusts to 47 mph, causing scattered power outages. Tree limb damage typically starts to occur when gusts exceed 40 to 45 mph. — *Roger Hill, Weathering Heights*

*You can see the weather in this syrup that was made on March 8, 9, 10, 11, 12, and 13 (from left to right.) On the 9th and 10th, highs soared into the 60s and nighttime lows never got below 40. This caused the syrup color on the 11th and 12th to go from a nice amber to a reddish deep brown, and the flavor to go from rich, sweet, and smooth to one with murky, bitter chocolate notes. Fortunately, freezes on the 11th and 12th and more reasonable (but still warm) daytime temperatures brought both the flavor and color back into line.*

# NATURE NOTES

**MAPLE SAP** looks clear when the weather is cold and the season is fresh; microbial concentrations are less than 1,000/ml. When temperatures get above 60, microbial colonizers reproduce rapidly and the sap begins to look like watered-down milk. Microbial concentrations can be in the billions, or even trillions, per milliliter. Yes, they affect flavor.

*March 27, 2020*

**AS THE SNOW DISAPPEARS, MEADOW VOLE TRACKS** appear. Voles have a greater capacity for population increase than any other North American mammal. Open almost any book about mammals, turn to the vole section, and you will read about one captive meadow vole that in a single year produced 17 litters, averaging five babies each time, for a total of 83 offspring. If the vole in this much-cited 1941 report had the usual 21-day pregnancy, she was not-pregnant for only eight days that year. (Meadow voles can breed year-round if there is an insulating blanket of snow.) Females are reproductively mature at about one month old, so think of the reproductive potential for voles that produce the maximum litter size of nine babies each time – and don't waste even eight days. Lots of people have done these calculations and arrived at numbers exceeding a million voles in one year from just one vole mother. For the whole Northeast, vole-to-vole carpeting, as a friend of mine has called it, wouldn't take very long.

Fortunately, this exercise tells us more about the horrors of exponential growth than it does about meadow voles. These dark brown, furry little creatures are 3.5 to 5 inches long, plus a short tail, and spend their usually short lives converting vegetable matter to protein-rich wildlife food. They are staples in the diets of hawks, owls, ravens, herons, weasels, coyotes, fisher, fox, bobcat, many snakes, and big frogs – those that enter water may even get eaten by fish. The average lifespan for a meadow vole is about a month. —*Virginia Barlow*

*Vole tracks*

# Beaver Bolts

Beavers are known for their ever-growing incisors, which allow them to cut trees down, eat the cambium (a nutritious layer just beneath the bark), and cut what's left into pieces they are able to haul and use as building material for dams and lodges. More often than not, it's straightforward work. Occasionally, though, not every step of the process is completed as usual. You can find still-standing trees with the bottom three or four feet (as high as the beaver could reach) of cambium removed. You might also see de-barked logs that have been left where they were felled rather than carried or floated to the dam or lodge as construction material. And it's not unusual to find standing trees where several times a beaver attempted but failed to cut all the way through.

Recently, John Twomey brought to my attention a tree felled by beavers unlike any other I've ever seen: one or more beavers had cut down a paper birch and eaten the cambium layer, leaving the tree clean of bark. At some point they cut into the tree every 18 inches or so, not quite severing the pieces, but leaving them connected by a core of wood that ran the length of the tree. If I didn't know any better, I'd swear they were bucking the tree up for firewood. —*Mary Holland*

**THE STATE CONDUCTED** a hemlock woolly adelgid overwintering mortality survey on March 18, 2020, and determined that 39 percent of the adelgids had died. This low number correlates with warm temperatures. During cold winters, mortality nears 100 percent.

**IF YOU'VE WATCHED BLUE JAYS LATELY,** you may have seen them bobbing up and down on a branch, extending their legs, then squatting, repeated several times. It may look like a person exercising, but for them it's about courtship and territory.

MARY HOLLAND

## AT HOME

# Getting Unstuck from a Sap Tank

Over the years I've felt the need to share the following hard-earned advice with my fellow sugarmakers. Paying heed could mean the difference between a successful open house weekend and utter disaster.

So you know those industry-standard 325-gallon plastic gathering tanks? Now there are two kinds – the kind with a little hole in the top that makes cleaning the thing impossible, and the kind with the larger hole in the top that makes cleaning a breeze. Kind of.

As you're cleaning this latter type with the just-about-large-enough-to-fit-in hole, you may notice a stray leaf or twig just below the opening. As the foreign object will be, inevitably, just out of reach, you'll push the tank on its side and then cram your torso inside it; herein lies the catch. If you're a man of average build, fitting into the hole is snug but possible. But since many of us clean our tanks on cold mornings, our frames will be made bulkier by heavy coats. As you slide head-first into the tank up to your waist, you may find, after you've grabbed the stray leaf, that you are, in fact, trapped. Your coat will make backing out impossible, and you'll look to all the world passing by like a large human wine cork with two wiggling legs. And being a New Englander who appreciates quality textiles, that coat's not gonna rip.

Claustrophobia will quickly set in, and you'll find yourself, after a frantic bout of struggle, wondering if this could really be it. You won't feel panic as much as intense shame, picturing an embarrassing photo of your limp behind in the paper under some snarky headline: Local Sugarmaker Proves Darwin Right! And you'll regret that time you laughed cruelly at your poor beagle who'd gotten his head stuck in a sap bucket (an act that prompted snide comments about a family tree with few branches).

Your problems will be compounded if visitors are dropping by the sugarhouse at just that moment. You see, people are unaccustomed to such sights, and there's no telling how they'll act. In a best case scenario, when presented with wiggling buttocks wedged in a sap tank, a passerby may simply grow uncomfortable and leave. But if you're unlucky, said passersby could be mischievous youngsters who might use your disadvantage to exact acts of cruelty (the stinging thwoop of a paintball comes to mind). Worse yet, these teenagers could be your own kids!

Beyond physical harm, there's a PR component to such mishaps that cannot be overlooked. It's our job as farmers to represent the industry well, and the sight of a man's bottom wiggling suggestively is not exactly pure or folksy; it could, in fact, be perceived as downright offensive. Have some empathy for the visitor who stops by for some delicious fresh syrup and instead gets strange noises and an unmistakably full moon (full, since by now the weight of your wet pants, coupled with the exertion of trying to free yourself, and the 10 pounds you've lost from a month of literally working your ass off tapping and chasing vacuum leaks, will have rendered your scrawny buttocks fully exposed). You'll just be able to make out the offended "I never" through the tank's polypropylene walls before being left alone to dwell on lost sales, terrible PR, and the irony that your "mooning" managed to simultaneously cover both the true definition of the word as defined in the *Oxford English Dictionary* ("to pass time in a listless manner") and the slang meaning!

Eventually you come to realize that the way out of your predicament is to crawl all the way inside the tank, where you'll be able to turn around, and, with embarrassing ease, crawl out head first, the way you came in. Free at last, you'll look around to see if anyone witnessed your idiocy. Afterwards, you may find yourself at a south-facing window, picking up the spring's first buzzing flies and guiding them away from the window glass, towards freedom.

—*Dave Mance III*

# *Beyond Syrup*

The pandemic was just getting going in March, which caused the Vermont Maple Sugarmakers to cancel their annual maple open house events. Probably you missed the sugar on snow, the maple cream, the candy, and all the other value-added goodies. Of course, you can always pick up a gallon of syrup and make these conventions yourself. Here's a cheat sheet to help. Remember, when heating syrup to a boil on the stove, rub the rim of your saucepan with butter. This will help keep the syrup from boiling over.

| Product | Temp. | Notes |
|---|---|---|
| Maple cream | 235 | Bring to temp, then cool immediately, without stirring, to 70, then stir, until cream forms. |
| Sugar on snow | 238 | Cool for a few minutes after bringing to temp, then pour, without stirring, onto snow. |
| Maple candy | 245 | Bring to temperature, stir hot for about 5 minutes, then pour into molds. |
| Coated nuts | 255 | Dry nuts in oven, toss with hot syrup as soon as it's at temperature. 1 qt. syrup coats 4 lbs. nuts. |
| Table sugar | 260 | Heat to temp, stir until your arm gets tired, stir some more until all the liquid is gone |

# Pruning Apple Trees

March is late winter in Vermont, nearly spring. Of course, not every day feels that way, but find yourself a nice sunny one and you've found the perfect time (an above-freezing day before leaf-out) to prune apple trees.

When apple trees are young, little pruning is required. The goal during the first five to eight years is mostly focused on developing one main (vertical) leader, and training several (lateral) scaffold limbs. Once the form of the tree has developed, though, pruning is required to keep apple trees healthy and productive.

Dr. Leonard Perry, horticulture professor emeritus at the University of Vermont, has an easy way to get started: Remember the two Cs and three Ds. "Remove any that are crossing and rubbing on each other (keeping the most vigorous of branches pointed in the desired direction), and those that are crowded (this allows more light and air into the center of the tree, increasing growth and reducing diseases)," Perry advises. "Then look to prune out any branches that are dead (discolored, no signs of buds, brittle), diseased, or damaged (such as broken by ice storms)."

Next, focus on the critical scaffold limbs, which are more productive and stronger (better able to hold up to wind and the weight of fruit) than the vertical leader. These horizontally growing branches "should be spaced up the trunk vertically 8 to 12 inches apart,

FORREST HOLZAPFEL

3 to 4 inches for dwarf trees," he recommends. "They should not arise off the trunk directly across from each other, nor directly above another branch."

While different apple tree varieties have different growth forms, as a general rule, when using the common central leader system of apple tree pruning, the main leader is pruned back by about 4-5 inches in any year where it has grown more than 18 inches. And any other competing upward growth near the central leader is also removed. This method may slightly delay fruit production in younger trees, but eventually ensures more branches and, thus, greater overall productivity.

"A common mistake of beginning pruners is to cut off too much of last year's growth, resulting in little to no fruit," Perry cautions. He adds that most apple trees produce fruit on spurs – the short (less than 4 inches), wrinkled stems that arise from branches. "So it is important when pruning not to damage or break these off," he states. "Spurs usually don't flower until the second year, and bear fruit starting the third year of their life." They can also live for 10 years or more on apple trees, so damaging them can have long-lasting consequences to productivity.

When pruning mature trees, if you come upon excess branches, just shortening them up is usually not the best approach. "Remove them at the trunk instead to avoid promoting excessive inner shoots called water sprouts," says Perry. He adds that it's also good practice to remove any clumps of shoots, which can develop on branches just below past pruning cuts. "And when cutting a branch back to the trunk, don't cut into the ridge of bark (the branch collar) from which it arises." Don't leave a stub, either; cuts made flush with the outermost collar will grow over the fastest.

Finally, while most apple tree pruning involves looking up, don't forget to also scan downward and remove any suckers growing up from the trunk of the tree.

FORREST HOLZAPFEL

## A LOOK BACK

# Log Drives on the Connecticut

### EVERYTHING TO BOTHER A RIVERMAN WAS THERE

At the turn of the 20th century, log drives, for river-bank viewers, were like having the circus come to town after a long winter and slow spring. If not the greatest show on earth, it was a close second. Caulked-boot rivermen ran rapids and dam sluices for bragging rights and a $5 bet. Pickers scrambled over gnarled fists of 20-, 30-, 40-foot-long logs, searching for the key logs that would unlock the jam. Dynamiters, as a last resort, blew the jam to smithereens – a once-in-a-lifetime story for grandchildren and a major economic loss for the drive.

Nowhere was this show greater than along 300 miles of the Connecticut River and the spider web of its tributaries – the Nulhegan, the White, the Black, the Upper Ammonoosuc, the Ompompanoosuc. There was no safety net. Caulked boots nailed to trees along the Connecticut memorialized the scores of men who drowned or were crushed by tumbling

logs. These long-log drives ended in 1915, but for half a century before that they fueled the sawmills and paper mills along the river. Two books – Robert Pike's *Tall Trees, Tough Men* and Bill Gove's *Log Drives on the Connecticut River* – best chronicle these men and their time. Pike writes of the drive:

*The Connecticut River was not only the longest in New England, it was the toughest. Everything to bother a riverman was there: falls, rapids, dams to be sluiced past, mill-owners to fight with, dry ledges to break a horse's legs on, freshets, droughts, ox-bows, bridges built on piers…God! How the rivermen hated those bridges! They would skillfully build jams against them, hoping to carry them away and never see them rebuilt. Sometimes they succeeded, as on May 7, 1890, when there was a tremendous jam of ice and sixty-foot logs that took away the old covered bridge at Upper Waterford, Vermont. It was a sight to behold – the great logs shot straight up into the air their full length, as the pressure built up, and the jam extended upstream nearly two miles. The bridge went out, and the next day the one at Lower Waterford was carried away. The latter was never rebuilt, but a one-span steel bridge with no piers replaced the Upper Waterford structure and lasted until the great flood of 1927. The old covered bridge at Hanover, beloved by so many Dartmouth students, sturdily withstood all the attacks of the rivermen, though many great jams piled up behind it.*

Should mill owners ever consider replacing log trucks with log drives, Gove's book would be a good reference. First, drives took money. Lots. Drives beginning in the rocky, snag-filled headwaters of the Connecticut started with 500 to 700 men, the number gradually diminishing as the river widened and calmed. Second, enjoy the tall tales of rivermen who could ride the bubbles of a bar of soap down rapids. More relevant were quick feet, balance, and endurance for months of 14-hour days. Equally important was a sense of how logs tumbled, rolled, jammed – wing jams, square jams, center jams, dry wing jams – and how they could be picked free. Third, know your water levels and booms – main, channel, shear, and fin – to restrain logs and direct their flow. Fourth, precipitous drops, such as at Bellows Falls, are good for dams and water-powered industry but they are an unending headache for rivermen who must sluice logs over these dams in high water or around them in industrial canals in low water.

In his closing, Gove captures the lure and drama of the last drive:

*The log drive of 1915 was a big one. In size, yes, but especially in the achievements and memories of rivermen all across northern New England . . . There wasn't much time for the sharing of tales of the old days, however, for ice went out in late March that year, and logs stacked streamside up along the Second Connecticut Lake began to roll into the cold lake water. Down across First Lake and over the sluiceway at the First Lake Dam rolled as much as 50 million board feet of logs. Tumbling on down the turbulent waters of the Connecticut River, the mass was joined by more logs from Dead Water Stream and Perry Stream.*

*Logs stranded on Guildhall Dam.*

*The drive arrived at Bellows Falls on July 25, with the Connecticut River still running at fever pitch; the boom, it turned out, couldn't hold them all back. Many broke through and many had to be stopped by another boom strung across at North Walpole… By August 8 the drive had cleared Bellows Falls, except for a few stragglers, and the men continued to move on down the river. But more troubles with log booms were still ahead. Arriving at Turners Falls, the logs massed together behind the boom that was customarily stretched across the dam in order to sort out the logs that belonged to the Turner Falls Lumber Company. But again, the pressure of the high water current was too much; the boom parted and eight million feet of logs were released, soon to jam against the Hadley bridge. The jam extended for 2,000 feet up the river and was wedged in tightly against the piers. Forty men toiled for three days to work the logs through a 200-foot wide passage between the two bridge piers.…*

What killed the long-log drives? Economics. Drives had become increasingly expensive with smaller logs, a result of heavy cutting, creating higher per-unit costs, Gove notes. Competent rivermen were also harder to find. Environmental concerns, lawsuits, and competing uses also played a role. Log drives damaged river banks and left logs in farmers' fields when the river receded. Bridges had to be replaced. Boaters sued for blocking their use of the river.

Log drives did not completely stop in 1915 and continued until the late 1940s with much shorter drives of four-foot-long pulpwood for paper mills in the upper Connecticut River basin. By then, the romance of long-log drives was all but forgotten.
—George Bellerose

*This excerpt is from a book George Bellerose is working on about the logging industry in Vermont. It will be published in 2021 and available through The Vermont Folklife Center.*

# INDUSTRY

## *Modern Maple*

Maple sugaring is an iconic part of Vermont and at the same time defies simple definition. Much of the imagery around the pursuit is still firmly rooted in the production methods of the late 19th and 20th centuries (think galvanized buckets and horse-drawn collection tanks). And yet the 21st-century commercial maple operation is a gleaming, high-tech affair, and the industry around it is buoyed by global forces.

*Raw sap (left), high-brix concentrate (right) after a pass through a reverse osmosis machine. The raw's about 2 percent sugar, the high-brix is 25 percent sugar.*

The story of how humans in this region first came to harvest sap from maple trees predates recorded history, but it was likely learned by indigenous cultures through careful observation of nature. For example, red squirrels *(Tamiasciurus hudsonicus)* are known to puncture maple bark in spring so they can harvest the sugar-encrusted deposits that then form. Other animals, such as the yellow-bellied sapsucker *(Sphyrapicus varius)*, could also have provided inspiration. As Europeans arrived in eastern North America, they brought with them metal vessels capable of more efficient evaporation and started practicing the craft commercially. Maple sugar was the

end product of the day, due to maple syrup's tendency to spoil if not refrigerated. Production of maple sugar was critical to farm income, as it provided farms with cash ahead of the planting season. To say that maple was an integral part of life in early Vermont is no throw-away line: A reference from 1809 estimates that roughly two-thirds of Vermont families engaged in sugaring. In 1810 Vermont's population stood at 217,713. This would mean that more than 145,000 people were making maple (though largely for home consumption).

The invention of continuous-flow evaporators and affordable metal containers in the late-19th and early-20th centuries allowed maple syrup to overtake hard sugar as the dominant marketable commodity. But as the agricultural economy declined in Vermont and farms were abandoned, maple production dropped dramatically. The late 20th century was a statistically stagnant time.

We're now in what you might consider maple's third epoch, and it's a period defined by a dramatic rise in production and expansion. The vast majority of producers still have tap counts in the hundreds, up to a few thousand, but some producers have expanded to have tens of thousands of taps. A few have hundreds of thousands. In 2000, only about 50 percent of the syrup made in Vermont was sold into the bulk market. But today, that number is closer to 87 percent. Marketing takes time and money, and many producers prefer to let others cultivate accounts and fill orders while they grow trees and fill barrels. As with many things, efficiencies exist at larger sizes, but many aspects of maple production cannot be automated and it remains a labor-intensive process.

Vermont leads the nation in many key statistics for maple production. In 2020, the state's sugarmakers had the highest total production (2.22 million gallons of syrup) and total taps (6.15 million). Vermont produced just over 50 percent of all the syrup in the US and led the way in terms of yield per tap (0.361 gallons syrup/tap). Syrup yield is affected by several factors, but none more than weather during the sap collection season and the use of modern vacuum technology. The weather cooperated in 2020, with March being a bit warmer than average and April remaining cool enough to prevent tap holes from being plugged with microbial growth. As a result, we saw the largest crop produced in 80 years. In general, Vermont sugarmakers saw lower than average sap sugar content. Producers reported

needing an average of 52 gallons of sap to make a gallon of syrup in 2020. This is about 20 percent off from the state's long term average of 44 gallons. The good number of sap-flow events during 2020 allowed sugar makers to overcome this challenge.

*Mark Isselhardt*
*UVM Extension Maple Specialist*

### VERMONT CANE SUGAR: CHANGING RETAIL VALUE & RELATIVE PRICE

| Date | Cane sugar per pound (cents) | Maple sugar per pound (cents) | Relative price (maple/cane) |
|---|---|---|---|
| 1800-1809 | 20.1 | 11.5 | .06 |
| 1810-1819 | 24.4 | 12.5 | .05 |
| 1820-1829 | 15.6 | 9.5 | 0.6 |
| 1830-1839 | 12.9 | 8.9 | 0.7 |
| 1840-1849 | 10.2 | 8.0 | 0.8 |
| 1850-1859 | 9.0 | 9.3 | 1.0 |
| 1860-1869 | 15.1 | 12.3 | 0.8 |
| 1870-1879 | 12.0 | 10.6 | 0.9 |
| 1880-1889 | 8.8 | 9.0 | 1.0 |
| 1890-1899 | 5.9 | 7.3 | 1.2 |
| 1900-1909 | 5.9 | 9.7 | 1.6 |
| 1910-1919 | 7.4 | 14.3 | 1.9 |
| 1920-1929 | 8.9 | 25.3 | 2.8 |
| 1930-1939 | 5.6 | 25.6 | 4.6 |

### VERMONT TOTAL SYRUP PRODUCTION

*(x1,000 gallons syrup equivalent)*

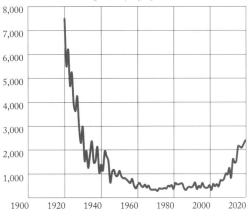

# Four–Season Pursuit

Besides being a maple scientist and an extension specialist, Mark Isselhardt is a photographer with a special eye for the beauty in a modern sugaring operation. The collection gives an indication of how sugaring is really a four-season pursuit, of course for the trees but for the sugarmakers, as well.

# *A Quick Q & A with Arnold Coombs*

Arnold Coombs is the seventh generation of his family to work in the maple business. Born in Whitingham, he still sugars with a cousin in Guilford, though the bulk of his maple work involves selling other people's syrup. As the director of sales and marketing for Bascom Family Farm – one of three major bulk buyers of Vermont syrup – he moves tens of thousands of gallons each year across the US and into 20 different countries. We caught up with him to get his thoughts on…

**WHAT HIS JOB ENTAILS:**

"We source from about 3,000 different sugarmakers, who bring their syrup in. It gets graded and put into silos. My job is to sell it, in everything from 1.7-ounce bottles to 220-pound totes."

**ON HIS MARKETS:**

"Our retail markets include health food and major grocery stores nationwide. We also do private label syrup for around 100 different clients throughout the world – we sell on every continent but Antarctica. We also sell into the industrial bulk market. This syrup goes into all kinds of products: yogurt, English muffins, Boars Head meats. Cheerios just added a new maple variety. What's great about the industrial market is that it's an outlet for syrup that can be too strong and dark to bottle."

**ON 2020:**

"We've seen incredible growth this year. Kids were home from school so there were more family breakfasts. I've been driving the production people nuts telling them they need to bottle more syrup."

**ON CONCERNS AMONG SUGARMAKERS THAT THERE'S TOO MUCH SYRUP BEING MADE AND THAT THE INDUSTRY IS GOING TO PRODUCE ITSELF INTO OBLIVION:**

"This is a complicated subject. I can say that we're seeing continued growth year after year. There was a record crop this spring, but 2020 will also end up being a record year for the packers. In my line of work, I'm concerned about not having enough next year, when we'll have a lot of new orders to fill. This is a tricky topic, though, and I don't want to seem unsympathetic to sugarmakers. Because we work closely with sugarmakers, selling equipment, Bascom's has a history of buying more syrup than we need. We'll find a home for it. We don't shut off our regular suppliers."

**ON WHETHER THE TARIFFS AND TRADE WARS OVER THE PAST FEW YEARS HAVE AFFECTED MAPLE MARKETS:**

"The EU has tariffs on US syrup, and there are no tariffs on my Canadian competition so we're mostly out of that market. We've stopped any marketing in China. It was a growing market. The Chinese glass we use is more expensive because of the tariffs. So yes, they've affected us. We've gone backwards because of all the trade junk."

**ON INDUSTRY TRENDS OUTSIDERS MIGHT NOT KNOW ABOUT:**

"We're seeing a good trend in the use of maple as an ingredient. We've published hundreds of thousands of recipe cards over the years that have been distributed by our vendors, and it's starting to pay off. People are now using cups of syrup at a time in cooking, as opposed to just using it as a topping."

REBECCA SIMMS

# *Maple Management*

**MAPLE MATH**

Pi day (3.14) falls right in the middle of sugaring season – and why wouldn't it, considering that sugarmakers tap based on tree diameter calculations, and tree diameter calculations involve Pi. If, God forbid, schools are closed again next March, and you find yourself homeschooling your kids again, you might take them out into the woods on 3/14 to study the tapping potential of the stand. First, identify the maples – a good lesson in botany. Then, measure the trees by wrapping a tape around the trunk at breast height. (If you don't have a flexible tape, use a rope, then measure the rope with a stiff ruler.) Divide the circumference measurement by 3.14 and you'll have the diameter. Best practices for a gravity operation hold that any tree over 10 inches can get one tap, any tree over 18 inches can get two. What's the sugaring potential of your woods? For more maple lessons, visit vermontevaporator.com.

**M**aking maple syrup is often presented as a single process from tree to bottle, but it is, in fact, two distinct activities: sap collection and syrup production. While the work in a sugarhouse clearly represents food production, sap collection is harder to define. Is it forestry, agriculture, neither, or both? A recent survey of professional foresters who work with maple operations indicates that less than 5 percent see sap production as a purely agricultural activity, while 30 percent view it as purely a forestry activity, and over 65 percent see it as a mix of both. Since the sap and not the tree itself is the object being harvested, it falls under the definition of non-timber forest product. Embedded in this definition is the fact that trees that will never make quality sawlogs can still be productive sap producers.

Sugarbush management is a poorly defined term that's evolved over the years. In the bucket days, the goal was to grow large-crowned trees with an open understory so the sap was easy to collect. Competing trees that were cut to achieve this goal would fuel the wood-burning evaporators. The plus with this approach is that large-crowned trees tend to produce sweeter sap. The down side is that over time this type of management steers a forest towards a monoculture and reduces its structural complexity, which makes it a less resilient place. It also doesn't allow for a next generation of trees.

The advent of tubing, significant energy savings through the use of reverse osmosis technology, and the transition to fuel oil as fuel source have changed how many sugarmakers manage their woods. A significant gap in the data prevents the making of sweeping statements about how Vermont sugarbushes are managed today. Most properties that can, do enroll in the State-administered Use Value Appraisal (UVA) program, which includes specific requirements relative to species diversity in a sugarbush. Monocultures are discouraged; a multi-generational, multi-layered forest is encouraged. And yet the UVA standards for sugarbush management, which generally favor a higher live-crown ratio, apply the same definition of acceptable and unacceptable growing stock used when clear straight sawlogs are the goal. Programs such as Audubon's Bird Friendly Maple program provide participating maple producers opportunities to model the best in sugarbush management. The rise of organic syrup production has also led to more stringent oversight of forest management practices. It is estimated that 50 percent of all syrup produced in Vermont has been certified organic. —*Mark Isselhardt*

MARION POST WOLCOTT

MARK ISSELHARDT

*These photographs give a sense of how things have changed in the sugarwoods over the years. Note the very ag-like nature of the old shot – the sugarbush was truly an orchard. The more modern shot, taken at Dave Gavett's sugarbush in Waitsfield, shows evidence of a recent thinning. Note how the tops were left high to discourage deer browse and create decent shade for seedlings. The wood debris and the intact duff layer will nourish the soil. Note, too, the multiple age classes of trees and the species diversity.*

# *The Trees Called the Dance*

Guy and I were rank beginners when we started sugaring. This would have been in spring 1975, the second spring at our homestead. We couldn't have gone about it more inefficiently, but every sugarmaker has to start somewhere. We used a small fireplace made of a few rocks with an iron grill on top for an arch. Upon that we placed two pots that could hold a few gallons of sap each.

We decided to start small and tapped only 19 trees. We'd later learn that 16 were sugar maples, one a red maple, and two were elms. We made seven quarts of syrup that first year.

As our operation grew, we moved down into the woods, judiciously placing ourselves on a small knoll in the heart of the maple grove. In every direction we snowshoed out paths to our tappable maples. The sugar shed we built was a three-sided shelter made of logs. We placed the 3x4-foot evaporator in front, out in the open, set on a rock fireplace. A step or two away, we constructed a woodshed, roofed over, that held four cords. We stacked the wood in four-foot lengths, leaving an alleyway down the middle where we could saw and split under cover. A big part of each day was keeping up with the wood. That, along with bringing in the sap, keeping the fire stoked to the maximum, monitoring the evaporator by adding sap as needed, and tending to the small fireplace next to it on which we finished off the syrup, were tasks that could engage many willing hands.

We settled on tapping 88 trees, in large part because we named each one, and 88 names fit conveniently in three columns on both sides of an index card. How busy we were was dictated by the flow of sap. If it was a light run, say the buckets were at most only a third full, it didn't take us long to zip around the sugarbush. But overflowing buckets meant we'd be boiling all night. Such events were unplanned; they happened at the whim and will of the trees. That's what made them so energizing and delightful – the trees called the dance.

One of us would dash up to the cabin for sleeping

bags, grab something for dinner, and breakfast, too. (We often used the fire to heat food. We were expert at toasted cheese for lunch and offering our guests tea with maple syrup for sweetening.) Meanwhile one of us was madly sawing and splitting wood while we still had daylight, enough wood to carry us through the night. Then we settled in, knowing the night would be clear and cold, but knowing as well that we'd be perfectly comfortable with the evaporator directly in front of the shelter – our stone hearth not so enclosed as to prevent it from throwing out a good deal of heat. Inefficient for boiling sap, but well suited to keeping sugarmakers comfortable.

Guy and I divided the night into shifts, and if we made sufficient inroads into the glut of sap, we could stop stoking the fire and crawl into a sleeping bag.

These were magical nights. The one on watch sat on the edge of the shelter in the dark, listening to the fire burn – big logs that crackled and popped and sparked and shifted, hard at work consuming themselves. You were alone with these sounds, and in the dark you found yourself paying attention to the hissing, sloshing, churning of sap at a rolling boil, with the kind of attention you didn't give to it during the business of the day. Every now and then you'd stir yourself to check the level in the pan with a stick marked for inches to see if you needed to add sap. If the answer was yes, you went into a side bay of the shelter and scooped out a pailful from the tubs. Adding cold sap cut the boil and changed the sound coming from the evaporator. But the roiling soon returned, a reassuring sound that signaled all was right in your world, deep in the forest, marking with these trees the earth's inevitable turn toward the sun.

We witnessed, over the years, on these nighttime vigils, several eclipses of the moon and, in 1986, the appearance of Haley's comet, coming into view on his 75-year rotation. In early April 1997, our all-night boiling corresponded with the appearance of the comet Hale-Bopp, who remained in the sky for several nights. And we could track the stars. There was rarely a breeze. These were cold, still nights with the temperature dropping below the freezing mark.

I remember how, at the beginning of my watch, the time seemed just to creep along. It took my mind and body a while to adjust to the slow pace – little to do other than adding wood and sap. Not enough light to read by. As the night progressed, I found myself taking in all the information I needed through my senses: the sound of sap busily bubbling, evaporating off that water, the sweetness of the air around me, as the sap thickened, and the smell of smoke, too. The syrup we bottled carried that smoky sweetness, preserving those days, and especially the nights, of our lives spent sugaring. When I was to awaken Guy I would find myself giving him another fifteen minutes, and then another. Not wanting to end this suspended state, fueled by the sounds and smells the sap and the wood made, not wanting to break out of a world created by these elements that seemed to close down the passage of time.

This weird and wonderful suspension, Guy told me, happened to him as well. And he, as I had, extended his watch, not wanting the spell to end.

But dawn, inevitably, pushed away the darkness, making room for day. The tree shapes grew visible, the maples we knew by name, sporting their buckets that we had painted green. No pinging, ringing drip of sap yet, still too cold. But we were up, one of us sawing wood, the other adding sap to the evaporator, stoking the fire, sparks flying upward. All of us in the routine: Mad Dog, Everest, those faithful sugar maples, and this year's rookies, Black Sheep and Galahad, all of our sugarbush swept up in the urgent work marked by the season's change, partners in the ancient golden harvest of sweetness and miracles. —*Laura Waterman*

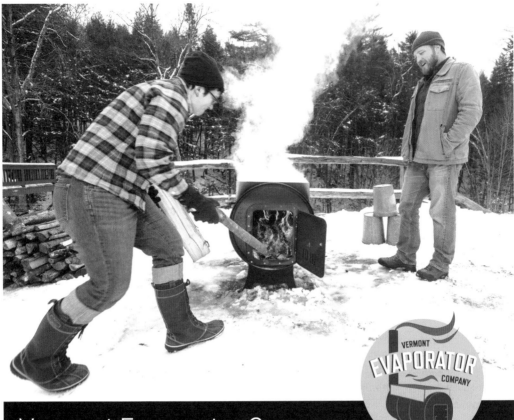

# Vermont Evaporator Company

*The Sapling Evaporator burns wood in an enclosed barrel chamber, which boils sap in a stainless-steel pan. After sugaring season, the pan pops off to create a grill, smoker, or wood-fired bread and pizza oven.*

Montpelier, Vermont
vermontevaporator.com

Kate Whelley McCabe grew up in a log cabin in the woods of New Hampshire. Her husband, Justin McCabe, hails from a farm in South Dakota. It was their rural roots that drew them to Vermont and led them to try their hand sugaring on their 10-acre property. Quickly realizing the limitations of boiling in a pot over a propane grill, and finding nothing on the market designed for modest backyard operations, Justin began tinkering with his own wood-fired evaporator design. With financial buy-in from family and crowd-funding support, Vermont Evaporator Company was born in 2015.

Maple is big business these days in Vermont, but we asked Kate what she appreciates the most about sharing the art with hobbyists.

*"We work hard at showing people how easy it is to make syrup in your backyard. Anyone with access to the trees can do it. And then we try to make the process even easier and more fun."*

And Kate still marvels at how much there is to know about sugaring beyond the usual "how-to" focus: "We have a blog that we use to contextualize sugaring by writing about history, science, current events, nature, industry, climate, culinary arts, and literature."

# Vermont Maple Sugar Makers Association

**Founded in 1893, the Vermont Maple Sugar Makers' Association** is one of the oldest agricultural organizations in the US. Since that time, the industry has changed quite a bit, but Vermont sugar makers are still committed to making the highest quality maple syrup found anywhere in the world. Our members take pride in creating amazing maple syrup and maple products, as well as caring for Vermont's working landscape for future generations.

The Association works to offer members benefits and education on industry research and updates, best practices, food safety regulations, product innovations, and much more. In addition, we serve at the voice of Vermont maple and share information with consumers across the county and the world. Vermont maple syrup contains an abundant amount of naturally occurring minerals such as calcium, manganese, potassium, and magnesium.

And like broccoli and bananas, it's a natural source of beneficial antioxidants. Antioxidants have been shown to help prevent cancer, support the immune system, lower blood pressure, and slow the effects of aging. Maple syrup is also a better source of some nutrients than apples, eggs, or bread. It's more nutritious than all other common sweeteners, contains one of the lowest calorie levels, and has been shown to have healthy glycemic qualities.

We love maple syrup on waffles and pancakes, but it can also be substituted in cooking and baking as a natural alternative to processed sweeteners. Try it in your bread recipes, in a peanut sauce to drizzle over tofu and vegetables, as a sweetener for cocktails – there's no end to the uses for this pantry staple!

*Vermont Maple Syrup – the official flavor of Vermont!*
**vermontmaple.org**

# APRIL

# April

## APRIL 5

In the morning there is a dusting of snow and more falling, albeit so lightly I have to look carefully to see it in the air. I halter Pip to the stem of a young birch and milk in the pasture, my right knee pressed into the soft ground, the small flakes melting into the heat of her flank. I can hear the mountain stream running strong with the melt that's still flowing out of the high woods. I can hear the steer, Saul, rummaging through the pile of hay I've heaped before him. I can hear the twin streams of milk hitting the bottom of the pail, and the change in tone as the milk accumulates. My nose is cold and I press it into Pip's side for warmth. It's the simplest of pleasures, the tiniest of comforts. But for now, it'll do.

## APRIL 15

In Monday morning's pelting rain, I'm on an errand run for essentials, this time passing a man gathering cans along the roadside. He is 60, give or take a few circles around the sun, and dragging a large garbage bag in the dirty snow, though he's leaving the trash where it lies: He's here for the money, five whole pennies at a time. The rain is beating on him. The cans are everywhere, scattered across the rotting snow like shells on a beach. Lots of Twisted Tea and Bud Light. Easy pickings. I pass what I assume is his van parked in a small pullout, a black Ford Econoline with a piece of hand-lettered plywood leaning against the rear bumper. Watch out for the Vermont Land Trust is what it says, and man-oh-man am I curious to know more. So curious, I almost stop. I even have my foot on the brake. But the rain. And, you know, the virus. So I carry on, counting the as yet ungathered cans as I drive, adding in my head, and wondering (because I can't help myself) what he'll spend it on. Gas for the van, I think (and yes: It really is 1.50 at Willey's right now). Maybe some Hot Pockets for dinner. Perhaps a six pack. Definitely, a six pack. So I add another 30 cents to the tally.

## APRIL 24

Snow falls. Wind blows. Overnight the skies clear and in the morning it is cold and sunny, the trees twitching in the diminishing wind like a cat's tail: back and forth, back and forth. I walk up the mountain road, intending to turn into the woods, but the sun full on my face feels so good that I keep walking, and before I know it I'm at the top of the mountain and heading down the other side. It occurs to me that I could just keep going, down, down, down into the valley below, and over the river, and not far beyond that a whole other state. New Hampshire they call it. Live Free or Die. It has a nice ring to it.

But of course I turn back (I always turn back). The sun no longer in my face, the wind rushing around me, the road slick where traffic has packed the snow to something like ice. Through the bare trees, I can see westward to the white-capped peaks of the Green Mountains. They don't look so big. They don't look so far. I bet I could be there by nightfall.
—*Ben Hewitt*

# April (Snow) Showers

The realities of Covid – of fear and shutdowns and closed schools and social distancing and home quarantines – were just beginning to settle in during April. What everyone could have used was some warm, sunny spring weather to make it possible to at least step out in the back yard and take in a little positivity. Unfortunately, the weather did not cooperate. The temperatures during April 2020 were meaningfully colder than normal, by a departure of 3.4 degrees. This cooler weather also turned out to be wetter, with 3.61 inches of precipitation (136 percent of normal) falling at the Barre-Montpelier E.F. Knapp Airport. In Vermont, April is a transition month between winter and spring, and this year it hewed closer to the former than the latter.

On average, temperatures on April 1 range between a high of 46 and a low of 26 degrees. Things warm up so that, by the end of April, the average temperatures range from a low of 37 to a high of 60 degrees. However, April 2020 basically leveled off, and it wasn't until around April 22 that temperatures began to creep upward.

The cooler nature of the month kept winter precipitation going, especially in the higher terrain. At the stake atop Mount Mansfield, a significant late April snowfall of over 10 inches brought total snow depth back to around 70 inches on April 27. This extra coolness back-loaded the snow cover in the Green Mountains, which hung on longer than normal, as spring hikers could attest.

The chilly and wet – and in some places snowy – nature of April was depressingly consistent; there were no warm-ups to speak of. Often, April can be exceptionally dry, with the snow melted out and dried leaves and grass fueling fire danger. With "April showers..." in mind, it may be surprising to learn that Vermont's prime fire season occurs during this month, from roughly when the last patches of snow

**AVERAGE TEMPERATURE DEPARTURE (°F)**
**APRIL 2020**

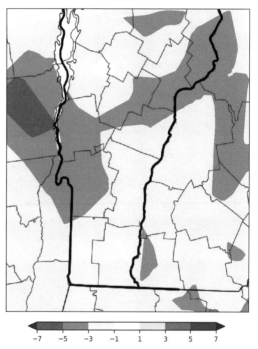

melt to leaf-out or green-up. That was not a concern in 2020, as the cool, moist weather kept conditions on the ground from becoming super dry.

April 2020 did provide an opportunity for some in the maple sugaring industry to extend their seasons. Optimum sugaring conditions occur when a slightly warmer than normal March is followed by a colder than normal April, which is exactly what we had this year. It's no surprise then that Vermont had a record crop.

Typically, at some point during April, we record our first thunder and lightning of the year, but not in 2020. Just as well, the month was stormy enough in other ways. —*Roger Hill, Weathering Heights*

# N A T U R E   N O T E S

## *Maple Sugar Content*

**MOSSES ARE GREENING UP** and tree trunks are the brightest things around now. *Lobaria pulmonaria*, a three-kingdom symbiotic organism consisting of a fungus, an algal partner, and a cyanobacterium, is common among the mosses on trees. It's also known as tree lungwort and is big and fairly easy to ID.

We made syrup this year at a ratio of 65 gallons of sap to 1 gallon of syrup. As a comparison, last year it was 51:1, which is closer to our long-term average. So things this year are significantly less sweet.

Why do trees vary in sugar content from year to year? There are so many variables that no one can say for sure. Two years ago our sugar content averaged 63:1, and I decided at the time that the low sugar content was related to a drought in 2016, which produced a stress crop of seeds in 2017, which depleted the tree's sugar reserves in the spring of 2018. Intuitively, this kind of makes sense. You can test the starch reserves in a tree's root system in the fall, and it's documented that the

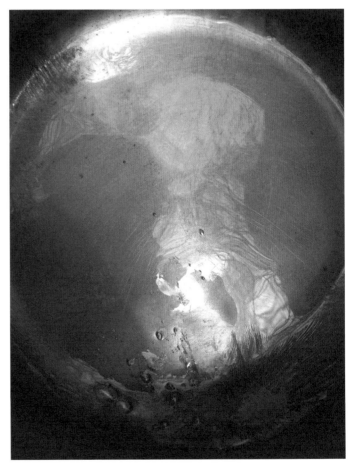

reserves vary from year to year based on stress. (Testing of this sort is not standard practice in the industry – it's mostly done in conjunction with an insect-related defoliating event, as it can give a sugarmaker an idea of tree health before the season so they can make the decision on whether to tap or not.)

We had a heavy seed year last summer, too. So maybe the same thing's at play again. But I have a new theory this year I'm toying with, and it involves nighttime low temperatures. What we're noticing, and it's backed up by another producer I know with a high-vacuum system, is that when you spot-check the sugar content of sap after a hard freeze, it spikes up to 2-plus percent, where it should be. But then as days go by without a freeze, the sap gets progressively less sweet. If we look at the last two weeks, which were the heart of this season, we had a hard freeze (below 25 degrees F) on April 8, followed by six nights where it either didn't freeze or just touched freezing. It froze hard on the nights of the 15th and 16th, recharging the trees, but then it didn't freeze hard again until the 22nd. So only three out of fourteen nights below freezing. When averaged, the low temperatures in that two-week window came out to 30.4 degrees F. Last year had consistently lower low temps. Nine of fourteen nights in the two-week heart of the season dropped below 25 degrees, and the overall average was 26.7 degrees F.

So now I'm wondering if these middling low temps might be a contributing factor to the low sugar content as well. I talked with friend Mark Isselhardt, the UVM extension maple specialist and a respected maple scientist, and asked his thoughts. He was buying the idea that the lack of hard freezes has an effect. He was skeptical of the seed theory. —*Dave Mance III*

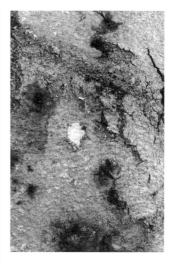

**OBSERVATIONS FROM THE HUNGER MOUNTAIN AREA** in Washington County indicate that beech bark disease may be more prevalent this year, possibly due to the warm, dry winter.

**APRIL 25 – SCARLET CUPS** fruit early in the spring – before there's much of any greenery. Small, just one or two inches across, this fungus lives on dead and rotting hardwoods. Sometimes the wood is buried in the leaf litter, making it appear to be growing from soil, but it isn't.

The cups of scarlet cup are shallow, and the brilliant red of the insides can be seen from quite a distance. Last year I gave several of these a little nudge and each time a cloud of spores filled the cup. I've since read that they make a puffing noise when large numbers of spores are released. It had never before occurred to me to listen to a fungus. —*Virginia Barlow*

AT HOME

## Pickled Ramps

One of the reasons that ramps, or leeks, or wild onions, or whatever you call them, hold a dear place in people's hearts is that they're relatively long-lived and predictable. Morels are mysterious and can't really be counted on. Fiddleheads sprint to maturity, so you'd better be on them. But ramps pop up dependably in April, and if you miss the early-season window when everyone's all excited about them, you can always go back in late spring and pop up some perfectly edible bulbs.

Back in the days of frugal living, pickling was a go-to technique for ramp bulbs. So that's what we did here. The bulbs were trimmed and packed in pint jars. We added a few dried chilies from last year's garden, a pinch of peppercorn, some herbs de Provence (fennel adds an especially nice note). We used white wine vinegar because it's what we had – different vinegars give things a different flavor profile, so it's up to your palate which to choose. Our brine recipe was 1 cup vinegar, 1 cup water, ¼ cup white sugar, ¼ cup maple sugar, 1 tablespoon pickling salt – you can scale up from there. Bring the brine to a simmer to dissolve the sugar and salt, then pour over the ramps. Cool and refrigerate, or process in a hot water bath for longer-term storage.

## Homemade Bug Spray

We're outside on the farm all of the time, and it's a requirement in our buggy area to have some sort of repellent. We use a DEET- or Picaridin-based product when we are doing high-risk jobs like haying, hunting, stacking firewood, mowing, or raking leaves. For everyday farm chores – horseback riding, dog walks, and jaunts to get the mail – we use a homemade, not-too-toxic spray.

It's easy to make up a big batch a couple times a year. I purchase amber or blue glass spray bottles on Amazon, essential oils from DoTerra, and other supplies at the grocery store. I like to triple the batch and have a bottle for each truck, the barn, and the front and back doors of the house…and a few extra bottles for friends. With essential oil-based sprays you do need to reapply more frequently than a DEET-based spray, but the plus-side is that they make you smell nice.

### HERE'S A BASIC RECIPE:

*2 oz of vodka*
*(witch hazel or apple cider vinegar also works)*

*2 oz of distilled water (if you're out, boil water for*
*5 minutes and use when it has completely cooled)*

*20 drops of cedarwood oil*

*10 drops of geranium oil*

*10 drops of lemon eucalyptus*

Pour the mixed ingredients into cleaned and sanitized bottles. When you're ready to make your bug spray, make sure the bottles and ingredients are not hot; essential oils are sensitive to heat and you want their bug-repelling force to be strong. I prefer to use spray bottle tops for easy all-over application. Give your bottle a good shake each time before you spritz. You can spray this over your clothing, hair, or right onto skin. Pay extra attention to the ankle and shoe areas.—*Kate Bowen*

# Grin and Pear It

In the spring of 2014 I began planting like the dickens with my oldest daughter Morgen, who lives next door with her husband and my two favorite (only) grandchildren. Thirty blueberry plants, some raspberries, two plum trees, a cherry tree, six apple trees, hazelberts (a cross between a hazelnut and a filbert), elderberries, gooseberries. And pears. When I was a kid, an uncle of mine had an old pear tree hanging on next to the milk house on his dairy farm in Hinesburg. The pears were the best I ever ate – I never had a store-bought pear that came close to them.

Today we have four pear trees that are doing quite well: a Golden Spice, two Ure, and a Waterville. The Waterville variety was started from a tree growing in an old orchard up in Waterville, Vermont, so we know it's tougher than wang leather. The Ures trace their roots back to Siberia, so pretty tough, too. Both started blossoming earlier this week. And if the frost is gone for good, I'm thinking we might get a decent crop this year.

Our pears have been some of the easiest trees to grow. They seem to have fewer insect problems than other fruit trees. Pollination can be tricky (part of the reason for this is that the blossoms aren't that sweet, so honey bees don't love them, especially compared to apple blossoms). But if you plant several complementary varieties together, it helps stack the deck. It typically takes five to seven years from planting to produce a full crop. And while we've only gotten a few pears in the last two years, right now I'm feeling optimistic. These trees have taken the worst that our tough West Bolton weather has thrown at them and come through it. Ain't lost a one. It makes me trust that there will be sunny, fruitful days ahead. —*Bill Torrey*

**SOIL FERTILITY**

**pss.uvm.edu/ag_testing**
This is a good site to visit if you're new to gardening. Or perhaps even if you've been at it for a long time. A half-cup of soil sent to UVM's Agricultural and Environmental Testing Lab, along with a check for $15, will result not only in a soil test report but also recommendations on what not to do as well as what to do. That in itself might be worth $15.

**www.uvm.edu/ vtvegandberry/pubs**
If you want to know more about garden soils, visit the site above and scroll down to the excellent "Managing Garden Soil Fertility" PDF by Vern Grubinger, an Extension professor at UVM. Your garden will likely benefit from the knowledge, and you might save some money, as he cautions against applying excessive nutrients. For one thing, mycorrhizae are discouraged when there is too much phosphorus in your garden soil.

KIM GOODLING

## *Sheepish Beginnings*

My husband and I came to Vermont over 30 years ago to embrace rural living and raise a family. Sheep entered our lives halfway through an 18-year stretch of homeschooling our children. We wanted our children to know what it was like to grow their own food, get their hands dirty, and care for living creatures. After a couple years of research and questions, we brought home our first flock of sheep and fully embraced all that animal husbandry in Vermont had to offer.

Through the years we learned as we went. As my husband says, "there is nothing more motivating than a sheep staring you in the face." Since our humble beginnings, I have been able to use what we have learned to help other individuals take a place of their own in Vermont's sheep legacy. With a little knowledge and basic equipment, raising sheep is totally doable. I've included some basic Q&A on the opposing page.

While it is important to do your research and understand what you are getting into before you bring your new flock home, you need to recognize when it is time to put the notebook away, grab your shepherd's crook, and go get sheep. As an older shepherd told me after I pelted him with questions for a full year, "Kim, quit asking questions and just go buy your sheep!" —*Kim Goodling*

## SIX BASIC QUESTIONS YOU NEED TO ANSWER
## BEFORE BRINGING YOUR FIRST FLOCK OF SHEEP HOME:

### 1. HOW MANY SHEEP SHOULD I PURCHASE?

Sheep need other sheep. I like to see at least three to five sheep when starting your first flock. The more sheep you have, the safer your flock will feel. The appropriate size of your flock will also depend upon how many acres of pasture you have available. In general, an acre should feed three to five sheep sufficiently, although it depends upon the quality of the pasture forage.

### 2. WHAT BREED OF SHEEP SHOULD I PURCHASE?

Each breed of sheep serves a different purpose. First, consider why you are getting sheep; this will help you narrow your search for the perfect breed. Do you want pets, wool sheep, or a dual-purpose sheep breed that provides both meat and wool? I always recommend visiting other sheep farms and attending festivals to meet different breeds in person and talk with their shepherds.

*Kim Goodling and a new Gotland ewe lamb named Nina. Kim offers workshops and farmstays at Vermont Grand View Farm to help others learn about keeping sheep.*

### 3. WHAT IS THE PREDATOR LOAD LIKE IN YOUR AREA?

Sheep are a prey animal, and if you have a heavy predator burden, you may need to invest in a guard animal to live with your flock. Ask local farmers about their encounters with predators to help determine whether or not you need a livestock guardian. There are several different livestock guardians, from donkeys to llamas to livestock guard dogs. Each works a bit differently, and it is important to learn as much as you can about the guard animal before purchasing.

### 4. WHAT DO I FEED MY FLOCK?

Sheep are easy keepers. Turn them out on a lush pasture and they are happy. Have your pastures evaluated for quality of forage and begin pasture renovations if needed before you bring your flock home. In winter months, sheep eat second-cut hay rich in protein. Some shepherds supplement with grain, whereas others are grain-free. You need to be aware of the changing nutritional requirements throughout a sheep's life span and provide extra feed when needed.

### 5. DO MY SHEEP NEED A SHELTER?

Sheep, in general, only need shelter during certain times of the year. They need shade from the sun, though this may be provided by a grove of trees. They need access to shelter during the winter months to get out of falling ice and snow; however, they still need access to the outdoors, even in snowy months. Lastly, depending upon the time of year you are lambing, sheep need shelter during lambing to protect the young from wind, subzero temperatures, and predators.

### 6. WHAT KIND OF FENCING DO I NEED?

Fencing keeps your sheep in and predators out. The ideal fence depends upon your terrain as well as your predator load. Consult with local farms and your local fence supply store when making fencing decisions. Several types of fencing are available, from portable electric fencing to sturdy woven wire fencing. If you are keeping your sheep behind an electric fence, the key is to have a high charge to ward off unwanted visitors.

A  L O O K  B A C K

*Reckoning*

THE BACKSTORY OF AGRICULTURAL EDUCATION IN VERMONT

Vermont's first farmers practiced agriculture the same way they practiced forestry, which is to say like miners: They took without any thought of giving back. Pastures were overgrazed; hill farms plowed and then stripped of soil by erosion; rivers were fouled. By the middle of the 1800s, people were calling for reform. Of course, if farmers were going to farm more intelligently, they needed to be taught a better way. In 1849, a resolution in the Vermont House called for the creation of "a department or school for the instruction of young men in those branches or natural sciences which have an immediate bearing upon the profession of agriculture." Bad agricultural practices were a nationwide problem, and so similar efforts were being undertaken in most states.

Enter Justin Morrill from Strafford. He was a member of the Orange County Agricultural Society, and so would have been well-versed in the need for ag ed. His wife, Ruth Barnell Swan, was an education reformer, so it's likely she was a behind-the-scenes influence, too. Morrill was elected to Congress in 1855, and he immediately began pushing for federal help with the issue. His efforts culminated in the Morrill Act, signed into law by President Lincoln in 1862. The act provided each state with 30,000 acres of land per congressperson, the sale of which would be used "to the endowment, support and maintenance of at least one college where the leading object shall be, without excluding other scientific and classical studies, and including military tactics, to teach such branches of learning as are related to agriculture and the mechanic arts, in such manner as the legislatures of the states may respectively prescribe, in order to promote the liberal and practical education of the industrial classes in the several pursuits and professions of life." If you lost the thread in that whopper of a run-on sentence, the act gave away land,

which was sold and turned into money, which was used to create schools where people could learn how to farm better.

It took a while for anyone in Vermont to notice the law. (That state's largest newspaper at the time, the *Burlington Free Press*, didn't even mention it until the session ended, and even then it was just a footnote.) But the powers that be at the University of Vermont saw opportunity, and by adding the title Vermont Agricultural College to the school's name, officially created a "land grant university" in 1863. They turned the federal land into seed money upon which they built their institution, leveraging the funds into more funds. Being a land grant college made them the point school in the state for future federal allocations, including money that created the Experimental

Station and the Extension Service. There are some really interesting nuances in the story that unfolded next – the question of how the money should be spent and who should benefit became a source of contention in the agricultural community for the next 70 years, and in fact the Grange and Dairyman's Associations were so dispirited by the school's ag department in the early twentieth century that they started a separate agricultural school in Randolph – but the simple fact remains that the Morrill Act was foundational to UVM and, over the long term, to agricultural education in the state. As you read the pieces in this very book written by Extension specialists, or when you send your garden soil up to get tested next spring, or if you are or were part of 4H, or if you go or went to UVM, then you have this connection to the Morrill Act. And Vermont's not an island – 52 universities all over the country were built on the Morrill Act. It is the backbone of what is today the public higher education system in America.

In any prior year, the story would have likely ended here: A neat and tidy piece about a forward-thinking Vermonter who helped lay a foundation for an educational system that would improve countless lives while helping society do better by the land. But 2020 brought a new reckoning where it comes to how we remember the past. And so we ask: where did the federal government get the nearly 11 million acres of land to give away? And the answer, of course, is that it was taken either by force or through coerced treaty with one of 250 indigenous tribes or communities living on those lands.

In March 2020, *High Country News* published a fabulous piece of journalism entitled "Land Grab Universities," which put a finer point on exactly where the land came from. If you go to landgrabu.org, you can see an interactive satellite map that lays out each of the almost 80,000 parcels of land in 24 states that made up the allocations. By their calculations, Vermont received 966 parcels of land (148,397 acres) in 13 different states. (Land in what is today Michigan, Minnesota, and Nebraska from the Chippewa, Sioux, and Missouri tribal nations, made up the majority.) When the land was sold, it netted the University of Vermont $122,626, or $1,971,455 when adjusted for inflation.

The point of these details is bigger than political correctness. It's about respect and healing in a year that's been short on both. The Morrill Act helped make America a smarter place. When we consider Justin Morrill and Abraham Lincoln in the context of their day, we see two outstanding public servants. Lincoln's famous "right to rise" line that politicians still quote today was uttered in the context of the Morrill Act. It's also true that Native Americans didn't do any rising in the wake of the land seizures. And that the act's funding mechanism was built on exploitation at best, and genocide at worst. In 2019-2020, Native American enrollment at the 52 land-grant Universities hovered around 0.5 percent. —*Dave Mance III*

*Chippewa lodges*

# I N D U S T R Y

## *Sheep & Goats*

The dairy industry – even with the serious challenges it's facing during Covid – is still the largest and most economically important sector of Vermont agriculture. Today, dairy accounts for almost 70 percent of agricultural sales in Vermont. But did you know that in the first half of the nineteenth century wool was bigger than dairy in our state?

The great Vermont sheep boom all began in 1810, when wealthy merchant William Jarvis brought about 200 Merino sheep to his farm above Bellows Falls. These sheep produced a much finer and more valuable fiber than was produced by the sheep breeds previously kept in Vermont. As a result of the Merino's introduction, the wool industry in the Green Mountains expanded exponentially. An 1837 report documented how the nearly 1.1 million sheep in Vermont that year produced more than 3.5 million pounds of wool; there were also 70 in-state woolen mills at that time working to keep up. There were ups and downs to Vermont sheep/wool market for several decades, before existential challenges came about in 1846 with the end of protective tariffs and the opening of the Erie Canal – these factors limited the price that farmers could receive for their wool and provided easier market access for (and competition from) larger sheep farms in the Midwest.

Between 1850 and 1865, the number of sheep in Vermont dropped by 25 percent. Demand for wool blankets and uniforms during the Civil War briefly increased demand for wool, but production also increased nationwide. The writing was on the wall,

*Daryll Breau in the milking parlor at Ayers Brook Goat Dairy in Randolph.*

COURTESY OF AYERS BROOK

and over the ensuing several decades, Vermont's agricultural focus shifted from sheep to dairy.

Today, Vermont's sheep industry is obviously only a fraction of what it was at its peak. The National Agricultural Statistical Services (NASS) tracks data on many agricultural products, including sheep. Because Vermont is a small state, its data are combined with those of other New England states and only broken out once every five years. The latest Vermont-specific NASS reports in 2017 showed that there were 704 sheep farms in our state, with 17,367 sheep. That year, 9,203 animals and 57,168 pounds of fiber were sold.

Wool fiber diameter and staple length vary widely among sheep breeds. Some Vermont fiber producers have developed successful and lucrative markets for their wool by catering to hand-spinners and having their wool processed into yarn. Others find that the price they receive for their medium-grade wool barely covers the cost of getting the sheep shorn. I am aware of two ongoing efforts to help fiber producers and processors find markets for their products: The Vermont Fiber Shed project is working to create an online directory of the actors involved in bringing fiber to market; and there's also a proposal to create a Vermont Yarn Sourcebook, which would be a binder of sample yarns and knitted swatches from Vermont fiber producers. There are also still a few small fiber mills in Vermont working with producers to create high-quality and locally produced yarn.

Vermont shepherds are able to produce a great lamb and there is increasing demand for lamb, especially in the Northeast. But producers face some challenges. Most lambs are born in the spring and are ready for market in the fall; this seasonality creates challenges, because consumers and restaurants want to buy lamb year-round. Lamb producers need support to produce the consistently high quality carcass that consumers demand. Producers also need a system to aggregate a steady supply of lambs, as well as access to processing facilities that are committed to small ruminants and support in their efforts to market and distribute lamb.

Goats are another small ruminant that offer many advantages for Vermonters interested in small-animal farming. Goats also have had a long history in our state. A humorous book published in 1983 by Frank Bryan and Bill Mares was titled *Real Vermonters Don't Milk Goats*. Actually, they do, and the goat dairy industry is a real bright spot in Vermont agriculture. There

are currently 46 licensed goat dairies in Vermont, and according to NASS, there were 3,553 dairy goats in the state in 2017. This sector is expanding rapidly to meet the demand from the state's two dozen goat cheese operations, which would like to avoid having to import goat milk into the state.

Miles Hooper owns and operates Ayers Brook Goat Dairy in Randolph with his wife, Daryll Breau. The dairy currently milks around 500 goats. Miles told me that "For many decades, goat dairy farming has existed in the hobbyist realm of agriculture because of the dominance of the cow's milk industry and the 'bigger is better' mantra. But now we are seeing a tremendous amount of activity and growth in our industry."

The Farm to Plate initiative (a food system plan being implemented statewide with a goal of increasing economic development and jobs in the farm and food sector and improving access to healthy food for all Vermonters) and the Vermont Agency of Agriculture, Food and Markets recently prepared a Vermont Food System Plan brief on goats in Vermont. One of the most surprising pieces of information in that report is that in the past five years, Vermont's annual goat milk production has increased from 2 million pounds to 3 million pounds. More growth is expected. The brief notes that "Due to the success of Vermont goat cheesemakers, an estimated 5,000 additional milking goats could be needed in the state." The report estimates that goat dairy farms have a viability threshold of 400-plus goats, meaning that just existing cheese processor demand could support more than 10 new goat farms in the state. This report offers a similar projection for meat goats. There currently are about 2.5 million meat goats being raised in the US, but another 750,000 are needed just to meet current demand. A brief about sheep will be released soon.

Vermont's smaller-scale farmers, including sheep and goat farmers, are competing against vertically integrated and international agricultural corporations, such as the large chicken and pork producers. But these mega-corporations focus only on delivering the maximum profit to their shareholders, and with no investment in local communities. I strongly believe that there can be a bright future for smaller-scale agriculture in Vermont if we make the necessary investments and continue helping consumers learn to value locally produced agricultural products.

*Dave Martin, President*
*Vermont Sheep and Goat Association*

# At Work Making Salame at Agricola Farm

What it takes to make a salame? Probably more than you can imagine (or want to imagine). You see, the job of the salumiere is only a small part. A good salumiere is humble, because her work is marginal compared to the work that the farmers put into the creation of the final product.

Making a salame starts in the barn, on cold winter mornings, inevitably when there is a storm. The patient sow works to get her piglets out, dry, fed, and warm while the human doulas jump swiftly to remove the little ones from underneath mom lest they get crushed.

Salame is made in September of the year before, when the farmer seeds the pastures with a combination of grasses, legumes, and herbs that will become an essential part of the pig's diet. It's made by picking up a bucket of food and running like crazy through the fields with a dozen pigs running after you while you lead them to the new pasture. Salame is made every Saturday when we pick up the expired fruits and vegetables from Shaws, and then giggle thinking of the pigs' reaction to avocados, cucumbers, and bananas (except for Salciccia: she does not like bananas).

We take pride in the fact that we process our own meat. A slaughterhouse close to our farm does the slaughtering, then a local delivery service brings the chilled carcasses to our processing facility in Middlebury, where we meet the meat. I know it is unthinkable for many people that I am now cutting the meat of the same animal that I have petted, fed, and cared for, but I am a farmer and a butcher and I have discovered that I can do that.

When the half-carcasses arrive, we lift them up and hang them in the cooler. I always spend time doing a carcass analysis, trying to figure out who is the pig that is now in front of me. Knowing their personality, the fields they grazed, their feed, and their personal history helps me make the link between the meat quality and farm management. I think this is the real secret of good pork.

We use only a few parts of the pigs for salame; the rest goes into fresh meat or sausage. The parts for the salame are the back fat and the lean meat. The back fat is the very hard fat on the back and the neck of the pig. The quality of this fat is key. The fat cells are what holds onto the flavor; they are what facilitates the curing and the aging process. Some farmers describe themselves as "grass farmers," meaning they put care into good grass, which is essential to the quality and wellbeing of the animals they farm. I leave that job to my partner, Stefano. I am a "fat farmer." Everything I do at the farm is for that hard, snow white fat that is so precious and limited. (The amount of salame we make out of a pig is almost exclusively limited by the amount of fat; we always have extra lean meat.)

The variation in fat quality is astonishing. A pig was ostracized and pushed away from the group? He'll have a soft fat, no good. (If you use it, it may smear and cause a crust on the salame that makes the aging process impossible.) Do you have a pig that was always lethargic and lazy or that favored high-sugar fruits over grains? You'll get a yellow fat that will become rancid and leave an acidic flavor in your mouth. Did the pigs escape their paddock and steal corn from the neighbor's dairy farm? (It happens.) Well, now you may have a lower-quality fat along with a slightly irritated neighbor.

At the butcher table, a surprisingly large amount of time goes into selecting the lean meat because it needs to be cleaned of any silverskin, tendon, fat, weird membrane. It takes me a whole day to select the lean meat that will fill 800 links of salame. After this, the salumiere needs to enter precision mode. We measure spices, culture starters (to promote the healthy bacteria that ferments the meat during the curing process), and nitrates and nitrites. (Yes, they are necessary. No, if used correctly, and if you do not eat more than one salame a day, they are not going to kill you. And no, celery salt is not a good substitute.) The sugar we add will feed the culture starter, which lowers the pH and contributes to the flavor. The amount of salt will facilitate the desiccation (the movement of the water from inside the link to the outside), which is key to a safe and tasty product. Too much salt will make the product very dry and very salty. Not enough and your product may not lose enough water and may rot. Fat repels water, so the amount and consistency of the fat

*The author and partner Stefano in the kitchen.*

determine speed at which the water leaves the link and therefore influence the aging process.

After grinding and mixing the lean and fat with the spices and other ingredients comes the part that is truly a long-lost skill: the hand tying. The casings are first stuffed into six-foot-long links, and then one of the three salumieri on duty makes sure the pressure inside the link is just right. Not enough pressure creates air pockets, which equals bad product; too much pressure and the link explodes and you have to start again. Then, with a few complex and swift moves, the links are tied in columns of four with a handheld spool of sturdy twine. Stefano loves this part of the process. We use a technique that was passed on to us by a salumiere in Turin, and we usually put on some traditional Piedmontese folk songs to relive this old tradition.

Until now we have talked about simple processes that require attention and care but not much technology. But when the links are ready for the curing process, we enter into the XXI century. We have state-of-the-art curing cabinets that control humidity, temperature, air flow, and resting times to the second. These cabinets are our jewels. And like everything that is sophisticated, we have a love-hate relationship with them. You see, I learned to make salame from a very old-timer, who would start a fire at the end of a cave

and then move it to the other end based on the way the meat was behaving. He would open a small window and block another one if he knew the wind from the east was coming, but would open both if the rain from the west was approaching. These cabinets work nothing like that, so Stefano and I had to re-learn. We had to read the meat and figure out that wind from the east actually means you must slow down the humidifier, increase the temperature, and do exactly the opposite of what you might do in a cave.

We check on our links every day during the sensitive time (the first week), and then the program takes them to the aging process, where they will sit until we feel they are hard enough and they have reached the right aging. At that point we select three random samples (okay… more like seven, since we end up eating a few now and again) and we send them to the lab where they are tested to confirm that the product is safe and does not have any pathogens. After the okay from the lab, the okay from the state inspectors (or USDA, depending), and the okay from our quality-control team (the "farmly" who eats too much salame for its own good), it is time to spend two days wrapping and labeling the salame.

And this is how the product comes to you.
—*Alessandra Rellini*

# *Engineering a Future at Haystack Farmstead*

W riters have this habit of turning farmers into martyrs: stoic, often unappreciated, salt-of-the-earth types who are practicing a vanishing way of life. There's a focus on toil – I'm hearing Paul Harvey's voice as I write this: *God said I need somebody to get up before dawn and milk cows and work all day in the fields, milk cows again, eat supper and then go to town and stay past midnight....* There's often, too, a fatalistic quality when we write about young farmers, torn between taking over the family farm and escaping in pursuit of a financially better future.

Brian Leach is probably too polite to roll his eyes at these tropes, but his words and actions betray that he has no time for them. Yes, many of the agricultural systems of the twentieth century are broken or obsolete – so how are we going to fix them? People who peddle in nostalgic stories have literary minds. Leach has a mechanical mind. If he's staring at the ceiling at 2 a.m. thinking about his future in farming, he likely has the components of agriculture spread out on an imaginary shop floor so he can clean them, replace the broken parts, and then reassemble the machine in a way that works.

Leach, 32, grew up on a Pawlet dairy farm that his father and older brother still run. Today, he lives down the road from the home farm and stewards 80

head of beef. Part of this diversification is practical: the riverbottom cropland grows corn for the cows, whereas the unused hillside pastures, best suited for grazing, were unspoken for. This gave him a niche. Raising beef, which is less labor intensive than dairy, also allows him to work in his shop (he has a mechanical engineering degree from UVM), both as a means of keeping the farms going and as an occupation that brings in steady money. It's hard to say whether he's a mechanic, an engineer, or a farmer – which is the point. In the old days before specialization, every farm was a diversified endeavor.

As we drive a buggy up the hillside toward the cows, he shows me the land – lovely layered hillsides framed by Haystack Mountain to the north and Scott Mountain to the west, the Mettawee herself wending through the valley like a green ribbon. And he shows me the cows – holstein, angus, wagyu-crosses; the holstein, a dairy breed, because that's what he had to start with; the angus a traditional beef breed to bring muscle; the wagyu a specialized, high-end beef breed with intensive marbling to give the meat a special touch. But really, he's showing me his system. That's what he wants to talk about. To pasture right you need to match the number of animals to the number of acres – too many animals and you'll get an ecologically damaged meadow that looks like a putting green; too few animals and you'll get a hillside full of inedible weeds. And you need a method that distributes the cows' grazing. Using portable electric fence, Leach creates temporary paddocks and moves the cows to fresh grass every day. He moves the watering trough, too: if your watering system is stationary, the cows beat highways to it and you lose productive land. He's got a waterline that runs along the bottom of the pasture, with headers and quick-connect valves every 200 feet. His trough is on skids and has a reinforced float system. "The cows' combination of size and curiosity is unbelievably destructive," he said, while attaching a steel guard plate to the intake.

It took him years to figure the system out and get it right. But now, when it's right, it means he's got less than an hour into the cows during the growing season, and the rest of the day to be productive somewhere else. Watching the cows graze, he said: "They're mowing, feeding themselves, and spreading manure on the fields. On a dairy farm those are three different jobs that a farmer has to do."

This freeing up of a farmer's time goes hand in hand with improved animal welfare. Dairy farms are

constantly dealing with foot problems – any human who works at a stationary job on a hard floor can relate. But on pasture this isn't an issue. "I only handle the steers maybe two or three times in their lives," he said. "It's kind of a Native American model, like when they followed the buffalo herds. I only exist in the animal's periphery."

Until now, the beef operation has been a break-even proposition. But with the infrastructure built, the systems refined, the herd at a size where he's not breeding all the two-year-old heifers, and the markets cultivated and stable, the operation is poised to start turning a modest profit. And his daily toil during the grazing season generally involves moving a fence on a gorgeous hillside. "It doesn't feel like work to me," he said. "Plus it's rewarding in that I'm meeting the needs of 80 animals."

This is another thing that some writers miss with their melancholy take on farming: to many who practice it, it's the opposite of drudgery. It's freedom. There are those who trade freedom for a job with financial security and stability. And then there are those who like their freedom too much to make such a deal. Looking at it this way shows the agency and power in the decision. A few years back, Leach took a job as a service tech at a microchip factory in Malta, New York, servicing robotic chip-making tools. It was a stressful industry and a stressful commute, "and for what?" he said. "To make the next gaming console run a little faster?" He couldn't connect with it, and was soon back on the farm doing something he loved.

Back down at the bottom of the hill, Leach takes me on a tour of his shop, where he's got an early 1970s-era International Harvester tractor in pieces. He pulls a sheet off the hydrostatic transmission. "You've got to take a picture of this," he said, his eyes lighting up. When he talks about farming and the land, he speaks with the deep familial love of someone who was born into this life. When he talks about transmissions and old equipment, he speaks with the more urgent passion of someone who loves their craft.

He's got two commercial shipping boxes in the shop that he's turning into mobile slaughterhouses. He's got a homemade walk-in freezer full of his beef and pork from neighboring Walnut Hill Farm. "When you consider the future of ag in Vermont," he said, "you see that the landscape is there. The people are there. All that's missing is infrastructure, and much of it basic and simple. It probably cost $5,000

to make this freezer, and it holds about $18,000 worth of meat. It's been transformational for two different farm families."

We look at a combine that's too small to be of any use on a large commercial farm, but is just the right size to harvest buckwheat with friends from Laughing Child Farm down the road – something he's doing that afternoon. The grain will be sold to Naga Bakehouse, an artisanal bakery in Middletown Springs. We see a similar vintage Massy Ferguson self-propelled windrower with a draper head for swathing grains. "This is worthless equipment on a large farm," he said. "But there's a ton of value to us. One windrow of premium grain can be worth $600 or $700."

"What's really exciting," said Leach, "is that a grain production system can work in concert with a rotational grazing system. You could almost make enough to buy a farm and support a family this way."

We visit briefly with his wife Breya and their two kids, Orrin, age two, and Rylan, age two months. I snap a few pictures of the young family, then he's off to harvest the buckwheat. There's not a hint of melancholy or hesitation in any of it; just strength and smarts and purpose. —*Dave Mance III*

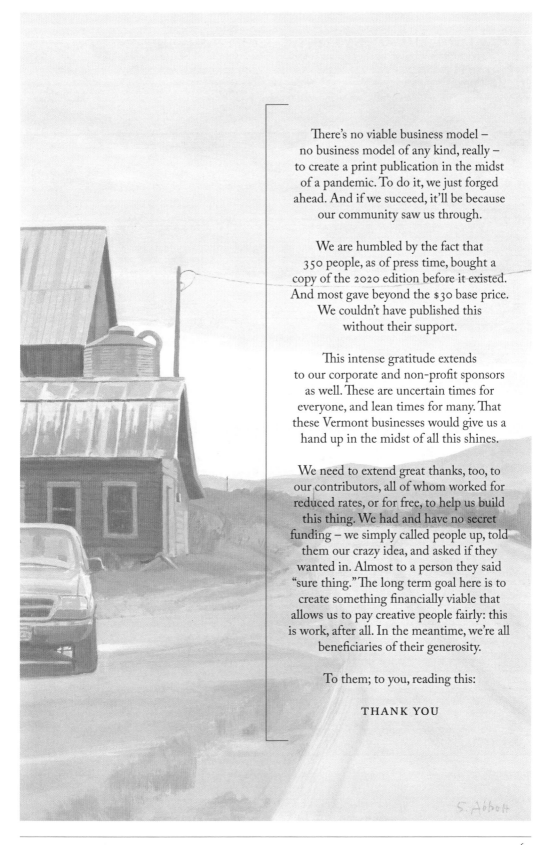

There's no viable business model –
no business model of any kind, really –
to create a print publication in the midst
of a pandemic. To do it, we just forged
ahead. And if we succeed, it'll be because
our community saw us through.

We are humbled by the fact that
350 people, as of press time, bought a
copy of the 2020 edition before it existed.
And most gave beyond the $30 base price.
We couldn't have published this
without their support.

This intense gratitude extends
to our corporate and non-profit sponsors
as well. These are uncertain times for
everyone, and lean times for many. That
these Vermont businesses would give us a
hand up in the midst of all this shines.

We need to extend great thanks, too, to
our contributors, all of whom worked for
reduced rates, or for free, to help us build
this thing. We had and have no secret
funding – we simply called people up, told
them our crazy idea, and asked if they
wanted in. Almost to a person they said
"sure thing." The long term goal here is to
create something financially viable that
allows us to pay creative people fairly: this
is work, after all. In the meantime, we're all
beneficiaries of their generosity.

To them; to you, reading this:

**THANK YOU**

# MAY

# May

It had been a mild winter, with temperatures staying mostly above zero. The ice went out early, leading to optimism about the onset of warm weather. But then winter decided it wasn't going anywhere. Cold days, high winds, and snow squalls were the norm through April. Snow-covered forsythia blooms are a dazzling sight, but not universally appreciated.

Robert Frost had it exactly right:

> *"You're one month on in the middle of May.*
> *But if you so much as dare to speak,*
> *a cloud comes over the sunlit arch,*
> *And wind comes off a frozen peak,*
> *And you're two months back in the middle of March."*

After one more snow – this one in the second week of May – my husband and I set off for a hike. It was a modest peak that we'd hiked before, one long-ago autumn. This time, instead of looking up and out at red and yellow leaves, we spent quite a bit of time looking down at the forest floor. Spring wildflowers were out in abundance, especially in the lower woodlands where our trail began. The woods were threaded by stone walls and a brook, and carpeted by trout lilies. Most of the flowers had yet to bloom, but some had half-open yellow blossoms. There were red trilliums, too, or wake-robins, the first I'd seen this spring.

As the trail rose, we began to see snow on rocks and roots. The steep parts of the trail were flowing, so we criss-crossed our way up, keeping our boots as dry as possible. There was more snow as we climbed, and I was glad I'd thrown my winter hat and gloves into my pack. On a snowmobile bridge, someone had drawn a heart and a face in the snow – probably some children who had arrived in the only other car at the trailhead. At the top, we had views to the south and west, and a peek northward to white summits. Ski runs stood out on the gray and green mountainsides.

After enjoying the view from the top and a spur trail, we headed downhill. Where the trail flattened out, there was a plank bridge in full sunshine. Down we lay on our bellies, with our heads over the edge so we could look into the stream. Last year's layered leaves were crystal clear in the cold water. My plan was just to contemplate the universe and savor the quiet spring woods; to simply be slow and be still. We got something more than that. Just as your eyes adjust in the dark and you notice more and more stars, our eyes adjusted to the microcosm below.

The stream was not just water trickling over leaves; it was a lifescape coming gradually into focus. Fuzzy green algae; egg masses in twiggy nooks; tiny, scooting arthropods; and a moving matchstick the same color as the oak and beech leaves. It was a caddisfly grazing its way along the stream bottom, scooping up an invisible layer of fungi and bacteria. The larva had built itself a protective case out of the available leaves, in a design that suggested the bands of a woolly bear caterpillar. Soon, I noticed a second caddisfly. And another…the more I watched, the more I found. Amazingly, the design was nearly identical on each case.

I had no desire to pick up a crawly caddisfly. But at a vernal pool, I picked up a transparent, grapefruit-sized jelly that contained the eggs of a hundred or so spotted salamanders, shining in the sun's rays. Later I would consult books and biologists. But right then I was just glad I had slowed down – and realized how seldom I do, and why I should more often. —*Laurie D. Morrissey*

# Winter's Last Gasp

May 2020 was a tale of two weather patterns, to borrow from Charles Dickens. The first two weeks were much colder than normal. High-latitude blocking up in the Arctic region pushed a jet stream and storm track south, delivering a long stretch of late-winter-like conditions in Vermont. The coldest stretch, between May 4th and 13th, featured highs that were only in the 40s and 50s.

The coldest daytime high was just 34 degrees on May 9th – that's 21.2 degrees below normal for that date. Snow was recorded on the 8th and 9th, with nearly 2 inches reported in many valleys and around 5 inches at the stake atop Mount Mansfield. The Valley of Vermont in our southwestern corner took the brunt of this storm, with totals in places exceeding 8 inches. This would be the last measurable snowfall of the 2019-2020 snow season.

*May 9:*
*Eight inches of snow on the level in Shaftsbury.*
*Higher elevations saw close to 10 inches.*

The second half of May – roughly from the 14th on – saw much-welcomed warmer weather. Daytime highs reached into the 60s, and warmed into the 70s from about the 18th to the 23rd. Things got even warmer, with a stretch of near-record heat on the 26th and 27th.

The early May Arctic air was very dry, as is usually the case. That meant that despite colder temperatures, we saw many sunny days. Consequently, the month averaged partly to mostly sunny with about 40 percent sky cover or 60 percent open to sunshine.

Thunderstorms were recorded on May 4th, 11th, 23rd, 24th, and 25th, with many people observing that these daily storms seemed to pop a little after the 12:30 p.m. time frame. Late in the month, a very warm and humid air mass migrated into Vermont; the overnight lows were only in the mid-60s, with higher humidity in the region.

Precipitation overall was below normal at 2.47 inches, or just 73 percent of normal – a sign, it turned out, of things to come. —*Roger Hill, Weathering Heights*

# NATURE NOTES

**MOST YEARS, PEAR THRIPS** are not that big a deal. But during drawn-out springtimes like this one, when the buds break but then cold weather delays leaf expansion, the damage can get ugly. In some cases, the tiny non-native insects cut the compressed leaf with their sharp mouthparts – when the leaf fully opens, the effect is similar to when you fold a piece of paper and cut a snowflake pattern into it with scissors. In other cases, they scrape and damage the plant tissue, which leads to stunted, curled, mottled leaves. We don't often see them because we don't often look; also because they spend most of their lives underground.

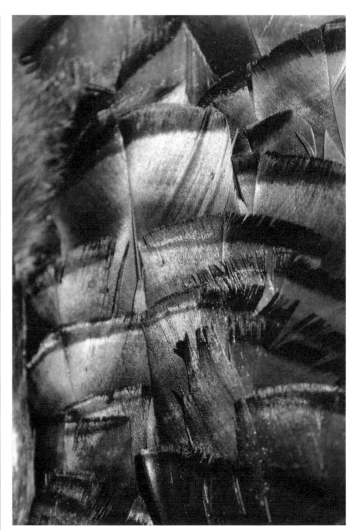

## *Turkeys: Not so Drab*

Wild turkeys have a reputation of being sort of ugly, especially compared to the flamboyant songbirds that take center stage this time of year. And yet any turkey hunter will tell you that, up close, a wild turkey's feathers are far more colorful than you'd ever imagine. Here's a closer look, courtesy of a turkey hunter who asked to remain anonymous.

## MOREL VS FALSE MOREL

There are two common "toxic look-alikes" that share the woods with morels. One is *Verpa spp.*, which have a cap and stem that's sort of like a morel on the outside but filled with cottony material, whereas morels have hollow interiors. Verpa caps overlap their stem and connect at the top, whereas morel caps and stems are seamless. But that might be too much information. Just remember that if there's cottony material inside, that's bad. We've heard of people eating Verpas on purpose, but most books suggest that you steer clear.

The truly toxic look-alikes (and "look-alike" is a bit of a stretch) are the *Gyromitra* species. (The one pictured here is *G. brunnea*.) They're sort of brainy looking in places, which might confuse a novice, but they're built much squatter than a morel. Mature, they're almost round – and any ridges and pits on the cap will not be uniform. You can see from the close-up photograph here that the stems are not hollow, so there's really no mistaking the two if you remember this.

*Above: Morel; below: False morel*

# Little Brown Butterflies
## and the Pandemic

BRYAN PFEIFFER

Although it is a prized sighting among North American lepidopterists, let's be honest: the bog elfin *(Callophrys lanoraieensis)* is not a particularly attractive butterfly. Brown with messy black and rusty markings, and no bigger than your thumbnail, the elfin displays none of the flash and glitter of fritillaries, for example, or even the emerald hues of its many elfin cousins.

And yet for two decades I have been searching for the bog elfin here in Vermont – without finding it. During my most recent expedition, I devoted three days to not finding any bog elfins. And what you probably do not know is that unlike many butterfly outings, a bog elfin search is no walk in the park or jaunt among the wildflowers.

In order to find this butterfly you must first get yourself to a bog in late May, which usually requires bushwhacking with a map and compass or GPS – all the while with a cloud of black flies attacking your head and neck. Your 62-year-old, arthritic right knee does not help – it is, in fact, worse than black flies on these bushwhacks. That is until you reach the bog, which is open, wet and squishy, and therefore better than ibuprofen. Bogs temporarily cure old knees.

And although you will find plenty of lovely pink, purple, and white flowers on the bog, you will not find nectaring among them any bog elfins. You might, however, find their close cousins, brown elfins *(Callophrys augustinus)*. That's a mating pair of brown elfins in the accompanying image. And the only reason I can bring you this photograph is because of the steadfast reluctance of bog elfins to show themselves, and the particular antics you must employ to find bog elfins (even when they are nowhere to be found at a bog).

Rather than prance about sipping nectar, bog elfins spend a good part of their lives sitting around on black spruce *(Picea mariana)* trees that grow from the bog mat. From those stunted-yet-lofty perches, bog elfins have no interest whatsoever in visiting with any human, much less one gimping along with a bad knee and trailed by a cloud of black flies. We are beneath them. Although I am somewhat reluctant to make the comparison, it's as if a bog elfin were up there dispatching its battalions of biting insects to attack even the most earnest lepidopterist, like the Wicked Witch of the West deploying her flying monkeys at Dorothy.

So, in order to dislodge a bog elfin from its perch, you must thwack black spruce trees with your insect net and hope to catch sight of it darting away. And you cannot perform this exercise casually. Remember, these are among the smallest butterflies on the continent. When you thwack the spruce, all sorts of stuff might come tumbling or flying off: bits of lichen or spruce cone scales, for example, or little brown moths (which, fortunately, are distinguishable because they fly with none of the dignity of a bog elfin).

Over the course of our three-day search, my partner on the expedition, Josh Lincoln, and I thwacked or tapped no fewer than 800 black spruce trees of all sizes on bogs across northeastern Vermont. Never did a bog elfin launch from any of these trees (at least none that we could detect). In fact, the only butterflies to launch were that mating pair (end-to-end) of brown elfins, which landed on the leaf of a Labrador tea *(Ledum groenlandicum)* for the photo. Josh and I also noticed another female brown elfin laying one of her powder-blue eggs on a leaf of a bog laurel *(Kalmia polifolia)*.

Though we did not notice any bog elfins, we had no regrets. I have a policy about bogs: No complaining on a bog. Ever. And at this point in this essay I am committing an unmitigated nature-writing cliché by telling you that my failed bog elfin expedition was in any event more about the journey. Yeah, we missed bog elfins. No surprise there. But on our first morning a bull moose sauntered close enough to us that we could smell him. A Canada warbler, gunmetal-gray above and highway-paint-yellow below, with a jet-black necklace, posed full-frontal for us and sang his fidgety song. A fisher emerged from the woods and practically bumped into Josh. And lucia azures *(Celastrina lucia)*, another thumbnail butterfly, flashed like little blue flames at our feet across the bogs.

But beyond the cliché, our expedition gave me something even greater than the journey: normalcy. As strange as it might seem for grown men to thrash around the woods and walk across bogs thwacking trees with butterfly nets, the bog elfin, mythical or not here in Vermont, rescued us for a three-day furlough from the pandemic. Once we cleared "civilization," Josh and I saw not a soul on or around these bogs. Nobody. For three days I could rub my eyes, pick my nose, not wash my hands, forget about the plague, and simply chase butterflies with a dear friend.

The coronavirus pandemic has broken so much of what it means to be human: to gather together with family and friends, to exchange love and ideas, experience and opportunity. Virtually every facet of our lives, every pillar of society and culture, has changed – perhaps for a long time. And yet nature remains among the few things in our world unchanged. Butterflies know nothing of the plague. They wear no protective masks. They dance on the winds carefree and sip nectar from shared meadow wildflowers and communal backyard gardens. Or just sit there atop black spruce trees in remote bogs.

To be sure, a bog in northern Vermont is the epitome of physical distancing. Even so, perhaps you yourself, seeking refuge, need not bushwhack so far and search high and low for a little brown butterfly. Maybe your respite is closer to home.

For centuries we humans have philosophized about the sublime transcendence to be found in the natural world. In that sense, the human mind is indeed a potent force, maybe even stronger than a plague. After all, to escape a virus I cannot see in my community, I found refuge in a little brown butterfly I never saw on a bog. —*Bryan Pfeiffer*

AT HOME

✖✖✖

## *Keep Roots Damp*

Christmas tree season comes in May, at least for growers in the state. At Meadow Ridge Farm, we plant about 800 trees around this time each year. Regardless of the type or number of trees you might be interested in planting, the rules we follow for transplant care can be applied to any bare-root stock.

Our transplants come to us in bundles of 100, packed in wetted sawdust and rolled in burlap to help ensure the bare roots – which no longer have soil to protect them – remain moist. The key is to keep them that way. We store the bundles on our cool garage floor in the dark and pour water over them every couple of days. When a bundle is ready to plant, we put about 20 transplants in each of several 5-gallon buckets that are half-full of water (again, to keep the roots wet), and rewrap the rest. The goal is always to minimize the time that the roots are exposed to sun or wind (this photo was just for illustrative purposes!). Even minutes can dry roots out on a hot, breezy day. Rewetting them at that point is useless – the damage has been done. So we lug the buckets of trees around the field, pulling one out only when there's a hole ready for it. — *Patrick White*

# Seed Sowing

Seed packets typically have a lot of information about seed spacing, thinning, distance between rows, and number of days until harvest. But soil temperature is what many seeds really care about. Here's what we learned from the High Mowing Organic Seeds planting chart, shown at right ("T" means that in our region transplanting started plants is the most likely way to succeed).

You don't need to go to a garden supply store to get a soil thermometer. Just poke a meat thermometer (or really any longish regular thermometer) four inches into the ground to find the temperature.

How long does it take for seeds to germinate? There's a big range, often listed on the seed packet, but soil temperatures at the high end of the germinating range produce seedlings the fastest. Carrots, for instance, take about 10 days to germinate when the soil is 60 degrees and a bit less than 5 days at 85 degrees. You won't see little spinaches until two weeks after planting the seeds if the soil is 45 degrees, but they'll be popping up in just five or so days if the soil is 77 degrees. Another reason to wait for the soil to warm up is that the longer a seed waits in the soil, the more time fungi and seed predators have to do what they do. If it's on the cold side, you'll also have to keep the soil watered for a longer time.

You may have noticed that celery is not on this list, and there's a reason for that. Those fussy seeds require diffuse light and night temperatures that are 10 to 15 degrees lower than the day temperature.

### SOIL TEMP
*(in degrees F)*

#### AS SOON AS THE GROUND CAN BE WORKED

| | |
|---|---|
| Beets | 60-85 |
| Brussels sprouts | 65-75 |
| Carrots | 60-85 |
| Kohlrabi | 65-85 |
| Parsnips | 50-65 |
| Peas | 50-75 |
| Radishes | 55-85 |
| Spinach | 45-65 |
| Turnips | 60-95 |

#### AFTER THE LAST HARD FROST

| | |
|---|---|
| Broccoli | 65-85 |
| Cabbage | 55-95 |
| Cauliflower | 55-80 |
| Cilantro, dill, parsley | 50-80 |
| Fennel | 60-65 |
| Lettuce | 40-80 |

#### AFTER THE LAST FROST

| | |
|---|---|
| Basil | 70-90 |
| Beans | 60-80 |
| Corn | 60-95 |
| Cucumber | 75-90 |
| Melons (T) | 75-95 |
| Okra (T) | 75-95 |
| Peppers (T) | 68-95 |
| Pumpkin | 70-90 |
| Summer/winter squash | 70-90 |
| Tomatoes (T) | 60-85 |
| Watermelon (T) | 75-95 |
| Zucchini | 70-90 |

*May 20, 2020*

❧

# Cooking Wild Turkey

You can see the remnants of a lovely spring meal in the accompanying photo. We opened things with shots of chaga-infused vodka. (Jelly jars full of violet-syrup-infused rhubarb juice for the kids.) We then feasted on freshly procured wild turkey (with trout lily and toothwort garnish), sautéed fiddleheads and nettles, potato leek salad and latkes. For dessert we had meringues drizzled with violet syrup and mugs of black birch tea. All in all it was a great success.

I don't feel like I have any particular expertise to share where it comes to preparing the vegetable, flower, and fungal portions of the meal. If you're new to foraging, you can find recipes ranging from decent to great online for almost any of this. If you simply substitute leek for onion and blanched nettles for spinach and fiddleheads for asparagus in your go-to dishes, you'll be fine, too.

I do feel like I have some hard-won knowledge regarding wild turkey, though, which I'll share. For years I tried, like a lot of people do, to cook it like a domestic bird. But this is the oldest mistake in the book. Some swear by tricks that let you get around this – like flipping the whole bird upside down as you cook it – but they've never worked for me. The breast meat is so lean, and the thighs and legs so sinewy and laced with bone-hard tendons that I can't see a way around treating the cuts separately. If you don't, you're going to have cooked breast meat and iron legs, or edible legs with shoe-leather breast meat.

Even when you recognize this, though, you've got to be careful. I've still had birds end up rubbery after separating and fussing and braising the meat low and slow.

I nailed the preparation of the spring turkey for this meal, and here's how I did it.

Step one was a brine. My go-to recipe is 3 quarts of water, ¾ cup kosher salt, 1.5 cups soy sauce, 2 cups brown sugar, 1 cup maple syrup, 3 heads garlic, 2 hands ginger, hot pepper flakes, and whatever herbs I'm feeling in the moment. But feel free to experiment. Heat the brine to a simmer and stir to dissolve the salt and sugar. Then cool to room temp before submerging and then refrigerating the bird. If you remove the backbone from the carcass, and separate the thigh/leg portions from the breast, you can fit a big tom into a three-gallon crock, which will easily fit in a fridge.

When it was time to cook things, I separated the breast meat from the carcass and the legs from the thighs. I drizzled the carcass with oil and put it in the oven to brown for about an hour – I'd use it later for soup. I took the thighs and legs and put them in a large braising pot, then poured the brine in until the meat was just submerged. All this liquid didn't feel right to me – one of the rules of braising is you don't want to drown the meat. But I drowned it, just like it was beef stew. I simmered it for about three hours. I then removed the meat, shredded it, and put it in

a casserole dish with some schmaltz (chicken fat) I had in the freezer. (To make schmaltz, next time you cook a chicken, render the fat, pour the liquid into a canning jar, and throw it into the freezer.) I then let the shredded turkey meat crisp up in the chicken fat for about 15 minutes in a 450 degree oven. If you've ever made pork carnitas, it's the same technique.

The breast meat I poached, using the same brine bath I cooked the dark meat in. The deal with poaching is that you do not want the liquid to simmer. You want it to be around 160 degrees. It took about an hour to cook. While the breast meat poached, I made a simple pan gravy.

The results were spot-on. Crispy, chewy dark meat and moist, succulent breast meat. The two textures complemented each other. My brother, having been subjected to rubbery wild turkey over the years, sheepishly brought hot dogs over for the kids, just in case the turkey didn't come out. They're still sitting, unopened, in the fridge.

Cookbook author Hank Shaw, who maintains a fabulous online game-meat cooking archive, was the one who inspired me to try these cooking techniques. The original source of my brine recipe has been lost to time. —Dave Mance III

# Danger Zone

USDA plant hardiness zone maps (planthardiness. ars.usda.gov) are based on the average annual lowest temperature at a given place, not necessarily the very coldest. It's at a certain temperature that many common garden plants, trees, and shrubs are killed. Some plants can't tolerate any frost at all; others are fine until even -40 degrees. But every plant has a limit to its cold tolerance.

On the 1990 hardiness map, much of Vermont was in zone 4. That's when the coldest nights

get to -30 degrees F. In 2012, when the USDA published its most recent plant hardiness map, more of Vermont was in Zone 5, where the coldest expected temperatures are -20. zones are separated by 10 degrees F, but now for every zone there's a further division – for instance, Zone 4A (-30) and Zone 4B (-25).

In the 25 or so years between publication of these two most recent maps, most of the United States got bumped up a half-zone, which equates to being 5 degrees warmer. Then there's the reality that the rate of warming

has increased in recent years.

In the last 100 years, the growing season in Vermont – the number of frost-free days – has increased by about one day per decade. Interestingly, most of these 10 extra gardening days are in the autumn, not the spring.

Climate change, on the other hand, is not an event – not a frosty or frost-free or a very cold night. It's more like a condition, deduced from an average of an almost infinite number of temperature readings, hot, cold, and middling. Here, we're a tad more than 2 degrees warmer now than a century ago.

# A LOOK BACK

## *A Narrative of a Tour Through the State of Vermont*

### FROM APRIL 27 TO JUNE 12, 1789, BY THE REV. NATHAN PERKINS

"y$^e$ people nasty."

Nathan Perkins was born in 1749, the great-great grandson of John Perkins, who landed in Boston in 1631. He would go on to spend 65 years as pastor of the Third Church of West Hartford, Connecticut, and earn two degrees from Princeton and one from Yale. Perhaps his most extraordinary accomplishment, though, was a nearly two-month solo journey on horseback through Vermont in 1789. This life-long city-dweller was sent to take stock of the new frontier – the land, its people, and the state of religion there. He liked only some of what he saw.

"As a diary, written for his own eye, it is hardly open to criticism," noted the Elm Tree Press in a 1920 printing of Perkins' rather blunt narrative. "Yet its frankness makes it amusing, and, apart from its historical value, it is a human document of no little interest. The writer was a keen judge of men and women, and recognized and admired the courage and endurance of the settlers of the new country...."

*New Haven – preached at a log house, – people serious and anxious to hear yᵉ word. – I was greatly worried & fatigued with riding, – poor living, nothing but brook water to drink, – & no comfortable victuals, – my nature almost exhausted, – went to Mr. Cooke's in New-haven, Friday & Saturday morning nine o'Clock, preached, in a log house, & yᵉ people wonderfully attentive. Slept, in an open log house, where it rained on me, in yᵉ night, & no keeping for my horse. Saturday 16th of May rode on after preaching to Moreton, – Pockock – mud belly deep to my horse, & I thought I should have perished: felt warm gratitude to heaven that my life was spared, – my health & strength continued, through such hardships & unwholesome food, – arrived just at night at Mr. Steeles my old parishioner, – was cordially welcome, & gratefully received at Hinsburgh. – preached 3th Sabbath in May, at his house, – a large audience for yᵉ wilderness, & deeply attentive. He lives well. Land good – gathered yᵉ church & organized them on Wednesday, preached a lecture & baptised a Child for Mr. Elisha Steele. Thursday 20 of May set out for Williston where governor Chittenden lives. – baptised five children, rode through yᵉ woods, 14 miles, yᵉ riding as bad as it could be, almost half of yᵉ trees in yᵉ woods blown down by yᵉ violence of yᵉ wind last year. Came to one Deacon Talcotts and he accompanied me to his Excellency's Governor Chittenden's. A low poor house. – a plain family – low, vulgar man, clownish, excessively parsimonious, – made me welcome, – hard fare, a very great farm, – 1000 acres, – hundred acres of wheat on yᵉ onion river – 200 acres of extraordinary interval land. A shrewd cunning man – skilled in human nature & in agriculture – understands extremely well yᵉ mysteries of Vermont, apparently and professedly serious. Williston a fine township of land, – soil fertile. And all yᵉ towns upon yᵉ lake Champlain & for three teer back yᵉ best sort of land. Not very heavy timbered, or stony or mountainous, well intersected with streams, & yᵉ streams full of small fish. – Two noted streams yᵉ Otter-Creek and yᵉ onion river – About 300 towns in the State of Vermont – 6 miles square – about 40 of yᵉ towns upon yᵉ green mountains – very cold – snow upon yᵉ top of them till June; commonly – good grazing land about half way up yᵉ green mountains – they almost end at latitude 44 1-2 – I go up as far as there are any settlements large enough to gather a Congregation – within thirty miles of Canada line – days perceivably longer – in reality 20 minutes longer. Moose plenty on yᵉ mountains over against Jericho, Essex & Colchester – people hunt them – eat them in lieu of beef – & get their tallow. Bears & wolves plenty – timber, beach, maple, – pine, cherry – birch & some oak and Walnut – about as many as 40 families, in a town, upon an average, about 40 towns totally unsettled – land extraordinarily good – from Rutland & Tinmouth clear to Canada line. Curiosities of yᵉ country – yᵉ innumerable high mountains 3 & 4 miles up them – 1-2 perpendicular. – covered with snow now three feet in depth – Lime stone in abundance scattered every where, but no good building stone – a lime pit of two acres in Sunderland – the lower end of yᵉ State poor compared to yᵉ North end – narrow & rough, – No cheese any where – no beef – no butter – I pine for home – for my own table. – Words cannot describe yᵉ hardships I undergo, or yᵉ strength of my desire to see my family – & to be with them. How affectionately do I remember them, hundreds of times every day, & shed a tear, in yᵉ woods – got lost twice in yᵉ woods already – heard yᵉ horrible howling of yᵉ wolves. Far absent – in yᵉ wilderness – among all strangers – all alone – among log-huts – people nasty – poor – low-lived – indelicate – and miserable cooks. All sadly parsimonious – many, profane – yet cheerful & much more contented than in Hartford – and the women more contented than yᵉ men – turned tawny by yᵉ smoke of yᵉ log-huts – dress coarse, & mean, & nasty, & ragged. – Some very clever women & men – serious & sensible. Scarcely any politeness in yᵉ State – Scarcely any sensible preaching – will soon settle Ministers in most of yᵉ towns – and in a few years will be a good Country, pleasant, & well to live in.*

# INDUSTRY

## *Seeds of Hope*

*"We're out of bulk cucumbers and squash. And strawberry plants.
And seed potatoes. And onion starts. We have a few asparagus left – that's it.
We've never sold out of everything this early in the 40 years I've been here."*

ELDERLY WOMAN BEHIND THE COUNTER OF A FEED STORE IN A SMALL TOWN

Reports from all over the region hold that there's been a surge in gardening this spring, an idea that shines in the midst of a pandemic that's killed 100,000 Americans in the past three months.

The conventional explanation is survivalist in nature: people are afraid of food shortages so they're taking matters into their own hands. We tend to see it more in spiritual terms. We shed our anxiety, or our grief, or our anger, by breaking ground. The world comes at us with waves of incomprehensible change, and so we look down to what moors us. We turn soil and turn inward towards something basic and primal and pure.

As World War I raged, more than a century ago, the poet Thomas Hardy wrote the verse at right in a poem called "The Breaking of Nations."

Our crisis looks and feels different. Yet there's still comfort in this rhythm.

*Only a man harrowing clods
In a slow silent walk
With an old horse that stumbles and nods
Half asleep as they stalk.*

*Only thin smoke without flame
From the heaps of couch-grass;
Yet this will go onward the same
Though Dynasties pass.*

As if 2020 couldn't get any stranger, mystery seeds from China began showing up randomly in some mailboxes during the summer. The source and type of seeds could not be immediately identified, and they should not have been planted. On a related note, in September retail giant Amazon banned the sale of foreign seed in the US.

# Vermont's Seed Law

Did you know that Vermont has a seed law, harkening back to 1908, that requires seeds be labeled truthfully regarding their identification, purity, and viability?

Companies that wish to sell seeds in Vermont must register with the Vermont Agency of Agriculture Food and Markets. Currently 115 companies are registered. Of these, 22 are located in Vermont. All types of seeds must be registered, including agricultural, turf, floral, vegetable, herb, tree, shrub, and hemp seeds.

Seed packages must be labeled correctly and include the name and kind of each seed, the lot number, and the name and address of the labeler or distributor, the percent of germination, and the calendar month and year the test was done (except for vegetable and flower seeds for home gardens, which may simply state the year for which the seeds were packaged and the "sell by" year). Agricultural and grass seed labels must also state the origin of the seeds, as well as the percent by weight of all weed seeds, crop seeds, and inert matter. If the seeds have been treated, this must also be stated on the label, along with any related cautionary statements (if the amount of substance used for treatment could be harmful to humans or animals). If seed is genetically engineered, it must be disclosed on the label along with relevant traits or characteristics. Marketplace inspections are routinely conducted to make sure seed dealers comply with labeling rules.

The Seed Law also requires seed dealers to annually report the amount of seed sold in Vermont in packages greater than 10 pounds. Around 4,000 tons of seeds are sold in bulk in Vermont annually. This includes agricultural crop seeds, turf seeds, and hemp seeds. The Agency of Agriculture does not track sales of seeds in packages less than 10 pounds.

In 2020, the legislature passed more stringent laws for establishing a Hemp Seed Program. In addition to registering as a seed dealer and following general seed labeling guidelines, hemp seed dealers must also state the name and type of each seed, whether the hemp seed was certified by a state or foreign country, and the percent of feminized seed, which is specifically bred to produce female plants, a desirable trait when growing for CBD. This is the first time that Vermont has required feminization to be listed on seed labels.

Vermont does not require seed dealers to report on the type of seed sold in the state, but it appears that the recent increase in the number of registered seed dealers is due to the sale of hemp seeds. Information from other sources indicates that feed corn and, to a lesser extent, soybeans, cereal grains, and grass seed for forage, fodder, and hay are the predominant agricultural seeds sold in Vermont.

Vermont's Seed Law may seem minor, but it is an important law that's been safeguarding our agricultural community and home gardens since 1908.

*Lisa Fantelli*
*Feed, Seed & Fertilizer Specialist*
*Vermont Agency of Agriculture, Food & Markets*

# From Small Beginnings...

## HIGH MOWING SEEDS HAS GROWN UP IN VERMONT

Tear open a packet of seeds, shake some out in your hand. What do you see? They're small, by all appearances inert. A grower, farmer, or gardener will probably also see possibility – a glimpse two seasons ahead at how much future life exists within. But have you ever thought back to where those seeds came from, and how they came to be in that packet in your hand? After all, there's just as much life in a seed's past as there is in its future.

High Mowing Seeds, based in Wolcott, is the only 100 percent certified organic and non-GMO project-verified seed company in the country. It began in 1996, when founder Tom Stearns was 19 years old. "We have been organic from the start," said Andrea Tursini, the company's director of sales and marketing. "So, from the beginning, we've been a little bit different than the norm."

While the organic component has remained unchanged, pretty much everything else about High Mowing Seeds – its scale, processes, technology, and customer base – have evolved and grown tremendously.

Stearns began harvesting vegetable and flower seed himself, all in Vermont, and selling it through a hand-drawn catalog. Those humble beginnings provided plenty of authenticity, but also came with limitations. The reality, explained Tursini, is that different crops grow best in different climatic conditions: "Lots of people assume that we still grow all of our seed here in Vermont. But if we were to do that, some of the seed that we would come up with would be very low quality."

Lettuce, for example, grows really well in the Pacific Northwest, where the summers are very dry. So these days, that's where High Mowing looks for its lettuce seed. The same approach applies to other crops: the company identifies partners in the very best production areas for a given seed and contracts with them. "This enables us to have a measure of control over who we work with; we want to work with people who are values-aligned, who produce high quality seed, and who understand our standards," said Tursini. "So seed is grown all over the world. It's really a global industry. If you want to have commercial quality seed...you have to make sure that you have the right climate conditions for growing that seed."

One reason that it can be challenging to produce seed for most crops in Vermont is our relatively short growing season. "Seed often takes longer to mature than the fruit or the vegetable does. So it'll be in the field for much longer. A crop such as tomatoes also requires extra processing and fermentation after harvest in order to produce viable seed," noted Tursini. Other crops even require overwintering before they will produce seed. There are a few crop varieties for which High Mowing still produces seed in the Green Mountains. "Things like melons, corn, squash, and tomatoes can all grow and mature and produce

*Company founder Tom Stearns,*
*with a whole lot of Shishito pepper seeds.*

*A 40-acre farm in northern Vermont is used to grow crops for seed harvest, as well as to test-grow seeds produced elsewhere. Here, Reemay is removed from a crop of honeynut squash.*

IMAGES COURTESY OF HIGH MOWING SEEDS

high-quality seed in Vermont," she said.

And Vermont is still very much the heart of the High Mowing Seeds' operation. For starters, every seed the company sells, no matter where it is grown, is brought into the company's Wolcott facility, providing the ability to check and confirm that everything meets its quality standards. "Seed is a living product. So it has a life cycle," said Tursini. "And it can remain viable for many years. But at a certain point, it's going to die. And we want to make sure that we're selling it within a viable life."

To that end, lab technicians at High Mowing conduct germination tests every four to six months, depending on the crop. They look for vigor as well as purity. There are also trial teams growing seeds out in the field. In other words, the seed doesn't arrive and just sit on a shelf – there's an active process running continuously behind the scenes. "Quality control, I think, is really the heart of our business. Organic seed in particular needs to be really solid with quality. People are not going to switch to organic seeds instead of conventional seeds if the quality isn't the same," said Tursini.

## AN ORGANIC START

Most people, when they think about organic produce, probably think of the organic processes under which a crop is managed. But High Mowing Seeds sees starting with organic seed as a critical piece of the overall puzzle. "That's because, in terms of an environmental impact, the seed takes so much longer to mature in the ground than the fruit or the vegetable does. So when you're producing seeds conventionally, it requires that many more pesticides, herbicides, fungicides to keep that plant healthy because it's around for so long," said Tursini.

High Mowing Seeds must continually bring to market varieties that meet the needs of organic commercial growers. "Organic growers want to use organic, but they also want to have varieties that work for them. So part of our work is to bring new and better genetics to the table that are specifically suited for those organic systems."

The process begins by identifying the "study question," Tursini explains. "We might be looking for a heat-tolerant broccoli that has some specific disease resistance. So then breeders – and we often work with

STORIES FROM & FOR THE LAND

183

*Seed germination tests are continually conducted in the High Mowing Seeds lab.*

university breeders – will work with companies that both breed and produce seed. They'll look at the suite of genetics and see if they can come up with a variety that meets our customers' needs." But breeding takes time, and success is not guaranteed. Once you've got material to work with, it still needs to be tested repeatedly in a variety of locations. (High Mowing Seeds sells across both the United States and Canada, so it needs varieties that are well adapted for a variety of locations.) "We trial it repeatedly at our own farm here in Vermont; we trial it with customers and in different places across the country. And then if we decide that it meets our needs, we'll add it to our catalog," she said.

Even if the company identifies a seed that works well for growers, it also has to be sure it can produce that commercially. "One of the things you don't want to do is bring a new variety to market that people love, only to discover that it's actually very difficult to produce seed for. For example, there are some tomatoes that we've been working on with a partner breeder that are very low in seed – which is delightful for the consumer, but not great if you're trying to produce seed to sell."

### THE COVID CRUSH

There are plenty of logistical hurdles involved in running a multinational company in the best of times, but those challenges grew exponentially when the coronavirus struck in early 2020. Covid reached American shores full-force in mid-March, but High Mowing Seeds began to see an uptick in sales a

couple of months prior, when cases were isolated on the West Coast. "Our commerce manager was saying, 'I wonder if this increase is because of Covid?'" Tursini recalled. "Then all of a sudden, in mid-March, everything changed."

About half of High Mowing Seeds' customers are commercial growers. The remaining 50 percent are split about evenly between home gardeners who order directly through the company's website and those who buy from the rack at their local hardware store or garden center. The company's busiest time of the year, traditionally, is January, February, and March. "So we were expecting to be on the downward trend at that point," she said. But when people began to recognize the ramifications of a national shutdown, and as national food chains became a concern, interest in locally grown food and in home gardening blew up. And so did the phone lines and ecommerce orders at High Mowing.

"We were running 300 to 500 percent higher than the same time period the previous year in terms of revenue. And in terms of number of orders, it was much higher than that, because there were lots of home gardeners purchasing smaller quantities," said Tursini. "We very quickly found that our operations team was overwhelmed." Technologically, the website was unable to handle that increase in volume. And the seed-packing team couldn't get seeds into envelopes fast enough to supply the demand. It was an industry-wide phenomenon. "Seed companies were

*Transplanting honeynut*

shutting down their websites, one after the other after the other," she says. "We held off absolutely as long as we could. But we did find that we needed to turn off ordering for two weeks at the end of April." That time was used to begin getting caught up on packing and fulfillment, as well as making complex changes to the website to enable "auto-scaling" technology that can accommodate spikes in traffic.

The seed industry was deemed an essential service by the State of Vermont, so employees who couldn't do their jobs from home were able to continue coming in to work, but this meant that High Mowing Seeds was forced to create and implement Covid safety policies – with no model to follow. "We formed a Covid taskforce…and tried to digest all the information that was coming from the state, CDC, and figure out how our business needed to adapt," said Tursini. "And we ended up having to create two shifts in order to have that physical distance and also navigate the increase in orders that we were handling at the same time." That was the first time we had ever had to run two shifts, and I think we will continue to do that at different times throughout the year as we need to."

The ramifications of Covid may be felt in the seed industry for some time, said Tursini. "Seed is a crop that needs to be planned at least a year ahead, sometimes two years. And I can guarantee you that nobody had Covid in mind when they were doing their crop planning two years ago. So, in some cases, supplies have been tight." Particularly, commercial growers have been encouraged to get their orders in earlier than normal.

While stressful on the entire team, Tursini said the experience of coping with Covid "was very illuminating. It really showed us where our limits are, and helped us to understand what we need to work on in order to navigate something like this in the future." Just as with the growers they serve, who may have needed to quickly find new markets for their produce, Tursini said that High Mowing Seeds was able to come through the experience successfully because it was able to pivot quickly. — *Patrick White*

*A seed counter precisely portions out seeds into packets.*

# A Pretty Good Start

The wider world is awash in anxiety these days, and so it's almost quaint to hear my 70-year-old father worrying about his seedlings. Not just a few, but 400. He stays up late reading about sapling development and nutritional guidelines; he wakes up worrying about whether they need more water during this late May dry spell. He proudly tells us about how this one grew a 9-inch-long tap root before it even sprouted, and how this other one already has not one, not two, but three leaf pairs. His grandson runs circles around him, and he proclaims that Niko is even more handsome than his seedlings, just as proudly, just as lovingly.

The objects of his affection are taking root in a very messy nursery. Dad had an overgrown spruce plantation cut over two years ago, leaving behind a sea of downed debris and brushy undergrowth. A few dead trees stick out of the melee like the broken masts of a shipwreck. When my sister first saw the site, she called it "Ragnarok," after an event that signals the end of the world in Norse mythology. Our forest management plan calls it a "seed tree cut with snags for wildlife." A biologist might call it bird heaven. After spending a few hours on a hot day there, I discerned it was also tick heaven.

Dad doesn't call it any of these things. He calls it a pretty good start. Where I see debris, he sees an opportunity. The fact that he can look at this desolate

*The author's son inspects a new crop of oak seedlings.*

landscape and see the spreading crowns of oaks and walnuts is a credit to his ability to see not just the future, but a future that he can shape for the better.

Dad's work life also involves shaping the future for the better, but in extremely hard-to-grasp ways. He promotes climate protection and clean energy policy, and the tools of that trade include seemingly boring written words on a subject that literally promotes the absence of something. That absence of something means less asthma, less acid rain and maple decline, less coastal flooding, fewer wildfires out West. But it can be a thankless task – one that requires connecting a lot of hard-to-see dots.

In his second love as forest steward, he's chosen another forward-looking task. But this one is more tangible. More relatable, too. Looking at bare land and seeing trees to climb in and eat from is the kind of thing humans have been good at for at least as long as agriculture has been around. The trees he's planting include oaks (white, red, and bur), horse chestnuts, sugar maples, black cherrys, hazelnuts, and black walnuts. He was awarded an Environmental Quality Incentives Program grant through the federal government to cover a small portion of the costs – a symbolic gift that encourages habitat improvement projects like this one. But in the end, this is a labor of sweat and love. Much of the stock he purchased from Forrest Keeling, a nursery catalog, or at the Intervale Nursery in Burlington. But he's also poured countless hours into sprouting his own oak babies: collecting acorns, germinating them, putting them in window boxes, and planting them carefully in the soil.

When I asked him why – why plant trees, why plant these trees? – he had a multi-layered answer that grew in complexity over the course of several days. At first, he said simple things: the land needs more hardwoods; right now it's mostly white pine, spruce, balsam, and cedar. Mast produced by the trees – acorns and walnuts and conkers (horse chestnuts) – will benefit wildlife. You can pay someone else to plant trees for carbon offsets, but this way you get to do it yourself. It's fun to have a project that gets me outside. Your sister promised to plant trees with me, so we get to do it together.

Then he said something that tied all those reasons together: Look at this house. It's 180 years old, and

*The author's sister hauls water to the oaks during a dry spell.*

the bones are still here. You can still see the marks of the axe blade on the beams in the ceiling. We still use the room that was the birthing and dying room for seven generations of Vermonters. The granite blocks that were laid for a dairy barn foundation are now the foundation of your mom's table garden. The two 40-plus-inch diameter maple trees out front were probably "marriage trees," planted by Sarah and Elias Tucker when this house was built to symbolize the strength of the marriage, and they're still here. This house has lasted a couple hundred years, and with the right kind of care, it might be good for a couple hundred more. The folks who built these stone walls left their mark on the land, and we can only marvel at how much work it took. Our work here is easier, but these trees will last a couple of hundred years, too.

This is his gift to the future. In a society where transferring wealth is taken to mean transferring money, Dad is passing on oak crowns, acorn-fattened bears, hazelnut-fattened children, less carbon in the atmosphere, a hardwood insurance policy (here's hoping the future won't need to cash it in), hands stained yellow-black from peeling walnuts, the idea that someday, down there at the edge of the woods, there could be a swing hanging from the stocky branch of a walnut tree. —*Meredith Cowart*

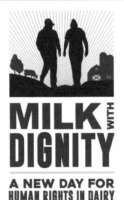

# JUNE

# *June*

On Saturdays during the novel corona crisis, I have indulged myself on Sunday mornings: no matter I'm (pinch me) 76, and no matter I've logged one "coronary event" in local hospital records, I cook bacon and eggs on that day.

This morning, as I tended the skillet, I looked up and out our kitchen window. I beheld a purple finch, a clot of wild iris, a hophornbeam still in rare bloom, a boulder striated with red quartz, and an oak whose leaves seemed exorbitantly large, given the youth of the tree.

I recognized that I'd taken these details for granted for many, many years, and, feeling somewhat ashamed, I summoned a cliché to scold myself: "You have one life to live" seemed apropos.

So I killed the heat. The breakfast treats could wait. I decided to take a tour of the house, and to proceed with a bit of deliberation. One of two living room windows looks downhill onto the little patch of playground that we fashioned when all our kids were small. A puff of breeze bent the weeds at its verges and set a swing in ghostly motion.

Next, I opened the door to the porch and gazed through screens, which blurred our pond and the beach we made back then, overtaken since by mullein and berry cane and vetch.

I watched a snapping turtle slog onto what remained of the beach's sand, intending to drop and bury her frail eggs, despite the fact that the day was raw, as many have been this June, a fact that will make the science-deniers scoff at what is lazily called global warming. Of course, we have also seen temperatures in the mid-90s, and, though I am scarcely a scientist, nowadays I suspect it's likely that anything historically "unusual" amounts to a portent of crisis.

It's not just Covid that has me thinking this way.

I remember when cedar waxwings clouded that same pond at certain easily predicted intervals in June, because various mayflies hatched as if on cue. No birds or bugs today.

We wear our sweaters. Earlier, we lit a fire.

A haze of smoke, which in such a chill should rise, sheathes the lawn instead like gossamer. —*Sydney Lea*

# Part Spring, Part Summer

Temperatures during June 2020 averaged exactly normal per climatology data at the Barre-Montpelier airport, but it was anything but an average month.

We started out very chilly, with temperatures dipping to 35 degrees at the Barre-Montpelier airport and many colder hollows seeing some frost on the first and second of the month. However a warming trend arrived on June 5, with daytime highs topping 80 – the first of many warm days to come.

Our weather in early June was still being affected by a common oscillation that began in the fall of 2019: cold frontal passages would introduce much cooler temperatures, followed by a few days of moderating – then rinse and repeat. The prevailing flow in early June stayed predominantly out of the northwest, where colder, modified-Arctic air was displaced by a dome of higher pressure located over Siberia. The Arctic itself was exceedingly above normal in temperatures, record setting, in fact; this due to a loss of Arctic sea ice and a warming climate.

The roller-coaster temperatures here in Vermont lasted into mid-June, before the weather pattern shifted to a more southerly flow. We experienced well above normal temperatures from the 16th to 24th. The warmest was 90 degrees, reached on June 20, but many days topped 85 degrees, including the 22nd and 23rd. Along with the warmth, it became increasingly humid.

Precipitation was extremely variable from location to location, as is typical with warm season convection. Summer thunderstorms can occur and unload a cloud burst in a particular area while neighboring towns bask in partial sunshine and only hear distant thunder. As one example, my location in Worcester continually landed right on the edge of storms, but we were never directly hit. Consequently, precipitation was far less than what was received at neighboring reporting stations. This created a lot of different levels of browning grass at a time of year when things are usually pretty green, and many gardeners were forced to water. This dryness, along with the slowness of green-up prior to June, may have contributed to increased bear sightings. Anecdotal reports indicate that the chilly, dry conditions in early June affected bees and beekeepers, too.

Thunderstorms occurred on six days in June: the 6th, 21st, 22nd, 23rd, 28th, and 30th, with a couple of these days recording storms that were strong to severe. Beautiful, puffy cumulus cloud formations were common. This, along with an anvil blow-off at the jet stream level, contributed to many gorgeous photo opportunities. —*Roger Hill, Weathering Heights*

ANGELINA RADOCCHIA

# N A T U R E   N O T E S

**MORE PEOPLE IN VERMONT** seek emergency treatment for tick bites in May and June than in any other months. In 2020, there were more bad tick bites than average, but not record numbers. Although there are 11 tick species in the state, the black-legged tick accounts for 99 percent of tickborne disease reported to the Vermont Department of Health. It's climate change that seems to be making a bad situation worse in our state.

## *Ghost*

This albino chipmunk was photographed in southern Vermont in June. We set up a game camera near its burrow and recorded thousands of photos and videos over a seven-day stretch. But it only appeared in about a dozen of the photos, spaced semi-regularly over the week-long span. Why? It could simply be that it's a young animal and not yet brazen enough to venture far. According to biologists Mark Elbroch and Kurt Rinehart in their book *Behavior of North American Mammals*, young-of-the-year chipmunks stick around the natal den for one to three weeks after first emerging, building courage, learning through play. There were several videos of a different young-of-the-year chipmunk chasing the white one, which seems to jive with this explanation. After the exploratory window, the mother bars the kids from the den and they disperse. Chipmunks are solitary animals, and with the exception of breeding seasons and the child-rearing window for mothers, they spend their lives alone.

Of course, another theory as to why the white chipmunk didn't come out much is that its eyes are bad. People with albinism are considered legally blind. So, if it is a true albino, and all the footage we've seen suggests it is, it likely has vision problems.

How rare are albino animals? According to the National Organization of Albinism and Hypopigmentation, one in every 18,000–20,000 people in the US has some type of albinism. A web search turned up an abstract from 1954 that estimated rates of albinism in gray squirrels in Maine at 1 in 10,000 – that's the closest we could get to estimated numbers for chipmunks. We'll never find an actual number, but safe to say it's pretty rare.

WE KNOW THE log driving history of the stream this 9-inch-diameter spruce log came out of, and we figure it was cut sometime between 1810 and 1868. We know it's of the era based on its tight growth rings. With a magnifying glass we counted 294 rings, which means the seedling that begat the log was born between 1516 and 1574.

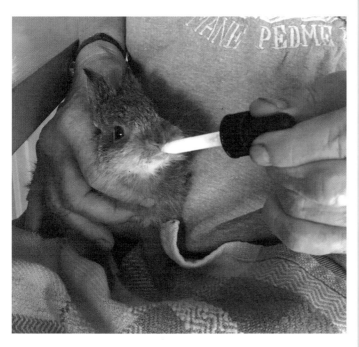

IF, BY CHANCE, you found a nest of snowshoe hare young, and you knew the mother was dead, and you figured you'd raise, wean, and release them, you might nourish them with a mixture of cat milk replacer and heavy cream from a dropper.

EARLY NEEDLE DROP in some white pines has been noted and puzzled over since 2009. Just after new needles emerge in the spring, the prior year's needles turn yellow and fall off. They're supposed to stick around and photosynthesize for a second year and this loss is stressing affected white pines, slowing their growth and sometimes killing them. Damage to susceptible trees seems to get worse every year.

In 2020 in Vermont there was a bit less of this so-called white pine needle disease than in 2019, but it's still bad throughout the state. This problem is more severe in the year following a wet spring. Because the spring of 2020 was unusually dry, perhaps there will be less of it in 2021.

Unlike many tree ills with a definitive cause, this particular ailment appears to be brought about by any or all of four species of fungus, only one of which is possibly non-native. The warmer temperatures and wetter weather of recent times may be allowing these normally weak pathogens to become more deadly.

# *Snapping Turtle Nest*

Two Junes ago, this turtle – or its relative – settled into a shady, moist corner of our yard. The thing is the size of a serving platter. My first thought was to be concerned about our cats, which might investigate and get their limbs snapped off.

On that first appearance, I consulted the local animal warden as well as an expert on turtles I found online. Their advice was to ignore it, and it would move on. It did. And we never saw an outbreak of mini turtles.

I dismissed the experience from my consciousness – that is until the snapper turned up the next year in the same place at the same time. And then, sure enough, last week, while I was bringing in the bird feeders, I saw a large lump in an open sandy area of the side yard that serves as our kitties' natural litterbox. It was the snapping turtle, digging down into the soft dirt with both of her rear legs, then pushing the sand out sideways. She was, of course, dropping eggs rather than poo.

The site is an anomaly in our heavily trafficked yard, where four 100-foot pine trees once grew. We had them taken out a decade ago to save the house from getting crushed in a blow-down, and the area has never fully revegetated. Hence its popularity as a litterbox. And, apparently, an incubator.

I watched her – entranced – for at least an hour. But the real-world question is: what do we do now? There's a pile of eggs smack in the middle of a daily transit path for humans, animals, and vehicles. Should I mark it with a stick and wait to see what happens? Internet research indicates hatching could occur as late as October. By then we will have transited the patch a dozen times with a lawnmower, not to mention daily foot traffic and weekly vehicle traffic.

I cringe at the thought of potentially cat-maiming creatures erupting from the soil as the cats squat above them, lost in concentration. I also cringe at the thought of what the cats – which, let's face it, are no angels – might do to these innocent turtles when they're interrupted.

Just another example of the endless, precarious balance between people and nature. —*Carolyn Haley*

---

*Editor's Note: We checked in with our friend David Carroll about this situation. Carroll is an author, illustrator, and naturalist who's been observing, and fighting to protect, turtles for 50 years. (His memoir is entitled "Self Portrait with Turtles," which gives you a sense of the devotion.) Here's our email exchange:*

Hi David,

. . . One of our writers filed a piece that details a snapping turtle nest that, unfortunately, is right in the middle of a heavily trafficked part of her yard. She wants to mow. She needs to drive a vehicle through there.

What would one do if they found themselves in this situation? And if there's an option to move the nest, what are the best practices one would follow?

**David Carroll responds**: Of course, the best option would be to welcome such an event and walk, drive, and work around the site; it is not such a huge area. Maybe have the compelling experience of seeing the nest hatch out. But she clearly wants her yard. Moving a snapping turtle's nest is a real project and has to be done correctly – all eggs kept in their present position, at the same depth. Maybe she has a naturalist, biologist, herpetologist friend who might want to undertake relocation.

Mowing over the nest would do no harm, driving would not impact it if tires did not directly run over it (and maybe the nest would survive even that). Stepping on it (hardly seems necessary) would not be harmful – snapping turtles lay eggs fairly deeply and usually reach back under a shelf of earth. The eggs are not likely to hatch until sometime in September, possibly into October, depending on how the summer temperatures go. Unless there are barbed wire fences along both sides of a very narrow pathway, leaving it up to fate with minimal thought beyond avoiding heavy impact or digging would seem the best route

to take. I'll show more of a bias (tilted heavily toward turtle): What good are, and how important are, lawns anyway? But then, our house insurance company has characterized our place as "overgrown" – maybe it's time to buy a ride-on mower?

My bias aside, I am grateful that she shows concern.

## POSTSCRIPT

**Carolyn Haley writes**: Thanks for getting David's response. Let him know that we observed two hatchings: September 14th and September 24th. The hatchlings were one or two inches in diameter. Counted four the first day, two the second; have not yet dug up the nest area to count shells. The two hatch groups appear to have come out of the same hole but took different routes downhill toward the pond. Don't know if any of them made it, but we each helped one across the open, dry, sunny heat of the driveway and scooted them into the grass in the right direction.

## A T   H O M E

### *Versatile Milkweed*

It's hard to think of another wild plant that has more uses for humans than milkweed. The young leaves and shoots can be eaten in spring – they're often referred to as "poor man's asparagus." This time of year, the flower buds can be harvested to make capers. Later in summer, the immature pods can be used to make a side dish that tastes somewhat like okra.

Milkweed is named for the sticky white juice in its stems and leaves, a slightly toxic, bitter latex that is neutralized when cooked. During rubber shortages in World War II, this latex was considered as a rubber substitute; in the same period, milkweed floss was used in life vests and other gear for US troops, substituting for kapok. It has been shown to be a better insulator than down.

The latex can serve as a natural bandage for wounds, owing to its quick drying and elasticity that doesn't wash off. It serves the plant by deterring insects and grazing animals with its bitter taste, though not so much the monarch butterfly caterpillar. Contrary to popular belief, monarch caterpillars are not immune to the latex – according to research cited in the book *Monarchs and Milkweed*, by Anurag Agrawal, about 60 percent of monarch caterpillars die when they eat it, either from toxins in the latex or because it seals their mouths shut. What's in it for the caterpillars is that those that do survive become toxic themselves to would-be predators.

Medicinally, milkweed is used as a folk remedy to treat warts and moles. (Many folk remedies are based on the "doctrine of signatures," which holds that plants that look like a body part can be used to treat that body part, making it no surprise that milkweed, with the wart-like projections on its fruit, has been used in this manner.)

Cherokee, Iroquois, and Rappahannock sources document its use as a laxative and diuretic; early American physicians used it to treat asthma and rheumatism, as well as for other maladies.

Its practical uses extend beyond medicine. According to Arthur Haines' book, *Ancestral Plants*, the stems make good cordage. The hairs attached to the seeds are also a useful tinder source. —*Carolyn Haley*

# Homemade Charcoal

The word senescence, which biologists use to refer to the process of growing old, has recently entered my vocabulary, and judging by the steady rate at which my nose hair is accumulating, probably not a moment too soon. I don't know if there's another word that relates specifically to neurological function and the aging process, but I should probably learn that, too, as I'm becoming increasingly curmudgeonly. The phrase "kids these days" has become a staple. A trip to the grocery store is just one big bitch fest. $15 for a bag of charcoal! Are you kidding me?!

After uttering just that phrase the other day, I decided to take matters into my own hands and make the damn charcoal myself.

STEP 1 was to call my brother and see if he wanted in. "Absolutely." Come to find out he's equally offended by the high price of charcoal. He scrounged a steel barrel and went down to his shop and cut some holes in the bottom. T and D Charcoal – nice, huh?

STEP 2 was to dig a pit that the barrel could sit atop with a little air intake chamber that would turn the barrel into a giant charcoal chimney.

STEP 3 was to put the barrel on the pit, fill it with hardwood offcuts that were too small or too irregular for the firewood pile, and get the fire roaring. When the smoke stopped and it was fully ablaze, we clamped the lid down, plugged the air intake, and let it smolder.

STEP 4 was to let the barrel cool for about 24 hours and then examine the product. About 30 percent of the wood was insufficiently charred; that'll go back into the next batch. About 30 percent was too fine; that'll get mixed with compost and used to amend the soil in the garden. The 40 percent that was left yielded probably $20-worth of store-bought charcoal. —*Dave Mance III*

# On Wood and Meat

Boutique charcoal made out of specific hardwoods is becoming a thing, but it's important to draw a distinction between charcoal and wood. Charcoal is largely pure carbon and is relatively smokeless – fully ignited it should burn at about 1,800 degrees F. While the charcoal itself will impart a slight flavor to food, the intense smoke flavor associated with good barbeque is created by adding wood to your coal bed. In other words, hickory sawdust or soaked hickory wood chips will produce more flavor than hickory charcoal. There's miles of room for experimentation, but some fundamental rules are that oaks, hickories, and fruit-tree wood (apple, cherry, pear) produce the most pleasing smoke flavors, while softwoods and their resins should be avoided. The following chart, from Harold McGee's *On Food and Cooking*, gives us a glimpse at specific trace flavors.

## WOOD COMPONENTS & SMOKE FLAVORS

| Wood Component % of dry weight | Combustion Temp. | Combustion by-products and their aromas |
|---|---|---|
| Cellulose (cell wall frame, from glucose) 40-45% | 540-610 degrees F | Furans: sweet, bready, floral; Lactones: coconut, peach; Acetaldehyde: green apple |
| Hemicellulose (cell wall fiber, from mixed sugars) 20-35% | 390-480 degrees F | Acetic acid: vinegar; Diacetyl: buttery |
| Lignin (cell wall binder from phenolic compounds) 20-40% | 750 degrees F | Guaiacol: smoky, spicy; Vanillin: vanilla; Phenol: pungent, smoky; Isoeugenol: sweet, cloves; Syringol: spicy, sausage-like |

# Haying in the 21st Century

The west side of Shaftsbury was among the first parts of Vermont to be settled, and the patchwork of fields and farmhouses that were established in the 18th, 19th, and early 20th centuries still dominate the landscape, even if the side fields of many of the old farms are now sprouting houses instead of corn.

Sean Shanny's barn sits out on the west end. It is not historic – it's a month old. Raised in six days by a group of Mennonite builders. Nor is Sean historic (he's a young-looking 59), nor is his "Three Dozing Dogs Farm," which he runs with his wife, Charlynn, and friend Ryan Hall. You might have guessed that from the modern-sounding name. Sean came to farming 10 or 15 years ago after spending more than 20 years in Boston working for Trip Advisor, making a living behind a computer screen.

In some ways it's important to lead with these de- tails – it's how he opened our conversation. You do so out of respect for the history around you, and for the men and women who have been carrying on the agri- cultural life for generations. "I've been playing farmer

for 10 or 15 years," is exactly how he put it to me.

But now that we've established the context and the humility, the truth is that I can't think of one farm on the west side of town that is still functioning in the self-contained, multi-generational kind of way that is so often associated with farming. And if you examine the agricultural fabric around here, you see that Shanny and people like him are crucial stitches that are helping to hold the whole thread-bare thing together. Shanny's operation will hay around 330

acres this year, a good chunk of this is land they took over when Henry Strohmeir passed away. Henry was the traditional dairy farmer of Vermont legend: big, with a gregarious personality. I don't know how many hundred head he milked, but his farm's footprint covered three or four towns. But his was a 20th century model – I don't have to tell you how hard it's been for dairy farmers of late. And so into this void comes Three Dozing Dogs with a 21st-century model.

Part of this modern model relies on a source of income that comes from off the farm. Shanny made some money in tech and then turned to farming; others keep their footprint small and run sideline businesses that subsidize their farming; others marry well, which doesn't necessarily mean an heir or heiress, it can simply mean a partner with a steady income, good health insurance, and low financial expectations from their spouse.

Another part of the 21st-century model involves keeping land costs negligible. While good riverbottom hay land might still bring $100/acre in rental fees, Shanny pays nothing for the 12 or more parcels that he cuts. In some cases, the landowners simply want to see their fallow land made productive. They're not making money, but they're eliminating the expense of brushhogging and getting the pride of contributing to the agricultural economy.

In some cases, Shanny's active farming makes their parcel eligible for a tax break through Current Use, which is the incentive. In some cases, the pitch is simply that he'll do right by the land. "I'm usually dealing with fields that started out in terrible shape," he tells me, "both structurally and in terms of soil health." Twentieth century corn-growing practices featured liberal use of herbicides and synthetic fertilizers, not to mention the fact that a crop of corn is a nutrient vacuum. All this left a lot of farmland impoverished. Hay's less taxing than corn, and Shanny's practices involve cover-cropping to rebuild soil rather than, or at least in addition to, fertilizing. He's also set up to rock-pick and smooth neglected fields to get them back into tractor shape. The idea that the fields and the soil will be more productive at the end of his five-year lease than they were when he started is attractive to landowners.

And the 21st-century farming model often means being specialized. Much of the work Three Dozing Dogs does is custom – custom baling, custom rock-picking, custom planting and harvesting. "A modern combine can cost half a million dollars and you use it for 12 weeks," said Shanny. So if you're a farmer, why buy and add to your debt load when you can just sub the work out to a specialized contractor like him?

The bulk of Shanny's hay work involves cutting,

baling, and selling directly to the farmer who owns the fields, so the hay never leaves the farm. The higher-dollar work (that term being relative, of course) is in square bales. This is boutique market hay that he cuts, stores, and then doles out to small-scale and small-animal farms that don't have the equipment to handle 1,300-pound round bales, and the high-end horse world. (Saratoga, New York, is only 45 minutes away; the Greenwich, Connecticut, region – which Shanny calls the "gold coast" – is 3 hours away.)

The catch with square bales is that they're labor intensive. In the old days, the extended farm family did the work. As extended farm families disappeared, farmers turned to neighborhood teenagers, a notoriously fickle demographic. There's an old saying around here that one teenager does one teenager's worth of work. Two teenagers do half a teenager's worth of work. Three teenagers do no work at all. Shanny reports that a work-around to this problem has been to have at least one girl on the haying crew who the guys could show off for (or be shown up by). But it still meant a relatively undisciplined and undependable workforce and a big labor cost.

So Shanny turned to an Amish-made hay accumulator instead. The machine sorts and stacks 15 bales at a time. (Picture a tractor-drawn Plinco board behind the bailer, where the hay falls down through a series of channels then drops in a neat grouping in the field for easy collection.) "In this system," said Shanny, "literally one person can hay."

The other aspects of making a real go at the hay business are basic and timeless. You need to make a good product. With hay this means appropriately sized square bales that break down into nice flakes; and tight round bales with an eye towards maximum utilization. (The hay in Shanny's round bales is chopped to 2.5 inches before being baled, so there's less waste when the animals eat it.) "Farmers and horse people talk about good hay," said Shanny. "So if you have a good product, word gets around." You've also got to time it right so the hay's at peak freshness; you've got to get it cut before it goes to seed so the farmers' barns don't fill with rats. You've got to store it correctly so it retains its color and shape. "If you can present a bale in March that looks like it's fresh off the field, you're in the money," said Shanny. You've got to take care of your repeat customers. Cut them bulk deals. Give them the first shot at hay when the crop's off and supply is limited. You help them, they help you.

"Can you actually make money at this?" I asked him bluntly.

"You can turn a profit if you stick to your guns," he replied. —*Dave Mance III*

**"HAY-CUTTERS"**

Time tells them. They go along touching

the grass, the feathery ends. When it feels

just so, they start the mowing machine,

leaving the land its long windrows,

and air strokes the leaves dry.

Sometimes you begin to push; you want to

hurry the sun, have the hours expand, because

clouds come. Lightning looks out from their hearts.

You try to hope the clouds away.

  "Some year we'll have perfect hay."

*William Stafford from* The Way It Is: New & Selected Poems *(1998)*

## *The Strawberry Fields*

At the farm, June hits like a storm. I am there seven days a week, and when work ends at four in the afternoon, I sit long into the evening by the riverbank sipping cool beers with Nick and Luke, growing stories like veins. My legs are strong from biking. My arms and back are deep tan. When I jump off the dock, soil runs off my skin and back into the river whose ancient flooding created the alluvial fields I plant, harvest, and sweat in. My body is never just mine, there are always traces of river and dirt, salt and the thin green sap of growing things.

At home, my mother scolds me if I walk into the house wearing my worn work boots. She makes me scrub the dirt out from under my nails before dinner. She has me leave my pants at the door. "Your skin," she says as my first sunburn flakes off, revealing a deep tan glow. "Your nails," she says as she sees me cut them low, scoping out soil from beneath their white crescents. To win her favor I bring her bags of vegetables and fistfulls of flowers, and gift by gift she warms to the idea of her oldest daughter as a farm girl.

But I have no time to think of nails and boots and gifts in June.

June sits in the very middle of the year when the days are longest and fullest. It is somehow both the start and the heart of the season. Rows of tomatoes, peppers, eggplants, melons, lettuce, corn, and squash have to be planted, while the earliest crops have to be picked, washed, packed, and delivered for sale. White strawberry flowers become green berries, and after a week of heat, flush from a light pink to a deep red. Suddenly it's strawberry season, and the farm is flooded with people picking them. The berries are the farm's highest-grossing crop, and their management, which is my job, drives my exhaustion.

Most years I have one day off in June, the day after our annual Strawberry Festival. I sleep in, my hands stained red from the fruit, my knees pocked with straw dust.

In June I am always the first one at the farm: both the houses on the property are dark. I get there early so that I can read the fields. When everyone wakes, they'll want to know what the berries are going to be like that day, what varieties are ready, how good the picking is. The phone line is flooded with calls as soon as the weather warms. It is my job to divine the fields and predict the future.

So every June morning begins with a survey of the strawberry fields, and I walk them religiously, like a monk to prayer. My course through the patch is a zigzag survey of each variety, deliberately random. Sometimes the front or back of a row can ripen at different times due to the slow shift of shade from the hedgerow, so I have to cover all four fruiting acres, back to front, side to side. The dew is heavy and my shoes and lower legs are soaked by the time I finish. Every few paces I stop and sink to my knees and lift a cluster of berries in my palm. I twist it side-to-side, checking for ripeness, firmness, and color.

Through this daily sampling, I develop a sensitive palate. Every morning I eat a few to register sugar levels on my tongue. A tart berry needs a few more days on the plant; an almost boozy, overripe fruit has to be picked as soon as possible. I read the weather report online every hour so I can forecast heat and rain and how the fruit will respond. Does the patch need water to grow fat or sun to ripen hard berries? Does it need a day or two of cooler weather to slow down a quickly ripening field, or does it need heat to raise sugar content? I weigh these things with the berries.

In the patch, I decipher how many quarts lie ripe in the field ready for picking, and how long the picking will last. The best fruit we harvest ourselves to sell at the farm stand and markets. These are usually the king berries, the first fruit set by the plant.

My staff of pickers works ahead of the pick-your-own customers who come later and harvest for themselves. I stick different colored plastic flags at the start of each row to indicate who picks there first. One color for U-pick, one for the crew. They flutter brightly. Walking out of the fields, wet, I fill out numbers on a pick sheet in the strawberry shack where the air is always cool and dusty. I write my notes in a journal: *Jewels great today, still picking Mesabi, will be open until Friday.* The pages are curled and damp from the dew. By the end of the summer the book will appear ancient, like a record from another time.

While I am out in the fields, the rest of the farm crew starts to trickle in. Their cars drift quietly through the fog, headlights illuminating the parking lot and rolling out over the banks of vegetation, casting rotating shadows in the straight rows. Luke, the field manager, turns on music in the processing area under the tin roof of the barn and the beat rattles the

beams. I can hear it echo off the pine trees across the river. The whiteboard in the washing area becomes a harvest list. The crew gather around the board, count out rubber bands, grab knives or scissors, and load harvesting totes into the back of the truck. Their bent-over bodies move slowly through the fields across the road from the berries. Occasionally, a crewmember takes the truck back up to the barn, the bed loaded with greens. Luke fills big metal sinks with cold water and washes the produce as it comes in, carefully completing the order forms from restaurants, stores, and the farm stand. He works fast; moving bunches from sink to sink and into black crates or wax boxes. The drumline of his music drifts down into the fields.

Nick, the equipment manager, starts up Yoda, the farm truck, its old engine whining as it cycles. I walk up as if drawn to the noise and, waving good morning, slip into the farmhouse to make photocopies of my notes. I leave copies of them like horoscopes on the

desk by the phone and on the farmstand counter near the register so that our retail staff can know what I learned in the fields at dawn. By our customer entrance, I switch out the closed sign for the open sign, slipping the hooks through the eyes. Words sway in the fog along the roadside.

With the patch open and my notes shared, I walk back down to meet our pickers. Years ago, Bill, the man who trained me, retired, and I've since become the strawberry crew leader. I hold up fruit for new members of the crew, just like Bill once held them up for me, and I tell them which berries are good and which are bad. I collect the picked quarts they leave behind in the rows and tally their numbers at the end of the morning. For hours I walk up and down the straw paths, tossing away bad berries, directing traffic, heaving heavy flats of quarts into the back of Yoda, scribbling quick notes, radioing up to the barn for more containers, moving flags to new rows, and watching the crew work around me.

In the morning everyone is quiet. But as the sun rises the crew starts to complain. There's more noise when bad bunches of beets or rotten lettuce come up to the barn, and I can hear Luke cursing and tossing plastic totes around. He turns up the music and works faster, yelling over it to the crew as they finish the harvest. When our picking is complete, the crew hitches a truck up to the flatbed trailer lined with transplants. A few people drop starts out of the tray onto the row and everyone else follows behind planting. Then they move pipes and set up irrigation and Nick turns on the old tractor by the river. The Rainbird sprinklers sputter then burst and cast long arches of river water over the newly planted rows.

By lunch, everyone has said every mean thing they could think of to each other. We all talk about quitting, starting our own farms, and doing everything our way. But as the heat increases, we settle. In June, we eat lunch by the river and Luke will often give us a full hour instead of the usual half so that the crew can swim and relax. We sit around on the steps of the cabin smoking cigarettes. A few guys slip off to suck on pot pipes behind the tree line. We take turns diving when the river is high, yelling out points like judges at the Olympics. When the river is low, we cannonball off the dock, exploding into the brown water. By the end of the month, only the current in the very center of the river is cold.

In the afternoons I go back to the strawberry fields while the rest of the crew weeds or keeps planting. Some days Luke surprises us at quitting time with popsicles or ice cream, or better yet, cold Coronas and a bag of limes. The crew piles into the back of a pickup truck and speeds down to the river, the tires kicking up silt. There we smoke in the shade, dangle our legs off the dock, lodge limes in the throats of cold beers, lick cherry popsicles or lie in the grass watching the big clouds roll away.

June is the month that forms friendships and alliances. There isn't any other way to get through. The crew bickers and comes together again, day and after day, until we build a mythology forged out of hard work. Stories about disasters averted, the coldest mornings or the hottest afternoons that we repeat until we've written sagas. In this way, we become the heroes of our own legends. They are little things mostly, tiny stories that only matter at the farm between the people who were there to see it and tell it. The afternoon, when all the gears except reverse failed on a tractor and Luke drove it from Alice's, one mile away, backward, looking over his shoulder. The day Luke and I planted strawberries while being chased by swarms of angry bees. There are stories of successes, too: the market when Robert and I sold $2,000 in strawberries and came back to the farm with a stuffed cash box. We showered $20 bills over Nick and Luke, who were drinking at a picnic table in the shade, and repeated the M.I.A. lyrics that had become something of an anthem, *all I wanna do is …  and take your money.*

In June the year is made or lost, so money is always on my mind. Bad weather can ruin the berry crop or bog down the tractors, preventing the fields from being planted and setting back the rest of the season. A crew might fail to come together and splinter and need mending for the next four months. Everything is magnified by that stress, so that joy in June is also bigger than it is any other month. Busy days and good harvests fill me with incredible pride. Overwork and sleep deprivation reduce my world to the point of simplicity. Food tastes better. Beer colder. Water on my skin is like a baptism, clearing away a day of toil and sweat.

*This piece was adapted from Megan Baxter's memoir, entitled* Farm Girl, *which will be published by Green Writers Press in time for Earth Day, 2021. The book chronicles her love of the land, as well as young love, ruined by addiction.*

# A LOOK BACK

## The Ackert Fern Empire in Danby

*Editor's Note: There was a time when wild ferns were big business in Vermont. A story, published in* The Vermonter *magazine in 1915, states that in the towns of Woodford, Searsburg, Stamford, and Readsboro alone, over 50,000,000 ferns were gathered annually. We went looking for a firsthand account of what life was like for a fernpicker, and found one at the Danby-Mount Tabor Historical Society. The piece, written by Chick Ackert, remembers the family fern business in the first half of the 20th century. Mr. Ackert passed away in 2012, and his words are reprinted courtesy of the Historical Society. The "fancy ferns" in this account are what now are called intermediate wood fern or evergreen wood fern* (Dryopteris intermedia)*, a very common and widespread fern. Some other Dryopteris species may have been collected at higher elevations.*

In the early 1900s, my grandfather, Peter L. Ackert, and his wife Sarah started a business to supply "fancy ferns" to florists, hotels, and fish markets all over the United States, and this continued for several generations. In the later years, they extended the business to include a massive inventory of pine, spruce, and hemlock cones, among others. During the reign of M. L. (Mort) Ackert, they became known as the world's largest supplier of these items. Mortimer was one of Peter and Sarah's twelve children.

The business needed millions upon millions of fancy ferns every year to satisfy the general public's fascination. These ferns only grew in the wild and couldn't be raised like vegetables. They only grew in specific areas of the Green Mountains, shaded by deep dark hardwood trees. They had to be accessible in massive amounts. Federal lands and the vast land holdings of the Central Vermont Electric Company became the prime areas where ferns were harvested around Rutland and Randolph.

*Peter and Sarah Ackert*

This was one of the few businesses that prospered during the Great Depression. Mort had the presence and ability to convince the powers that ruled this domain to allow the many large, starving families he employed to gather ferns on their land. He also built a large cold storage warehouse to maintain these very fragile ferns at a constant temperature of 33 degrees. Danby became the central area, then Merle "Zib" Ackert annually set up in the Chittenden area. Arthur "Dodd" Ackert did the same for his part of the business in Randolph.

*Fern bundles; inside the Ackert cold storage*

One must remember that fern picking was hard, demanding (because of the bugs and the heat of summer) piece work, paid by the bunch. So the original work force was the family and the extended family and their friends. Gramp, however, was prepared: he started a crash course of annual on-the-job and one-on-one training. There was a modest investment by the family – twine, and their time, but that was it. This Depression-era business took off like gangbusters.

Picking areas were cherished and there were a lot of unwritten rules, like don't never-ever go into someone else's area. There was plenty of area all over the Green Mountains, so this wasn't much of a problem. The hard part was telling fancy ferns from seed backs, brakes, daggers, and water ferns. Most pickers did quite well for the times. People today wouldn't believe what so many did for so little pay, but back then it was a minor miracle. Get up early, go into your local mountain, apply what you had been taught, work hard, bring your packs of ferns into a fern camp, and walk out that day with your earnings in your hand. That was the magic of it all! It's also difficult for people to grasp just how many, for so many seasons, found this a way of life.

Each summer after school was out, Merle "Zib" would set up quarters in the old Chittenden Hotel, a one-time stage stop on the way from Rutland to Pittsfield. This building had a dance hall upstairs and a number of rooms. The season would start off slowly and build up gradually until the end of August when it got really busy as school was about to start and the State Fair was in town.

Fern pickers had to build themselves one or two pack boards, two feet wide, three feet high, with shoulder straps and rope to tie down the ferns to be packed out of the woods after picking. Five thousand ferns per pack (200 bunches) was considered a reasonable load. I have carried out 10,000 on one pack, but that's how I and many others literally ruined our backs. But of course, we all bragged and loved being in the great outdoors, at least on the good days. My dad always

went in for 10,000 ferns every day, rain or shine. The best figure, bragged my uncle Robert, "Toots," was 27,000, but Dad said he had several of the girls helping him while he bunched them. My brother Johnny claimed 17,000 and the best I ever did was 14,000.

No fern picker ever got rich, but I never knew one to starve, either. When the season started the demand was not great, so the price always started low: 40 cents per 1000. That's right, year after year, 25 ferns to the bunch, 40 bunches to the 1,000. Fern pickers can't just grab handfuls of ferns and pack them onto a packboard and bring them out and get paid. Oh no. What you did was find a patch, a big patch of ferns in an accessible area, pick 'em, one, two, maybe three at a time, place them face up, one at a time atop each other until you have 25 atop each other, each fern being 15 inches tall, not counting the 5- to 6-inch butt (handle). Then rub all the feathery fern parts off of the butt, then grab the very sharp knife you had dangling from string from your belt and cut the ends of the butts even. Then take the end of the fern twine dangling from your pocket and put twine through the end of the butt, make 3–5 turns around the butt ending by again pulling string through the butt, break off the twine, and "Eureka!" one bunch, one fortieth of a thousand, one cent at 40 cents per thousand. But don't worry, by season's end the price will be up to three cents per bunch, $1.20 per thousand, less for bug-eaten or damaged ferns (and the fancy fern is very fragile).

For us Ackerts, that was just the beginning of our second half of the day. After we brought in the ferns, we had to pack them in moss lined 3.5 x 3.5 x 1-foot fern boxes in preparation for trucking to the Danby storage. Often at night, George Stone would ride up with Art White and pick up the ferns. Sometimes John Francis, a son of Dad's good friend Roy Francis, would play his guitar and sing real late. He was good, even at 79. —*Chick Ackert*

## Keeping Vermont's Forests as Forests

Vermont's forest products industry generates an annual economic output of $1.4 billion and supports more than 10,500 jobs in forestry, logging, processing, specialty woodworking, construction, and wood heat. The environmental and economic viability of Vermont's forested landscape depends on a healthy forest and wood products industry.

### A *healthy and productive* forest is a well-managed forest.

As stewards of our forests, professional loggers and foresters manage our forests to be healthy and productive, as well as resilient to invasive species and severe weather events.

### *Craftsmanship* is part of our heritage.

Wood products from Vermont represent the core values of the Vermont brand: authenticity, craftsmanship, quality, and a connection to nature.

### *Wood heat* is a local, renewable resource.

80 cents of every dollar spent on wood heat in Vermont is retained in the local economy verses 22 cents spent on heating oil or propane.

### *Forest-based recreation* doubles economic impact.

Hiking, mountain biking, camping, fishing, bird watching, and skiing on Vermont's forested land adds an additional $1.9 billion to the economy and supports another 10,000 jobs.

**VERMONT FOREST INDUSTRY NETWORK**

The Vermont Forest Industry Network brings together people from throughout Vermont's forest economy. Our Steering Committee includes representation by the Vermont Woodlands Association, Vermont Forest Products Association, the Vermont Wood Works Council and Renewable Energy Vermont, along with government and non-profit partners.

**vsjf.org**

# JULY

# *July*

A mellow afternoon, a lazy July afternoon, a quintessential Lake Champlain afternoon, perfect for bobbing in a kayak, cultivating aimlessness, temporarily forgetting about The Dreaded Virus and The Teetering Democracy and The Warming Climate and The Rest. I lower the paddle, stow it across my lap, listen to the *drip-drip-drip*. The faint breeze nudges me north, along the shore's sweep of cliffs and dangling cedars, around the bulge of Hills Point.

Here is a large bay on the Charlotte-Shelburne border, a bay unlike any other – a bay dressed in feathers.

Wait… *what?*

Some boaters I've met call double-crested cormorants "ratbirds." While I appreciate regional variation in ornithological nomenclature, this nickname is obviously meant to denigrate. So often with humans, when offered too much of a good thing, we become lazy and bored, letting our awe and gratitude diminish until we're filled with apathy or, worse, ill will.

Double-crested cormorants are common on Lake Champlain, as rats are common in a sewer, I suppose. Between the size of a mallard and a Canada goose, with a bright yellow-orange throat set against gleaming black plumage, they're physically conspicuous. They're behaviorally conspicuous as well, regularly congregating to feed en masse. It's this kind of dense foraging party that I've discovered, and that I couldn't be more thrilled to have discovered.

The breeze – steady, soft – enables a furtive approach. Easing in close, individuals begin to separate out from the great undulating fabric of feathers, the gargantuan buoyant birdquilt. Double-crested cormorants gather in groups exceeding two thousand on San Francisco Bay, but I've never seen more than a couple hundred at once on Lake Champlain. I divide the scene into a grid, count the birds in a nearby zone, then multiply.

*Whoa.* That rarest of occurrences – math sending a tingle zipping up the ol' spine.

At least eight hundred birds float in front of me, maybe nine hundred or a grand. There's only one way to get a better estimate, but I don't kid myself that scientific accuracy is the magnet drawing me in. What I'm about to do will be fun, plain and simple. Like all naturalists, I'm an adult intoxicated with a child's curiosity. Sniff and lick. Peer and poke.

The breeze nudges me closer, closer, closer, and I try not to breathe, try not to move even my lungs.

Cormorants with green eyes twist their necks to preen. Cormorants dive, stay under for ten seconds, stay under for twenty seconds. Cormorants emerge with silvery morsels, toss their heads back, and gluttonously gulp. Cormorants cormorant – the coinage pops into my mind, the goofy verb attempting to capture this presence, this power, these guttural croaks and gentle rustlings.

Five, four, three feet away…

Finally, a bird on the edge reacts, rearing up with quick, slapping wingbeats, stretching forward, elongating, transforming into a dark arrow shot south – sharp beak, fletched tail. The bird beside it follows, and the next bird, and the next. As the leader flies, practically skimming the bay's riffled surface, it pulls a thread and the quilt slowly, smoothly unravels into a single-file line.

For as long as I can remember, there's been this part of me that doesn't think, but *feels* – it doesn't know, but boy does it ever *know*. Sadly, this is the same part of me that routinely crumples beneath the crushing weight of confusion and sorrow, the relentless *ugh* and *argh* of twenty-first-century existence. Shit is real these days, really real. The Dreaded Virus. The Teetering Democracy. The Warming Climate. The Rest. But cormorants, a quilt of them unraveling, disappearing around the bulge of Hills Point, knitting together again on some bay beyond the reach of a puny human's vision – that's real, too.

And that is *here*, that is *now*, that is *this*.

And this is July – height of the breeding season on Lake Champlain, home of the glorous ratbird.

—*Leath Tonino*

# It Was a Dry Heat

July is Vermont's hottest month of the year, and July 2020 was even hotter than normal by a substantial 4.1 degrees in central Vermont.

The above-average warmth was consistent statewide. Temperature oscillations due to routine warm and cold fronts continued, though in a much more muted fashion. Near 90 degree temperatures on the 2nd yielded to lower 80s on Independence Day. The coolest day was on the 14th, when the high reached just 70 degrees. The warmest was the 19th, when temperatures hit 90 in the Barre-Montpelier area. Several other locations (notably in western Vermont) saw even warmer readings.

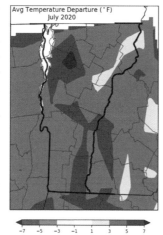

As in the month of June, July's rainfall was quite variable from place to place, which is somewhat typical thanks to localized convection caused by summer thunderstorms. Interestingly, those areas not receiving the "gully washers" began a dry feedback loop, where drought begets drought, and by later in the month, abnormally dry to moderate drought conditions were noted. Soil lacked moisture in a big way, hurting vegetable farmers, many of whom had to irrigate. Few home gardeners have irrigation systems, and many needed to water by hand frequently.

The lack of moisture made it easier for the weather to remain warm on many days – something certainly noticed by farmers and anyone else who works outdoors. But the warmth was perhaps even more noticeable at night. In fact, minimum temperatures during July rose faster than daytime high temperatures – something we've seen world-wide as the climate warms. This phenomenon is what exacerbates the onslaught of heat waves in a dry feedback mechanism. Case in point: the month's warmest minimum temperature was 72 degrees, recorded on July 20.

Spring into early summer 2020 was also warm and dry across parts of Europe and Siberia. Much of this was related to extensive broad anticyclones blocking ocean moisture sources. The effect here in Vermont? Water levels of ponds, rivers, and streams – not to mention Lake Champlain – dropped precariously.
—*Roger Hill, Weathering Heights*

*Comet NEOWISE was visible to the eye on clear nights during much of July.*

# NATURE NOTES

## Broad-leaved Helleborine

**THE YIELDS OF TIMBER-PRODUCING TREES** such as ash and poplar are increased when they grow with speckled alder and can share in the nitrogen fixed by the alder's bacterial partner.

Many orchid species use deceit to attract pollinators, but broad-leaved helleborine *(Epipactis helleborine)*, if it were a person, would be considered to be especially duplicitous.

Darwin noted that although this orchid's flowers have abundant nectar, only wasps visit and pollinate them. No bees.

Jennifer Brodman, a researcher at the University of Ulm, in Germany, figured out why. Oddly, helleborine flowers don't produce the kinds of organic molecules that are emitted by most plants to attract pollinators; instead they send out scents that other plants use to signal insect attacks. Kind of like alarm bells, they signal other plants to up their defenses when insect damage reaches a certain threshold in the neighborhood. Cabbage family members emit these same volatiles to call in predatory wasps when they are being eaten by cabbage worms.

But helleborine is not under attack at all. It's seeking pollinators. And, indeed, these compounds do attract wasps – predatory insects expecting to find a tasty caterpillar meal. Instead, the summoned wasps begin to drink the helleborine's nectar, which makes them so sluggish and bumbling

**A FARMER** across the road is rehabbing an old corn field with buckwheat this summer and the crop is just breaking into flower. It smells 80 percent sweet and lovely and 20 percent dank and sour.

that they sometimes even fall to the ground. The nectar is laced with several narcotic compounds, including a small amount of oxycodone. In addition, some of the fungi and bacteria that are transferred to the flowers by visiting wasps convert the nectar's sugars into ethanol. No wonder the wasps get tipsy. It's not known for certain what role these drugs play in the relationship, but it is possible that keeping a wasp in the flower longer may increase pollination success.

Helleborine's pollen is borne in sticky packets called pollinia, and these – often several of them – become glued to the wasp's head as she drinks. Having a pollinia party hat does not keep wasps from seeking out and pollinating other helleborines. Helleborine flowers are dull, with little of the pizzazz that endear us to most other orchids. They often grow in dense shade, so using odors instead of showy flowers to attract pollinators is a good strategy.

A common European species, helleborine was first noticed in the US in 1879. Its devious ways appear to be effective. Since being introduced, it has spread to most of the US and much of Canada.

**ACCORDING TO THE CHINESE ZODIAC CALENDAR,** 2020 is the Year of the Rat. That sounds about right, so far. But at least in our old farmhouse, it's the Year of the Earwig. We've been inundated, and they seem to be multiplying exponentially. After doing a little research, I now realize that isn't far from the truth. Female earwigs lay as many as 60 "round, pearly" eggs in shallow soil, and, unlike most insects, they guard their eggs and watch over the hatchlings until after their second molt. The little ones reach the adult stage in about 70 days. It also turns out that earwigs prefer hot, humid environments – so the recent weather has been perfect for them, and perhaps that's why they're so plentiful and active this year. "Their invasion of houses begins sometime in July," according to UVM Extension's website, and I can confirm that invasion has begun. Our friend Marian Cawley in Corinth suggests trying an oil trap – a cup or laundry soap lid filled with oil and buried to the rim in your garden. Flavor it a little with soy sauce or something tempting, and it purportedly works like a charm. —*Patrick White*

## AT HOME

❧

# *Foraging for Color*

Last year I asked a simple question: could I make homemade finger paints for my one-year-old using ingredients found in my kitchen? Thus began an ongoing quest for salvaged and foraged paints.

Using beets, turmeric, and paprika, I found that I could easily make bright magenta, yellow, and orange finger paints. The teal to purple to pink effect from a color-changing purple cabbage pigment rounded out a simple kid-friendly palette.

Buoyed by this success, I found myself wondering what other paints I could make with salvaged and foraged plant material. I started with foraged berries, which have a reputation for easy extraction and colorful potential.

My first attempt was in early summer with strawberries. I boiled the berries and let them soak to leach out the color compounds, then strained out the chunks. I boiled down the bright red juice, which turned into a thick syrup. I added salt and vinegar as preservatives before bottling and labeling my new paint. Using the same technique, I moved on to blueberries, thimbleberries, and blackberries. My biggest challenge making berry paint came from my daughter, who, as my foraging partner, was liable to eat most of our findings.

Berry watercolors are thicker than conventional watercolor and aren't as stable. The strawberry dulled from orange-red to an orange-brown, the blueberry varies from purple to royal blue depending on what paper it's applied to, but the thimbleberry and blackberry are relatively reliable variations on maroon.

While I was still seeking wild colors, a friend and fiber craftsperson mentioned that lichens can provide bright and stable pigments.

Lichens should always be collected as salvage, not directly harvested, due to their slow growth. I began scouting for reliable sources of discarded lichens and quickly discovered two local sources:

*Collecting fallen rock tripe with my daughter at The Dome climbing crag.*

*My notes and swatches as I tested concentrated colors on parchment paper.*

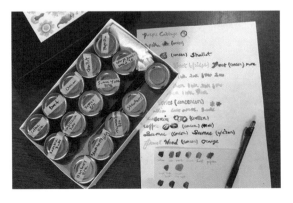

*Using ferns as masks for berry watercolor art on Arches watercolor paper, birch bark, and wasp paper.*

*Nature journal page showing a rock tripe lichen, notes on the biochemistry and color swatches of the pigment, and test art inspired by the magenta color of the resulting paint.*

firewood and rock climbing crags. Many of the firewood logs from our property have circular patches of shield lichen, some of which can provide red-brown to purple colors, while rock climbers actively scrape lichen from established routes, often rock tripe, which also provides red to purple colors.

Lichen colors are more difficult to work with because they are extracted and digested with ammonia for several months for full color development. Dyers traditionally used human urine; I found some leftover household cleaner. The extract should start as orange-brown, but when some of my rock tripe solutions quickly became a rich burgundy, I had to try it. It painted onto watercolor paper as a color-stable light magenta.

By late summer I had collected a dozen colors, but most were dark browns and maroons. Looking to fill in the gaps in my foraged paint spectrum, I experimented next with sumac and jewelweed, following the same boiling water extraction technique as for the berry watercolors. Fuzzy red sumac drupes gave me yet another brown, or a strong gray when cooked down in a cast iron pan. Both orange and yellow jewelweed concentrated into an orange-brown similar to the color of shallot skins.

With the summer foraging season coming to an end, I now had sixteen little jars of homemade watercolor paint ready and waiting for what looks to be a fun fall season of experimental artmaking. —*Rachael Sargent Mirus*

Rock lichen Watercolor Experiments

Lasallia umsilicate lichen

umbilicate lichens can be used for burgundy to purple

from gyrophoric acids

Thimbleberry

painted with Lasallia purple, umbillicaria burgundy, orange from shallot skin, and brown from beet

# *Save Those Heirloom Tomato Seeds*

**SEED SAVING**
Seeds can be classified into three categories based on their level of complexity in saving.

**BEGINNER**
bean
lettuce
pea
pepper
tomato

**EXPERIENCED**
corn
cucumber
muskmelon
radish
spinach
squash
pumpkin

**EXPERT**
beet
swiss chard
cabbage family
carrot
escarole
frisee
onion
radicchio
turnip
Chinese cabbage

If you are interested in seed saving, saving your own tomato seeds is a great place to start. First, make sure that the varieties of tomatoes from which you want to save seed are open-pollinated and not hybrid. Their seed packet should indicate this. Hybrid varieties will not be good for saving seed because the offspring from their seeds will not be true to type.

Carefully watch your tomato crop. Keep a keen eye out at the beginning of the season for the plant that looks the healthiest and produces fruit the earliest. With that in mind, also notice the way the plants fruit. As you sample your tomatoes, decide which ones taste the best. Keeping all of these factors in mind, choose one of several of the best tomatoes to save seeds from, knowing you will get the same variety next year and that it will become ever-so-slightly more adapted to your garden.

As tomato seeds have a gel casing around the seeds, they need to be processed using a wet method. By slightly fermenting the seeds, you inoculate them against disease. Don't be intimidated by the following wet-process method: it is very simple.

Harvest your favorite tomato when it is fully ripe on the vine.

To process, take your tomato, (or tomatoes), into the kitchen and scoop out the seeds into a glass jar. Make sure to label the jar as all tomato seeds look similar.

Add a little bit of water to the seeds and tomato pulp, stir, cover loosely with a dishcloth or cheesecloth, and place in an out-of-the-way location.

Allow to sit and ferment for, on average, four to five days.

Make sure to stir one to two times per day. A thick, white layer of mold with bubbles will begin to form on top and will produce a strong, bad smell. Don't allow the seeds to over-ferment as this may cause germination.

After fermentation has occurred, scrape off the moldy layer. Add water to the jar and swish. Wait 10 seconds for the seeds to settle. Good seeds will sink to the bottom while bad seeds and debris will float to the top. Pour off this liquid, the bad seeds, and debris and rinse again.

Repeat this process until you have just good seeds and until the rinsing water is completely clean.

When you are finished, pour off all the liquid and spread the tomato seeds on wax paper, a paper plate, or a coffee filter to prevent sticking. Label each tomato variety again.

Allow the seeds to dry for one to two weeks in a non-humid location out of direct sunlight. Make sure the seeds are completely dry before storing.

*Cedar Circle Farm Staff*
*cedarcirclefarm.org*

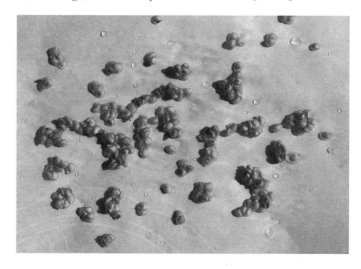

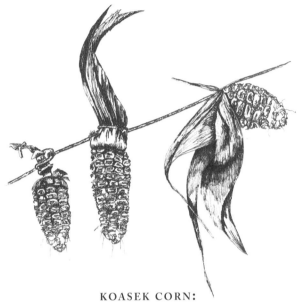

KOASEK CORN:
A HISTORY OF STEWARDSHIP & SURVIVAL

## The Little Corn that Could

Small ears of corn hang from the rafters of a log home in West Braintree. They will spend the winter inside, and the golden-brown kernels will be returned to the ground in the spring to grow again. Each year, the cycle of seed-saving is repeated, allowing the crop to be renewed from one season to the next and from one generation to the next.

For the Koasek Tradition Band of Abenaki – one of four tribes of Native Americans recognized by the state of Vermont between 2011 and 2012 – this corn is sacred and a key element of harvesting and planting ceremonies. The Koasek had been the keepers of the corn for the past millennia. But this particular corn, in this particular part of Vermont, had been "lost" for three hundred years; the people and the plants separated. It was only through a string of unlikely stewards that they were able to be reunited.

Abenaki food systems were disrupted by the arrival of settlers who pushed the Abenaki off their land, introducing crops, growing schemes, and germs from Europe. Abenaki people were seen as a threat to the early settlers, and the indigenous people of Vermont struggled to preserve their food ways and traditions that were increasingly under attack.

While there were conflicts over land and culture,

there were also instances of cooperation, which were key to the corn's survival through tumultuous times. Koas stories recount how Abenaki farmers gave Koasek corn to Jesuit settlers around 1675 in the spirit of sharing with new neighbors. These early Jesuit settlers began growing the corn and, for the next three centuries, served as its stewards.

Carroll Greene, a direct descendant of the early Jesuit settlers, was part of this lineage. He was vocal about his love for Koasek corn and spread it around to his neighbors, among them Sarah and Charles Calley. The Calleys had moved to Vermont in 1980 as part of the back-to-the-land movement that gained momentum in the 1970s, and they were interested in the state's agricultural heritage.

The Calleys found that Koasek corn thrived in the hills of Newbury – the small stalks sweet to eat, resistant to pests in the field, and more gentle on the soil than modern, commercially available corn that strips nitrogen from the earth to fuel its large stalks. "It's a sturdy corn, and delicious," said Sarah Calley, who continues growing it today.

For the 40 years the Calleys have been growing Koasek corn, they have guarded their crop against cross-pollination, keeping the corn pure. Cross-pollination is a threat to heritage crops as it can alter their genetic makeup and lead to hybrid varieties. If mixed with genetically modified corn, farmers can even lose the right to grow their own due to patents protecting GMO crops.

Learning about the history of the region and Native American agriculture, the Calleys eventually realized that they were growing an indigenous corn variety, but it wasn't until 2007 that Sarah Calley met then-Chief Nancy Millette Doucet and realized she could return the corn to its original keepers. In a ceremony, the corn and the Koasek people were officially reunited after many years apart.

At the Koasek Tribal Garden in West Braintree, Chief Shirly Hook continues this rich tradition, growing the sweet corn that is small but mighty in its perseverance. The corn takes over the house in the fall, when Chief Hook brings it inside to dry. "My parents used to do that, too," she recalls. This year, Chief Hook's daughter Amy Hook-Thierrien is planting a garden of her own for the first time.

There is reciprocity between plants and their people, each one taking care of the other, ensuring their survival and flourishing for generations to come.
—*Amanda Gokee*

# 2020 *Fishing Report*

I t was the summer of Covid, of low, warm waters, and hatches that were sporadic or had fisherman wondering if their timing was off on almost every outing.

The usual fishing spots were full of out-of-state cars, even on weekdays, and once untrod stream banks had well-beaten (although unlittered) paths along them, in places remote enough that it seemed technology had made it easy for distant travelers to find.

Still, fishermen were friendly, rivers were pristine if not low due to near drought conditions, and while dry-fly fishing didn't rule the day, at least not as it had predominantly in past seasons, there were still wild and well-stocked fish to catch on streamers and other attractors.

In my area, the consensus was that the reliable Battenkill didn't produce many prolific hatches, and if it did, the fish didn't rise, or perhaps this was due to aforementioned bad timing on our part.

In a state with so many great fishing options, it was still possible to find solitude and great fishing if one was willing to think outside the box. June marked the season peak in terms of fishing, and October its beauty and solitude. —*Owen Duffy, Fisherman, Shaftsbury*

STREAM AND BROOK FLYFISHING, MIDDLEBURY

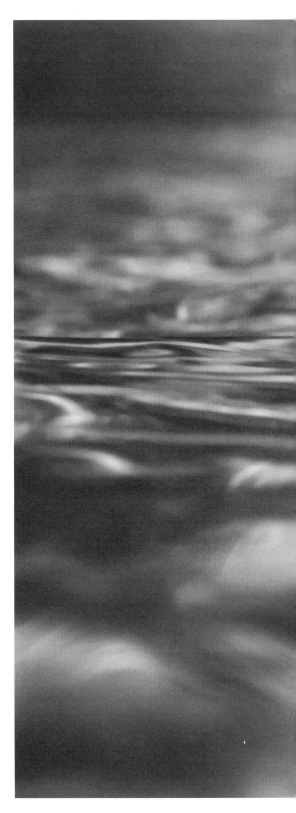

## A LOOK BACK

# Vermont's Potato Mania

*There was a man I once did know,*
*And he was wondrous wise,*
*He raised potatoes very fine*
*And dug out all their eyes.*
*And these he sold for piles of gold,*
*For so the story goes,*
*He gave a blessing on them all,*
*And called them Early Rose.*
*And such a time as men did have*
*To watch them night and day,*
*I vow! Before I'd have such work*
*I'd throw myself away.*

These lines, written by Mrs. A.E. Stanley of Hubbardton, are the beginning of a ballad she composed about the excitement caused by the Early Rose potato, developed by Albert Bresee, also of Hubbardton. Mrs. Stanley was known to sing the song in the years after Vermont's "Potato Mania."

Much has been written of the tulip speculation in late seventeenth-century Holland when, at its peak, a single bulb sold for more than 10 times the annual income of a skilled worker. A less well known but equally compelling story is of the potato craze that started in Hubbardton in the 1860s. *The History of Hubbardton, Vermont,* points out that "At one point a bushel of [Early Rose seed] potatoes would buy a farm or a good team of horses." Potato breeders had to post armed guards in their fields around the clock to keep poachers from their precious crops.

Before the pioneering work of Albert Bresee, the potato was a tasteless and unappealing tuber, prone to diseases and poor harvests. Its vulnerability led to the infamous

famine in Ireland in the mid-nineteenth century. The ravages of the potato blight on the Emerald Isle caused the starvation of over one million people and a massive exodus that saw the population of Ireland reduced by 25 percent. Clearly, a hardy and palatable potato was needed.

The potato's origins are in South America, and it was first introduced to Europeans by conquistadors who began propagating it in sixteenth-century Spain. From Spain it migrated to Italy and then to the rest of Europe. It was unknown in North America until 1719 when Irish immigrants brought the potato to Londonderry, New Hampshire. Its passage from South to North America took almost three hundred years and two ocean crossings.

Few, if any, attempts at scientific breeding or hybridizing of potatoes occurred before the work of two amateur agronomists: Chauncey Goodrich and Albert Bresee. Goodrich's efforts in New York state were aimed at producing a crop that would not be ravaged by the blight that had caused such misery in Ireland.

Although the potato was a staple

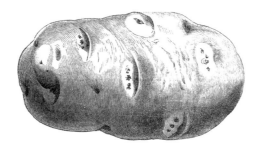

food crop in mid-nineteenth-century America, its propagation was subject to increasing numbers of diseases similar to the one that caused famine in Europe. Agronomists believed that the potato had become weakened by years of propagation from pieces of tubers (eyes) instead of seed. In Utica, New York, Reverend Chauncey Goodrich, chaplain of the New York State Lunatic Asylum, believed the stock could be rejuvenated from original seed. Toward this end, he obtained (with a substantial investment) seeds from the potato's original habitat, Chile. From this original planting he grew a plant that he named the Garnet Chili. This fabled tuber, with its light red flesh and silky-smooth skin, was an immediate success for all tastes.

Albert Bresee, on his farm in Hubbardton, used Goodrich's stock to invent the first commercially successful variety – his justly famous Early Rose. Its appearance on the market was a true phenomenon, especially when it became apparent that it passed on its positive qualities (blight resistance, flavor, and early maturity) when used as a foundation for further hybridization. Harold Bailey's *Vermont in the Potato Lineage* calls Albert Bresee "the Justin Morgan of the plant realm," and farmers reportedly paid $1,000 per pound for true seed for his new variety.

The Early Rose was described in a catalog from 1870:

> *Although this valuable variety has been but two years before the public, it is already as well known as any variety now under cultivation in the United States, and it has been the subject of more unanimous and universal praise than any other potato ever offered to growers. . . . The tuber is of large size, eyes shallow, skin thin and tough, flesh white, solid and brittle; boils through quickly, is very mealy, and has a delicious flavor.*

As this new potato caught the fancy of the nation, tales of its means to wealth and prosperity assumed the cachet of legend. Lyman Draper warned in 1870: "Beware of the potato fever. It is during some years and in some districts, more malignant than the potato rot. It affects the dealers more than the tubers, and in general breaks out in the eye – of the former. Printer's ink aggravates the infection. It soon makes its way to the pocket."

*The Caledonian*, a newspaper published in St. Johnsbury, was particularly taken with the stories of speculation and rapid wealth accrued from buying and selling the Early Rose and other new potato varieties developed by Mr. Bresee:

> *The potato mania, which seems to have taken hold of all classes, the mechanic, manufacturer, merchant, and gentlemen of leisure, as well as the more slow and plodding farmer, increases rather than diminishes. We haven't much faith in speculation, so far as benefitting the agricultural community is concerned, but in this case it is probable that it will be of ultimate benefit as it is likely to stimulate the production of new and valuable varieties. Within the last few weeks Mr. Bresee's No. 4 has sold at extraordinary prices.*

Reports continued to be received from around Vermont extolling the great prices paid for these hybrids. In April of 1869, *The Caledonian* noted lucrative potato sales in Brandon:

*The potato fever is at its greatest height in Brandon and Mr. Cyrus Jennings, the Early Rose man, is reaping a rich harvest. During last week he sold 35 barrels at $35 and $40 per barrel, five bushels Bresee Prolific, No. 2 at $60 a bushel, 1 potato of No. 4 Prolific at $30 and two of the No. 6 species at $10 each.*

The prices paid for single potatoes would seem extravagant even in today's dollars. In October of 1868, *The Caledonia*n reported that Mr. Hiram Linsley, from Rutland County, raised one plant, which produced eighteen potatoes. He sold ten of them for $615, or an average of $61.50 per potato. He subsequently paid off his $500 mortgage.

Bresee accrued so much wealth from the Early Rose that his farm was considered among the best maintained in Hubbardton, but his good fortune didn't last. A subsequent town history remarked upon his enterprise, "After developing four varieties, Bresee suffered so much theft and raids on his field that he transferred further experiments to D.S. Heffron of Utica, New York.

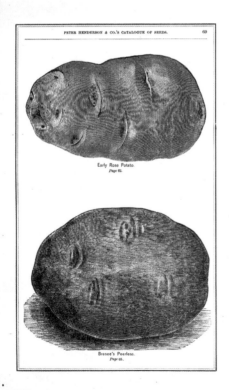

PETER HENDERSON & CO.'S CATALOGUE OF SEEDS.        69

Early Rose Potato.
*Page 62.*

Bresee's Peerless.
*Page 65.*

While many were eager to jump on the potato bandwagon, there were also voices urging caution and common sense. An editorial in the *Maine Farmer* urged caution after being shown a single potato, which was wrapped carefully in tissue paper in a nice box, for which the owner had refused $50:

*While we do not say the introducers of the potatoes and other seeds, roots, vegetables, are deceiving the public and filling their own wallets, we do think a little prudence on the part of purchasers will not be amiss, and that it is best, at any rate, to invest moderately in such stock. If part of the care and attention bestowed upon new and much lauded varieties were given to old and good, but neglected sorts – we think farmers would be quite as well off as they are now.*

As Bresee's new varieties became established, prices for the new hybrids fell precipitously as there was soon enough of the seed to satisfy demand. More than one farmer, late to the party, found his investment vanished as the popularity of these new potatoes became rife throughout the country.

Below are the concluding stanzas of Mrs. Stanley's ballad, "Early Rose Potatoes." —*Paul Heller*

*So men, they traveled day and night,*
*Without regard to health,*
*To beg or borrow, buy or steal,*
*This secret to princely wealth,*
*And very lucky was the chap,*
*For so the story goes,*
*Who in his travels could obtain*
*A peck of Early Rose.*

*At length their feeble faltering steps*
*Showed labor all in vain;*
*The Doctors shook their heads*
*And said: "Potato on the brain.*
*The patient must be quiet kept, "For so the story goes,*
*And ne'er allow his mind to dwell*
*Again on Early Rose."*
*So nicely humbugged folks did get,*
*I laughed both night and day,*
*To think that men of common sense*
*Should throw themselves away!*

# ANATOMY OF A COMPOST PILE

LEAF
LITTER

FOOD
WASTE

SHORT PAPER
FIBER

HORSE MANURE
WITH BEDDING

WOOD
CHIPS

**THIS PILE CONTAINS ABOUT 500 YARDS OF FINISHED COMPOST,** made from five different ingredients. The basic recipe for compost is 4 or 5 parts Carbon to 1 part Nitrogen, but every composter uses different mixes and ratios, based on their feed stock, to end with a product that has a 65 percent moisture content. It takes food waste about a week to break down into dark sludge, and it takes the whole blended pile about 3 or 4 months to achieve a compost-like consistency. At 7 to 10 months, the bacteria stop working and the pile cools to an ambient temperature. At that point it's considered cured and ready for sale.

INDUSTRY

## *"Vermont is a Model for the Country"*

### COMPOST REPRESENTS A NEW FRONTIER
### IN RECYCLING & ENVIRONMENTAL HEALTH

Compost production at farms, community sites, certified facilities, and in backyards is steadily increasing, largely due to the mandated organics diversion in Vermont's Universal Recycling Law (Act 148). Unanimously passed by the legislature in 2012, the Universal Recycling Law provides a framework for the goal of getting food waste out of landfills. The ban on landfilling food scraps was phased in between 2014 and 2020, beginning with those producing greater than 104 tons of food scraps per year and expanding to require all Vermont residents to divert food scraps from the landfill.

Composting at all scales benefits the environment. Organic materials emit potent greenhouse gases when they're landfilled, but those methane-producing anaerobic bacteria can't survive the compost pile, turning a liability into an asset. Gardeners, farmers, and others use compost to build soil health. This reduces the need for synthetic fertilizers and pesticides, lowers runoff of stormwater and agrochemicals into watersheds, and helps minimize the loss of topsoil from erosion, all while improving resistance to drought, insects, and diseases.

There are economic as well as environmental benefits from compost. Jobs are created at each stage of the organics recovery cycle – from collection to production to use. On a per-ton basis, the process of making compost employs twice the number of people as operating a landfill.

In 2020 there were 11 certified food scrap compost facilities in the state, in addition to many on-farm composting operations. Thirty-seven food scrap hauling businesses now provide collection services to businesses in approximately 80 percent of Vermont towns; more than 25 of these haulers also offer residential curbside service, and over 100 transfer stations now accept residential food scraps. Even before

the residential food scrap mandate was implemented, Vermonters sent over 15,000 tons of food scraps to certified processing facilities (composting and anaerobic digesters), and composted an estimated 27,000 tons at home.

There's raw energy to be captured in compost, too. Some farms are using heat recovery compost systems to heat greenhouses and hot water. As of 2019, anaerobic digestion of manures and other materials (which captures the methane as a renewable energy source) generated enough electricity to supply 3,200 customers and removed 73,000 tons of methane from the atmosphere each year.

Vermont is a model for the country with its state-wide ban on sending organic materials to the landfill. While significant strides have been made, much still needs to be done to establish efficient collection systems, ensure that materials are free from contamination, and support compost production at every scale. And we must continue to educate people about the true potential of compost (including its erosion control and water quality benefits) and to provide reliable markets for compost. The environmental, economic, and community benefits of compost will only be realized if we apply it to our soils. —*Natasha Duarte, Composting Association of Vermont*

# A Closer Look at Execution

*It's easy to feel powerless in the face of the big, global environmental problems of the day. But whatever else Vermont's new food waste ban is, it's an action. A verb. An example of people doing something. We talked to* Vermont Almanac *board member Chuck Wooster, of Sunrise Farm in White River Junction, to get a farmer's perspective on all this. Turns out he's in the process of building a compost facility at his place.*

"The classic organic model is you raised animals and vegetables together. The left-over veg was fed to the animals, the animal manure fertilized the veg – it all made a ton of sense. But things are more linear now. Consumers for sure, and also farmers, have lost track of the old circular system. People talk about eating a fake-meat burger as if it's good for the planet. You're getting herbicide-soaked GMO soybeans out of the Midwest. And meanwhile, how are those farms going to fertilize the vegetables? With natural gas and oil.

Here, our vegetable operation has gotten big and our animal operation's gotten smaller because the economics of meat are so terrible, so we're buying more and more organic fertilizer. This is expensive, and it's also kind of antithetical to what we're really after here, which is a sustainable model. I would love to be putting tons and tons of compost – literally tons and tons – on our fields. You can use all the commercial fertilizer you want – and we're using a lot of it. But it doesn't give you the soil texture, the organic matter, the carbon sequestration that compost does.

We're also a CSA, and we're always trying to figure out ways to encourage people to join. One of the cool things about our compost plan is that it will allow members to bring their veg waste with them – we'll take it and then they'll take home some new veg. This resonates strongly with our customers. I think the most exciting thing here is this educational piece, actually. We're able to show people how vegetables grow, how farms work, how animals fit into it, and how carbon is managed in the real world. We're calling our compost shed our 'carbon management facility.' There are going to be solar panels on the roof. The whole thing is going to offset the carbon emissions from our farm."

*The new carbon management facility at Sunrise Farm.*

*Screening compost at Casella's Long Trail Composting Facility.*

*In Natasha Duarte's introduction to this story, she writes: "much still needs to be done to establish efficient collection systems, ensure that materials are free from contamination, and support compost production at every scale." We caught up with Trevor Mance, another* Vermont Almanac *board member, who's the Food Waste Project Manager at Casella, Inc., and asked him to tell us more about this work.*

"When it comes to efficient collection systems, the biggest challenge from a hauling perspective is a lack of density." If the first house on a street hires us to pick up their food waste, but the next house does home composting, the next house grinds, the next house throws it in a hedgerow, the last house feeds it to animals, there's just not enough economy of scale to make a collection program profitable. And it doesn't help that out-of-state companies are coming in and competing with Vermont hauling companies for the big anchor stops.

Another challenge is figuring out markets for the end product. Compost is no different than dairy farming: just because you put on more cows doesn't mean people drink more milk. So if we're making more compost than ever but not selling it, then you'll start seeing prices drop.

A big elephant in the room is the PFOA issue. Food scraps can have PFOA in them: it's just an uncomfortable reality. So the industry is at work figuring out how to keep it out of the compost we sell. Man-made problems are something the composting industry has a long history of dealing with – the last one involved persistent herbicides in the Pyralid family. With that we figured out that high-carbon wood ash effectively locks it up, but it's an additional cost and can be hard to source. A big challenge of this line of work – whether it's hauling food waste or household garbage – is that society doesn't want to acknowledge its environmental problems until the end. We ignore that there's PFOA in the paper that wraps fast-food hamburgers, in dental floss, in waterproof clothing, but we get upset when years later it's in our food and water and soil. Instead of going to the manufacturers and saying: you can't use this stuff, we go to the compost manufacturer or the landfill and say: you've got a problem here.

All that said, it's an exciting time. We're at the beginning of real change. Infrastructure is coming along, public understanding of the impacts of their waste is growing, and businesses are investing in technology to make this happen. [Casella has a new de-packaging machine that allows us to take packaged food waste and separate out the organics, which then go into an anaerobic digester to generate clean power, and then finally to land application.] We expect to process over 4,500 tons of waste in the first year through this machine, a number that we hope will grow into the tens of thousands of tons in future years. There's great hope here that we can effect change that will help the land and forests and water in Vermont and beyond."

# Composting at Home

There's seemingly no shortage of ways in which 2020 has been an aberration. In Vermont, add to that list the fact that residential composting has suddenly become all the rage.

"This spring, all of the solid waste management entities were slammed in a way that none of us have ever seen," says Cassandra Hemenway, outreach manager with the Central Vermont Solid Waste Management District. "I mean, in our field, when are we ever slammed? It's not like it's a super-popular thing!" Supplies of composting equipment flew off the shelves and people had to wait months for stocks to be replenished. Waiting lists formed and grew at an unbelievable rate. "We got to a point where we had sold out of some things and had to stop accepting new orders," says Hemenway. "And our workshops, which had to move online because of Covid, were getting 500 to 700 people signing up. Interest in composting just went through the roof."

Hemenway says that Vermont isn't the only place where composting exploded, as home gardens went in around the country in response to concerns about food shortages – and many people found themselves at home with time on their hands in the midst of a global pandemic. But that reality, along with the fact that Vermont's long-anticipated food scrap ban went into effect on July 1, has made composting a particularly hot topic here.

### THREE CRITICAL TIPS

"People who have never composted before typically are afraid that it's going to smell bad and that it will attract animals," says Hemenway. "That's not necessarily true at all – but those are their fears."

There really are two basic strategies to prevent smells and animals, she notes. The first is to be sure to add three times as much "browns" (materials high in carbon such as leaves, dried grass clippings, or wood shavings) as food scraps to your compost bin. And to do this every single time you add your food scraps. "That does two things: it covers up any smells there might be in the food scraps, and it also provides 'food' for the microorganisms," says Hemenway. She explains to those just starting out that the composting process only happens because there are trillions of microorganisms decomposing the food; without

A two-bin compost system, with dry storage for browns.

food, air, and water, those microorganisms die. And that's when things start to smell bad. "Providing browns is really the single most important part; if there was only one thing anybody ever wanted to know about composting, it would be to pay attention to your browns," emphasizes Hemenway. That means designing your compost area with sufficient storage space beside your bin to hold those browns; personally, Hemenway simply uses a large trash can with a lid to hold wood shavings and leaves.

A close second in order of priority is to remember to turn your pile. "It doesn't have to be every day; it doesn't have to be every week; it doesn't necessarily even need to be every month. But you need to make sure that you add air to the pile, either by turning it or poking it with a stick," says Hemenway. Another technique is to layer the compost pile with sticks or corn cobs, in order to create air pockets in the pile. Regardless of which approach you use, the key is to monitor your pile; over time, as it decomposes, things will settle. That's when air needs to be reintroduced.

Another "magic trick" to successful home composting, says Hemenway, is to use hardware cloth to line both the bottom and sides of your bin. This very stiff screen (for compost, the ideal size is quarter-inch or half-inch mesh) keeps animals from digging underneath and up into your pile, and blocks even small rodents from chewing through it. "You have to be sure you install it in a way that there are no gaps for small animals to squeeze through, she advises. The hardware cloth will thwart larger animals, as well, like skunks and raccoons. Bears, not so much.

Another important note: Hemenway advises that until you are a pro at composting, leave meat, bones, and fish scraps out of your home compost pile.

Here are a few additional composting considerations found in the Central Vermont Solid Waste Management District's comprehensive guide (available at www.cvswmd.org) called *The Dirt on Compost.*

## DIFFERENT APPROACHES TO COMPOSTING

The publication reviews seven different approaches to composting: the pit (just dig a hole at least one foot deep and throw your food scraps in); the trench (sort of an extended version of the pit, typically done in a garden where you bury your food scraps in rows); a trash can (pretty self-explanatory, just be sure to drill air holes); the pallet bin (an enclosure with walls built from old pallets and lined with hardware cloth); the tumbler (a commercially available, fully enclosed device in which small batches of compost can be produced, though it may need to be finished in a separate bin); a multi-bin system (separate bins constructed with untreated lumber that allow material to be transitioned through the various phases of composting); and the commercial compost bin (popular and available in many styles, these bins allow you to start composting right away, but look for one at least three feet in diameter and ensure there are plenty of air holes).

## HOT OR COLD?

For those who want their compost to be ready quickly (in as little as three or four weeks), intensively managed "hot compost" is the way to go. This requires starting with a larger pile (at least 3x3 feet) and investing in a compost thermometer to tell when to turn the pile (when the internal temp drops to 100 degrees). "Cold composting" is a more passive alternative and a more common one for the majority of residential composters, who don't generate enough food scraps to hot compost. Expect it to take about six months to produce compost in these smaller, less intensively managed batches, and be aware that weed seeds and pathogens won't be killed because the temperatures are lower – so don't add weeds or diseased plant materials to the pile.

## CONSIDER WHY YOU'RE COMPOSTING

Vermont's scrap ban has expanded the number of people contacting solid waste management districts for information, but compost isn't always what they're interested in – especially those who don't have gardens and thus aren't necessarily interested in generating high-quality soil. "It's a real mix," says Hemenway. "Some people are definitely all about the garden, but there are also people – especially now, – who just want to keep their food scraps out of the trash." (Before passage of the food scrap ban, an estimated 20 percent of all landfill waste in Vermont was food scraps.) For those people, a Green Cone is a great option, she explains. These commercially available devices aren't composters at all, but rather digesters. These units are mostly buried in the soil and require full sun to produce heat, but require no ongoing maintenance (or browns). Simply dump your scraps (including meat/bones/fish) in. Because the digesting process isn't necessarily rapid, depending on the amount of food scraps you generate, your Green Cone may fill up over time. —*Patrick White*

CVSWD

*Cassandra Hemenway leads a pre-Covid composting workshop at the Community Garden in Montpelier. For 2020, live workshops were moved online and were attracting as many as 700 viewers.*

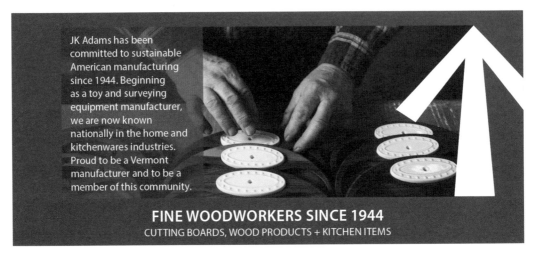

# Rooted in Vermont

### CASELLA CONTINUES SUSTAINABLE GROWTH

On a chilly day in early April 1975, Doug Casella began picking up garbage from a few customers in the Rutland and Killington region with a pickup truck he had bought with money saved from jobs he'd had as a kid in high school. Because the service was good, the small enterprise grew, and John Casella joined his younger brother a year later to help run the business.

The brothers, influenced not only by the unique history of Vermont frugality, could also see the future – and in 1977 built Vermont's first recycling facility. It was an inspired vision, one that anticipated the opportunities around resource renewal as well as viewing waste management as an integrated set of services – collection, recycling, transfer, and disposal.

Today, Casella Waste Systems, Inc. is helping thousands of customers in more than 40 states manage their waste, as we build the infrastructure that makes modern life possible.

Our company is rooted in the timeless values of Vermont and has grown because of our steadfast belief in creating and sharing value with our employees, customers, and communities. We started this business providing an essential service to our friends and neighbors and we're honored to continue to do that very same thing 45 years later. ◆

# AUGUST

# *August*

On the other side of the narrows things will be different.

I grew up on an island, and there were narrows directly across from our home. The water currents were different on either side, as were the winds above the water. I can remember sailing my little sunflower sailboat through the narrows, having to tack very slowly and tediously to move forward. One side was very calm and protected from the wind by the Island herself, but little ripples of waves forewarned what was coming. On the other side was a broad lake where the winds were often fast and furious. I remember the waves crashing over the edge of my little sail boat. The narrows were a space where I collected my thoughts and got prepared for the change ahead.

The metaphor of going through the narrows can be applied to the Covid pandemic, as we watch human systems break, not to be seen again for a very long time. Going forward, life will be different. It will be hard. The change will be gradual for some and fast for others. We need to accept this change – those that don't might not make it through.

Traditional Ecological Knowledge tells us that while journeying through the narrows into the new world it is essential that the old ways – stories of survival, the old songs of prayer, the generations of skills passed down of knowing and being with the land – survive. They will guide and give us strength, help us to understand the difference between a want and a need.

In my family, in Abenaki tradition, I was taught very early in life to value the five Rs: respect, responsibilities, relationships, reverence, and reciprocity. Our respect for the land and water was a direct connection with our survival. Reverence and reciprocity followed: we were taught to nurture and nourish the land. Fishing was an almost daily responsibility. We took what we needed to feed our family and share with the elders living down the road. Family was the center and came first; extended family and elders next. These relationships sustained us.

Some say Covid may never leave, some say it will be gone soon. We need to be prepared either way. The stay-at-home orders have limited driving, which in turn has cleaned the air in many places. In some cities, skylines have become visible that haven't been seen for many years. Less pollution for now: we need this when we cross the narrows.

The Coronavirus has led to a need for fresh food. Gardening has come back. Children are learning to harvest off the land, reclaiming traditional ecological knowledge. Along the way they are forging family bonds and getting good, old-fashioned exercise. By reclaiming the old ways they stand a chance of getting through the narrows better than they were before.

Empty beaches, forests, meadows, and roads have led to more animal habitat being reclaimed. More turtles are laying more eggs on beaches because there are fewer intrusions from people. And more animals are taking back the natural spaces they need to live healthfully. If life goes back to "normal," the fear of humans will return and animals will retreat to their little corner of space we have delegated them to live in. Alternatively, as we travel through the narrows to a new world, we could develop a good relationship with the plant and animal people, one in which we see each other as related kin. I know what I want, do you?

When we make it through the narrows, it will be up to us to create a new normal and a new world. Wouldn't it be nice if, in the midst of everything, we could seize the opportunity to change. —*Judy Dow*

# Hit-and-Miss Rain

The summer's big disparities in rainfall continued into August. Large portions of central and eastern Vermont were in moderate drought, and things became even drier across southern portions of the Champlain Valley. There was also a prevalent hopscotch effect of rain east of the Green Mountains.

Temperatures ran just barely (0.2 degrees) cooler than average. Cooler weather was on hand for the start of August, with temperatures only topping out around 70 on the 4th, but things ramped up shortly thereafter with an August peak temperature of 88 degrees on the 11th. After that, a slow cooling took place through the 19th. The next period of warmth was not quite as hot as the previous one; a high of 83 was reached on the 24th. Thereafter a cool pattern ensued, where four out of the last six days of August reached only into the 60s.

Thanks to the minimal, hit-and-miss rainfall, groundwater levels – which had already fallen from the late winter into the spring – continued to drop. The evidence was seen in nearly dry streams and rivers. Surface water temperatures were very warm – in many cases between 70 and 75 degrees. So if you could find water, the swimming was rather pleasant.

Tropical Storm Isaias tracked into northwestern Vermont on the 4th of August, cutting north-northeastward from the Lake George region of New York to around Addison before exiting into Canada

*This map shows The Evaporative Demand Drought Index – a tool used to examine the atmospheric evaporative demand ("atmospheric thirst") of a place over time. This unit of measure is often used as an early warning system for extreme drought conditions and fire weather predictions.*

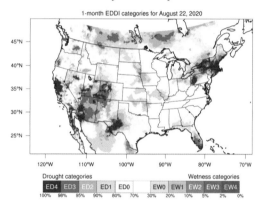

around Enosburg. The remnant moisture made for the wettest day in some time with 1.5 inches recorded at the Barre-Montpelier Airport. That one-day rainfall contributed nearly half of the month's total precipitation. It was a good soaking rainfall, moderate to even heavy at times. Runoff was at a minimum, with a very thirsty, dried-out landscape eager to take it in. The soaker proved very beneficial, but nowhere near a drought-buster. —*Roger Hill, Weathering Heights*

*August 6, 2020. As the nights get longer, and temperatures get cooler, warm valleys exchange moisture with the cooler air above, creating valley fog like this over the Victory Basin.*

# NATURE NOTES

## Yellow Grub

**ALTHOUGH WOODLANDS** are preferred habitats, red-bellied snakes are also found in fields, bogs, and wet meadows, as well as along the borders of marshes, swamps, ponds, and streams. They are small and secretive snakes and spend most of their time hiding under rocks, logs, boards, or debris, or within rotted stumps. Slugs make up the bulk of their diet, along with earthworms, sow bugs, soft-bodied insects, and small frogs.

Taking a three-year-old fishing is chock full of lessons. There are predictable ones: ichthyology, self-sufficiency, cause and effect. ("If you throw all the worms in the water, honey, we won't have worms to fish with.") And then there are the random lessons you don't expect to learn, let alone teach, like the ones involving the parasitic yellow grubs that you might find in perch meat. These animals have life cycles that, coolly enough, involve the blue herons that were flying over us while we fished and the snails we noticed on the bottom of the lake floor under the bridge we were fishing on.

In this photograph you can see the cysts that were in the perch fillets. The grubs *(Clinostomum marginatum)* are inside. Humans aren't part of the parasite's life cycle, and the insects die when you cook them, so the meat is still edible, if not exactly appetizing.

The parasite starts its life in an egg in a heron or a bittern's throat. The egg is either regurgitated into the water as the bird feeds or shat out – reputable sources vary on that detail, which could be an indication that both methods of expulsion are possible. Once free of the bird, the egg hatches and the miracidium, as the little organism is called, finds a snail to infect. The parasite goes through several larval stages in the snail, then leaves the snail to find a fish. It infects a fish, then gets passed to a fish-eating bird when the fish is eaten. Once in the bird's throat, the adult lays eggs and the life cycle starts anew.

IT'S HARD NOT TO NOTICE FALL WEBWORM WEBS. This insect, a moth native to North America, is now found in temperate forests around the world. It feeds on more hardwood species than any other caterpillar, but around here it has a strong preference for black cherry. The webs are at the tips of tree branches, unlike the spring eastern tent caterpillar, which makes its nests in tree crotches. This year fall webworms have shown up earlier in the season and they are so abundant that everybody's complaining about them. They're not that harmful to trees, but most birds are put off by the caterpillar's long hairs, even if they could get through the webs to consume the caterpillars. Roadsides, yards, and field edges get the most webs because these caterpillars like the sun's warmth.

THE CORN IN YOUR GARDEN, and many of the grass species in your meadow, grew well despite the dry weather because they evolved in arid environments. Corn, and about half of all grass species, practice $C_4$ photosynthesis, which allows them to make more sugar out of less water than their conventional counterparts. Though they make up only one percent of the world's plants, $C_4$ plants account for five percent of the globe's biomass, and because they are so efficient, they are responsible for 30 percent of all the carbon that plants remove from the atmosphere. Doubling $C_4$'s market share to 10 percent of the earth's biomass could make a significant dent in the excess atmospheric carbon that we're emitting from burning fossil fuel.
—*Chuck Wooster*

THE GREGARIOUS WHIRLIGIG BEETLE is usually zooming around with a bunch of other whirligig beetles. Their speed is remarkable. Also remarkable are their compound eyes: each eye has both a top part that can see above water and a lower part for below water.

AT HOME

BILL TORREY

# Brush Hogging for Dummies

I'm proud to say that I'm a sixth-generation Vermonter and a second-generation brush hogger. My dad first introduced me to this activity when I was around 11 years old. For those not familiar with a brush hog, it is a two-bladed mower mounted on the back of a farm tractor. If you can run it over with your tractor, this thing can cut it. Dad had purchased 32 acres of land in West Bolton with a variety of terrain – woods, scrub fields, and beaver ponds. He bought a five-foot-wide Sidewinder brush hog to go behind his 1953 8N Ford tractor. The brush hog's blades are driven by the tractor's PTO shaft, and on an old 8N

that does not have live hydraulics, the PTO shaft can continue to drive the tractor forward by the momentum of the spinning blades even after the clutch pedal is pushed down. My dad learned this quirk when he ended up buried to the axles in a beaver pond. Once he was extricated from the pond, he acquired an overrunning clutch device that mounts on the shaft and this solved the problem.

Soon he commenced to reclaim the grown-over fields and woods roads with his much loved tractor and brush hog. For dad, it was almost like a sport to see what he could hog. But, as he pointed out, not a spectator sport. Stuff would be thrown out the back and sides of the brush hog at amazing speeds and directions. On one occasion when he was hogging he hit something substantial and broke a blade. I heard the racket and went to check it out. As I wandered around in the area where it happened, trying to find the busted off piece, he asked me what I was doing. "I'm looking for the broke blade. Maybe you can weld it back on," I replied. "Thanks for the effort boy, but I believe you're looking in the wrong county."

When I began working in the woods, I bought a 60-horsepower four-wheel-drive tractor. I soon purchased a brush hog and started to take hogging jobs while I wasn't logging. Savvy woodland owners know the importance of retaining their forest openings – they supply critical edge habitat and open areas for songbirds, deer, and turkeys. I always tried not to mow until August to allow birds to be done with raising their young and fawns to be up and moving more with mom. If possible, I tried to make just a couple passes around the field and let it set for a day. This sort of warns the critters of what is coming and gives them time to vacate the premises. Waiting until as late in the summer as possible also saves the milkweed for Monarch butterflies to use.

I learned some things about brush hogging the hard way, just like my dad did. Like that it pays to walk areas before mowing if you suspect there might be hidden drainage ditches or rocks, which you can mark. Even in places that I've mown year after year, I still walk with a roll of blue masking tape and fold a small piece of it back on itself on a stem of goldenrod or timothy to mark an old stump or rock. I've found it's better to take the time to do that than to shear a pin or break a blade. For a job well done, slow down the speed of the tractor but not the RPMs of the tractor's engine. Plus, if you get in trouble, and you're going slow, things happen slowly. And for the love of Mike, sharpen the blades now and then. Nothing looks worse than a hogged field that looks like it has been fluffed instead of mowed.

I now live on those 32 acres dad bought. When he passed away I sold my brush hog. Now I use his old Sidewinder, which is still in amazingly good shape despite being nigh onto 50 years old. I always grease the PTO shaft universals and check the gearbox for oil before each season of use, just like dad taught me. And I can't help but smile every time I mow my way past that spot in the beaver pond. — *Bill Torrey*

# A Game Warden's Perspective on 2020

Complaints about bears doubled in volume in 2020 compared to previous years. There are more bears, but not that many more, and the problems are mostly due to an increase in bad human behavior. Bears are territorial and once the most preferred habitats are taken, only less optimal places are available for the surplus population. That's what sends bears to garbage cans and bird feeders. Over time, there's also been a cultural shift among bears, and nowadays sows are teaching their cubs to rely more on humans.

Another cultural shift is occurring in the game warden mission itself. Wardens have traditionally been thought of as an arm of law enforcement, although responding to animals that are creating a nuisance or have been injured has always been a big part of their job. To more accurately reflect this reality, the division has been renamed the Warden Service.

Many people stuck at home due to Covid have discovered, or rediscovered, the pleasures of being outdoors and the benefits of finding food close to home. Participation in hunting and fishing has increased by about 30 percent this year, following many years of a slow decline. —*Mike Scott, State Game Warden*

*Warden Kyle Isherwood with a rescued bear cub in April.*

# Hack and Squirt

A fond memory from the summer of 2020 was participating in a work conference call while sitting in an old aluminum chair someone had left in the woods. I was perched in a breezy, shady spot on family forestland in southern Vermont – we'd retreated there from the swelling number of Covid cases in Georgia for some serious social distancing. My ears joined my coworkers, but my eyes took in the sunlight-filled stand and my mind soon followed.

Seeing the green glow of light, I felt the accomplishment of the crop tree release work I had done there several years ago. It warmed the heart because I'm participating in a multi-generational relationship with this land (our children are the ninth generation to tread here) and I'm witnessing the influence I've had on this site. It stimulated the mind because this treatment is right at the intersection of my passions for Appalachian hardwoods and financial investment-driven forestry. Radial growth can be accelerated by as much as 50 percent when you release the crop trees. When that accumulation occurs on stems of high-value species, the value appreciation can be tremendous.

*The painted maple is the crop tree.*
*Note hatchet marks on incised ash and beech.*

The stand originated from a clearcut following a harvest in the late 1960s that funded the travel of my great aunt and great uncle to Hawaii. As a Master of Forestry student at Yale in 1996, I had cruised this stand for a mensuration class project. At three decades old, the stand was thick with pole-sized birches, maples, and beech, but there were a fetching number of cherry, oak, and ash stems. My great aunt gave me a portion of the woodlots during my final year at Yale (she died during a storm about a week before graduation), and in 2005 my wife and I bought from my uncle the portion of the woodlots that included this stand. I told my wife about the potential: "It's a diamond in the rough!" She modified that characterization to "diamond earrings in the making." Within a couple of years I gave the stand its first nudge towards diamond status.

While working in West Virginia, I became interested in the research by Arlen Perkey and others who were developing the concept of crop tree release. This method of reducing stand stocking contrasts with standard thinning in that one is not concerned with overall tree count or spacing. The emphasis is on finding the best trees and removing competitors. Recognizing that a mature hardwood stand is often comprised of only 50 to 100 merchantable stems per acre, this technique ensures that the best trees are well represented – typically by selecting 20-40 per acre for release. An organized method for selecting the trees at this rate is to begin at a corner of the stand and pace out a tenth-acre square. Pace a third of a chain, turn a right angle, and pace another third of a chain; from this point you can visualize the tenth-acre and pick out the best two, three, or four stems in the area. For my objectives, "best" means the ones of the form and species that will develop into the highest-value sawtimber. For others, it may be the crowns with the best potential to produce mast for wildlife. For a less structured approach, it can be enjoyable to drift through the stand and release promising trees as you encounter them.

My first treatment of the stand came when the trees were about 40 years old. I released the crop trees

*Openings in the canopy following a treatment. The crop trees will soon seize this new space and light.*

by girdling their competition, but some competitor trees did not succumb to the girdling, even with double incision. I applied a second treatment 10 years later. This time I used the hack-and-squirt method developed by Jeff Kochenderfer and others. A hatchet is used to incise the bark (about one incision per inch of diameter), creating an opening in which to squirt herbicide. Glyphosate (generic formulation diluted to 21 percent active ingredient) is my preferred herbicide due to availability, low cost, and effectiveness across most species (maple is notoriously resistant). My preferred season of application is late summer, when the temperatures are cooling but there are at least several weeks before the leaves begin to fall. The herbicide is more effective when applied during the growing season, and the tree's translocation of nutrients to the roots as fall approaches boosts the efficacy.

Crop tree release is a potent method for improving stand value. Hack and squirt empowers a landowner to actively participate in the silvicultural process by marking the trees and applying the herbicide. It allows you to improve a stand without the stem damage you get with a commercial thinning or the hazards of felling or girdling trees with a chainsaw. An ancillary benefit of this method is the production of standing dead wood. With the arrival of the emerald ash borer just around the corner, I'm pleased to have an above-average number of snags and presumably an above-average number of woodpeckers. —*Christopher M. Elwell*

*The Elwell family.*

A  LOOK  BACK

## *See You at the Fair*

Agricultural fairs have been a late-summer tradition in Vermont for more than 150 years. In the beginning, they were sponsored by a county's Agricultural Society, and were the place you'd go to hear lectures, meet salespeople, show off your livestock, and swap notes. As the world became a more connected place, fairs became imbued with a circus sensibility: they were the place you'd go to see an elephant, a snake charmer, a burlesque show, among other wonders, real or manufactured. The Ag bit never went away, but by the turn of the 20th century, the midway had already become as big a draw as the cattle judging.

The fair is still a huge part of twenty-first-century rural life. And we missed it this year. We missed it terribly. The following portraits were taken at Vermont fairs in 1936 and 1941 by photographers Carl Mydans, Arthur Rothstein, and Jack Delano. Here's to the idea that next year the fairs will be back, and order will be restored.

*Essex Junction*

*Tunbridge*

*Rutland*

*Morrisville*

*Rutland*

*Tunbridge*

*Rutland*

# Saffron

Jette Mandl-Abramson of Newbury wasn't unhappy being an organic market gardener, but her husband, Zaka Clery, wanted to do something more interesting, so she was looking around. And when she read an article about growing saffron in a 2016 UVM alumni magazine, the idea appealed to her immediately. She contacted the subjects of the magazine story, Arash Ghalehgolabbehbahani and Margaret Skinner, at the North American Center for Saffron Research and Development formed by them at UVM. Beginning as far back as 2012, those two have been into, you could say obsessed by, saffron. Ghalehgolabbehbahani is from Iran – as is about 90 percent of the world's supply of saffron – and when he first visited Skinner's entomology lab he asked why no one in Vermont was growing saffron. Many experiments and field trials later, they've learned that just about everybody could be.

As everything you read about saffron points out, it's the most expensive spice in the world, at $3,000 to $9,000 per pound. And no wonder: it takes about 4,000

flowers of this fall-blooming crocus to produce an ounce of saffron because it's only the tiny female part of the plant, the thread-like stigma, that is harvested and dried. An entire acre of established crocuses will yield roughly three and a quarter pounds of saffron. A newly planted bed will produce much less.

Mandl-Abramson and Clery started one of the Saffron Center's experimental plots in 2017, had good luck, and in 2020 planted 120,000 corms in a half-acre of fenced field. They expect their harvest to triple in each of the next two years. Saffron corms are planted in late summer and bloom in October and November. In spring each corm produces several new corms, and then the plants are dormant for a few months. Replanting is typically necessary every six or so years.

Zaka Clery has his heart set on having nine acres of crocuses, but this year's experience has convinced Mandl-Abramson that five acres is her max. Each corm has to be planted about seven inches deep, and planting has been a workout, especially on the hands. Despite eating well, she lost six or seven pounds during the planting season. They've had lots of help

from friends and may need more at harvest time.

At present saffron is mostly used in cooking, but it has potential medicinal uses, as well. It's said to fight cancer and colitis, help with weight loss, improve one's digestive system, and reduce macular degeneration in some circumstances. Saffron can be tested in a lab for several compounds: crocin imparts the color, picrocrocin provides the flavor, and safranal the aroma. Interestingly, the quality of saffron grown in Vermont equals or exceeds that in other countries where it's been grown for centuries. And if marketing these little threads becomes difficult, you can wait it out. Saffron retrieved from tombs in Mesopotamia was tested and found to be just about as good as new.

The UVM Saffron Center holds annual conferences each year, which draw people from all over the US and many other countries. Many technical publications and research results can be accessed through the center, addressing issues from plant spacing to corm size to rodent control. Now, any of us can stick a trowel and some corms in the ground and add flavor and color to our risotto. —*Virginia Barlow*

JOHN DOUGLAS / FLYING SQUIRREL

*Zaka Clery and Jette Mandl-Abramson*

# Don't Bargain with Your Farmer
# From the Window of Your Audi

Green is the color of springtime: baby vegetable plants, new leaves on trees, emerald grasses. And cold hard cash.

Sunrise Farm is a CSA, which stands for Community Supported Agriculture. Individuals and families "join" our farm in the springtime, paying in advance for the upcoming season of vegetables, which usually runs from May through October. Watching the bank account burgeon in May can be as thrilling as watching the bees stash dandelion honey in their combs – both are signs that the lean days of winter are past. I can log into my bank account some mornings in April to the lovely news that more than a hundred thousand dollars is now sitting there. I feel a surge of pride at my business acumen and entrepreneurial success.

But only for the briefest of seconds. Because like honey in a hive, the size of your cache in May doesn't make a damn bit of difference if the stash is gone in December. Winter is when swarms starve and farmers throw in the towel.

Before the spring flood of cash has even crested, it's started ebbing away. Normal springtime expenses include seeds and fertilizer, replacing or repairing equipment, and restocking supplies. This is part of why the CSA model is so effective: your members are investing in you at the exact moment that you need the money. But it's also why the CSA model can be illusory. You feel flush in spring, and forget that every week from that point until the end of the year, you and your employees will need to eat and be paid. And all the money has already come in. Even in the best of years, those six figures in the bank will be reduced to five or even four by Christmas. Foolishness in May leads to being a fool in December.

The tension for me, as I feel the cash rush through my fingers, is that it's food we're talking about, not some sort of gadget or optional entertainment. People need to eat. It's fundamental, and I feel awkward charging people money for something that they can't live without. Especially people who look like they could use a helping of tasty, fresh vegetables. This is when I realize that perhaps I'm not really cut out for the entrepreneurial life after all. If there were a

way for me to pay myself and my employees a decent wage while giving all of our food away for free, I'd be a very happy farmer. (Well, that and getting rid of all weeds.)

In the actual world, I often have to deal with the opposite problem: people who can easily afford the prices we charge yet want it for free anyway. Or at least, demand a discount or complain about the cost. I call them the "Audi bargainers."

It's not the Audi part that makes me angry – it could be a Lexus or a Tesla or even a tricked-out F350 – it's the people who drive such cars who come into my farmstand asking me to give them a lower price.

We Americans like to think that we're shrewd bargainers who know how to get a good deal, yet we have very few opportunities to exercise our birthright. Maybe a President's Day sale on TVs, or a mattress clearance sale. Beyond that, it's hard to feel much competence as a bargainer, especially on stuff that counts. Good luck negotiating for a home mortgage, or college tuition, or health insurance.

So folks turn their constitutional energies toward bargaining for the little stuff, and nothing is an easier target than food. It's for sale everywhere, with stores and vendors on all sides, and everyone knows something about the cost of food. Or thinks they do.

If, from your perspective, one carrot or pork chop is interchangeable with another, you can unleash your zeal exclusively on price. And if you don't get the price you want from your local farmer, you can indignantly claim that local food is way too expensive and that hard-working people shouldn't be expected to pay such exorbitant prices. Then you can slip back behind the wheel of your Ford Expedition and drive off.

In 2020, you can buy a brand-new set of very reliable wheels in this country for something like $25,000. Call it a Honda Accord or a Ford Escape. This car will completely meet your transportation needs and do so in no small amount of comfort, being much more reliable than anything your parents had to choose from and almost unimaginably good from your grandparents' perspective. And yet, if what you see driving on the road these days is any indication, lots and lots of people spend twice that amount of money on something much fancier.

The math here is simple. If you spend an extra $25,000 on a car that you drive for 5 years before trading it in, that's $5,000 of discretionary spending per year that you're throwing into your car. In the small-farm world, $5,000 is a large amount of money. If you instead decided to throw that extra cash into food, upgrading all of your meats and vegetables from the bargain-basement supermarket schlock to the best stuff your local farms had on offer, you would be making a real difference in your local community. You'd also still be driving an excellent vehicle and have money left over to load up on craft beer and artisanal cheeses.

In doing so, you'd also be doing hard-working people a favor, and I'm not speaking only of the farmers here. There are lots of people who genuinely cannot afford to spend even a dime extra on food, and you can tell who these people are because they don't drive Audis. Or Accords or Escapes, for that matter. But the local farm economy is so fragile and the margins are so thin that there's no way that small farmers can afford to drop their prices to meet these peoples' needs. Only if enough people are willing to pay the going rate will the local-farm economy become strong enough to help subsidize the folks who desperately need but can't afford nutritious food.

Lest it seem like I'm busting on the owners of fancy cars, believe me, I'm not. I have many loyal and devoted customers who drive fancy cars and who come faithfully to my farm every week to buy what we have, at the prices we're asking, and then buy extra to share with their friends or visiting family or to send to the local food shelf. It's thanks to them that my farm remains in business, that I get to hire wonderful employees every year, and that the farm-to-table movement has been so successful in this country for the past two decades. We literally could not be doing it without them, the folks who put their money where their mouths are. —*Chuck Wooster*

# A Quick Tour Around the State

There are around 1,000 produce farms in Vermont; they generate over $50 million in annual sales, employ thousands of (mostly seasonal) workers, and give us healthy, locally produced food that doesn't have a planet-wounding carbon footprint. Farms range in size from a few acres to a few hundred acres, and produce is sold through 70 summer farmers' markets, 17 winter farmers' markets, 65 CSAs, 91 pick-your-own farms, and hundreds of farmstands. Those numbers are from a 2020 Food System Report that was published by the Agency of Agriculture.

We couldn't figure out how to publish a profile that represented a season that was unprecedented – farms' experiences were all over the map in how they dealt with Covid. And so we decided to take a random tour around the state to check in with some of the men and women who make their living growing produce.

In mid-March, the crew at **EVENING SONG FARM** in Cuttingsville made the difficult decision to stop attending farmers' markets. And so during the 2020 growing season, they sold their vegetables through the farm's CSA – shares were picked up outside the barn – and by pre-order deliveries to Rutland and Ludlow.

"Our farm is lucky to be fine for many reasons," said owner Kara Fitzbeauchamp, "but the biggest reason is our CSA members. Having 225-plus families getting their veggies from us every week is incredibly supportive."

In late August, Kara's husband Ryan was invited by the Northeast Organic Farming Association of Vermont to testify during a Vermont Senate committee meeting regarding use of CARES funds for the agricultural sector. Currently, the way the legislation is written, non-dairy farms have to show losses between March and October to be eligible for

CARES funds, which doesn't take into account how farms like Evening Song need to operate.

"Not including payroll, our farm spends nearly 75 percent of our budget during December through February; meanwhile, 50 percent of our sales occur between May and August," said Fitzbeauchamp. "We can't think of a single farm anywhere that hasn't had to pivot drastically in terms of marketing, production, and food safety to meet the needs of the pandemic, which has come with unforeseen large expenditures."

Why do veggie farms typically fall out of the scope of most government programs? "There are incredibly long answers to that question, but to greatly overly simplify it: veggies aren't a commodity crop," said Fitzbeauchamp. "Our farm is extremely lucky to have several layers of resiliency, but Ryan was motivated to advocate for veggie farms throughout the state, since many are having a harder time."

*Evening Song Farm found ways to adapt in 2020 in order to serve its 225-plus CSA members.*

*Harvesting potatoes at Clearbrook Farm*

In years past, Rosemary and Gerard Crozier made lunch every day for the crew at **BERRY CREEK FARM** in Westfield. But because of Covid, they can no longer get together in the kitchen and shoot the breeze over lunch. It's bring your own, and Rosemary misses the camaraderie.

They have had more CSA members this season, and have sold a lot of cheese, maple syrup, and other mostly organic products, but Rosemary's most-often used word for 2020 is "exhausting." The need for constant sanitizing, monitoring their customers' compliance, and keeping up with endless new guidance about Covid has been stressful. Rosemary has woken up at two in the morning worrying about whether she remembered to sanitize the portable toilet.

They are near Jay Peak, and weddings and events used to be a big part of their summer business, but not in 2020. Their wholesale accounts, too, dropped dramatically. Berry Creek Farm has been in operation for nearly 30 years, with a farmstand and a pick-your-own berries operation, as well as a CSA. They're hoping for better times ahead.

2020 was **CLEARBROOK FARM'S** 26th season, and owner Andrew Knafel said they've never been as consistently busy as they were this summer. It was a lift to get the farmstand Covid ready, for sure, but the greenhouses were empty by the first week of June; the crew was fabulous; the winter CSA has a long waiting list.

Weather challenges were also overcome. "If you can irrigate, dry is good," said Knafel. "We had our best garlic in ages; solid tomatoes; awesome greens." The dry seemed to affect the flavor of the melons, making them extra sweet. So too the winter squash. "We probably had 40 percent more yield with winter squash," he said. The one notable crop on the off-side of the ledger was onions, which for whatever reason struggled.

The farm cultivates around 45 acres of land in Shaftsbury, about half of which is in veggies and small fruits while the other half gets cover-cropped.

*A common 2020 chore at Berry Creek Farm: monitoring for Covid compliance at the farmstand.*

*Manager Brian Stroffolino runs the curbside pick-up table at the Hartland Farmer's Market.*

Planning for this year's **HARTLAND FARMER'S MARKET** was a challenge, as there initially were no state guidelines beyond a mandate that they could not operate in an open-air setting. "Given the resources that our small market had, and with help from a community member, we decided to create an online ordering platform from scratch," said market manager Brian Stroffolino. "We put all of our time and energy into creating and implementing what is essentially a pre-order, curbside-pickup model."

Stroffolino reports that both vendors and customers were pleased with the online platform. Customers felt safe and grateful for the access to local products; vendors preferred the model because it reduced the amount of time spent preparing for the market and eliminated excess products at the end of the markets – only products that were pre-sold were brought to the market.

"Our overall market sales were equivalent if not better compared to previous years," said Stroffolino, "even with fewer vendors. The average order size increased, with customers purchasing more at each market. Many vendors experienced increased sales, in part because customers were even more adamant about seeking out local produce and products during the pandemic. Average order sizes were larger than in years' past, which I speculate is due to the fact that customers could more easily purchase products from all our vendors through our online platform."

Bob and Kim Gray began **4 CORNERS FARM** in Newbury over 40 years ago and it's still going strong. Maybe stronger. Pete and Charlie, two of their three children, now work on the farm full time, as does Pete's wife, Marie, who manages the farmstand.

Covid has presented some challenges, but sales at the farmstand have been a bit higher than normal, as new customers – it seems the pandemic has led many people to develop a new appreciation for good, local food – have joined their existing customers. And there's more home cooking these days, too. Though the Grays

considered curbside pickup, it never came to that. The farmstand is the ground floor of a very large barn and is wide open to sun and breezes and it's not hard to keep shoppers well-separated. And, yes, masks are required.

4 Corners Farm a well-loved, beautiful place where almost every imaginable vegetable that can be grown in Vermont is on display. The pick-your-own strawberry and blueberry patches were as busy as ever in 2020.

Seven workers from Mexico with H2A visas worked at 4 Corners this year; one of whom has been coming to the farm seasonally for 20 years.

*Sales (and masks) were up at 4 Corners Farm during the 2020 pandemic.*

2020 was **HONEY FIELD FARM'S** first season, and it's probably safe to say that a pandemic was not in the business plan. Eight months later, owner Valerie Woodhouse says she's amazed at what they were able to accomplish.

In response to Covid, we created an online store for customers to pre-order organic vegetable and herb starts for their gardens," said Woodhouse. "We advertised . . . and wound up doubling our production plan and fulfilling over 350 pre-orders from April-June. It was such a hit that we are continuing this tradition next year too."

The farm's also rightly proud of the contributions it was able to make in the name of local food security. Woodhouse and her team donated veggie starts to community gardens, family centers, and to the food restoration organization Willing Hands. They contributed over 1,000 pounds of produce to restaurants and community centers in New York City who made free meals for their communities. They worked through the federal Farmers Feeding Families and NOFA's Farm Share programs to get produce to those who were experiencing economic hardships. And they collaborated with the garden club at a local retirement community under lockdown to provide weekly deliveries of veggie and herb starts, annual and perennial flowers, and fresh produce all season.

As far as a growing report goes, the veggie starts and bedding plants were great; cherry tomatoes, zucchini and summer squash, fall broccoli were all glorious. Some root crops had trouble germinating in the dry weather and never sized up. Cukes never thrived.

COURTESY OF HONEY FIELD FARM

*A year to remember: the 2020 crew at Honey Field Farm.*

**SOMEDAY FARM** in East Dorset is a family-owned business. Someday sells poultry (turkey and chicken), as well as fruits and vegetables including berries, carrots, and potatoes. Scout Proft is the caretaker. The farmland has been in her family since 1937.

Covid has created problems for businesses all over the country, and Someday Farm is no different. But there were some positives. Scout said that Covid made locals more aware of what local businesses do for a small town. People stopped taking for granted how much they get out of the house to run small errands like going to the farmstand. Because of this, and the number of second homeowners and tourists that are currently in Vermont, there has been more traffic on the road by Someday Farm.

On the negative side, Someday Farm has had fewer customers, but the customers they still have are buying larger amounts of food. Interestingly, turkey sales have gone down. It is assumed that they haven't been as high as usual because people don't know what they are going to be doing for the holidays.

What a year. But Someday Farm powered through and they are excited for 2021. —*Madelyn Robillard*

*Scout Proft at Someday Farm.*

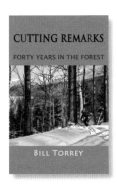

# Sunrise Farm

Route 5 South
White River Junction, Vermont
**sunrisefarmvt.com**

*Certified organic vegetables and
pastured lamb, chicken, and eggs.
Available year-round through our
on-farm CSA and at local food co-ops.*

Chuck Wooster started
Sunrise Organic Farm LLC
as a part-time business
in the spring of 2000,
focused on growing organic
vegetables for a small group
of CSA members. Over two
decades, the farm added
lamb, chicken, beef, and
maple syrup, and expanded to a second location.
The CSA now feeds 350 families each summer, and
vegetables are grown year 'round.

**We asked Chuck: Why Vermont?** He spoke of the long
tradition of successful, independent, small farms, and
an equally long tradition of living close to the landscape.

*"Vermonters see small farms as worthy businesses
and appreciate the flavor and quality of food
grown locally. It makes Vermont an ideal place to
grow and expand the local food movement."*

The Community Supported Agriculture (CSA) model
aims to strengthen Vermont's rural traditions.
"The CSA moves food buying out of the bland retail
environment and returns it to the outdoors and
the community," Chuck said. "Buying and eating
food becomes a relationship with your friends and
neighbors rather than just a financial transaction."

# SEPTEMBER

# September

In early September, the mornings have a kind of tender feel: cool after the heat of August, the grass shining with dew. The sunrise is still a yellow-pink glow above the easternmost hill when I set off with the dog for the first walk of the day. We head down through a neighbor's hayfield, skirting a patch of corn, sending up a flurry of sparrows.

The corn has not thrived in this dry summer. The stalks are thin, anemic-looking, the ears stunted. Still, the birds come back each morning.

One morning I am thinking about Mink the bear, whose body was found in the woods near Hanover the previous day. I'm trying to imagine how she made her way home after being captured and transported to northern New Hampshire. Her journey back would not have been an easy one, but necessary. On her return, Mink became something of a folk hero, loved in spite of her "nuisance" status. Her death leaves a marker in time.

When I was young, spending time on my grandparents' farm with my cousins every summer, we children marked our last evening together with a ceremony that involved a procession up and down the lane, carrying flowers and singing (in retrospect, quite medieval.) This would be just before Labor Day, when we were saying goodbye to our long days together. Goodbye to swimming at Cindy's – the swimming hole named after a forgotten person – and to weeding the immense vegetable garden, getting chased by an indignant rooster, singing "Home on the Range" and "Danny Boy" with my grandfather. It was our version of summer camp.

I don't remember what we sang in our farewell ceremony; the only requirement was that it must be sad. The next morning, we would be off in our family cars, going back to suburban homes separated by hundreds of miles. It would be forever before we saw each other again, before we lived so freely on the land.

Mink and the three cubs she left behind are still on my mind as I make coffee in the kitchen. I glance out the window and see four ravens strutting about at the edge of the corn, and beyond them, my footprints in the damp grass – a meandering trail leading back to the house.

By mid-September we are desperate for rain. The nearby stream has become a thread of water trickling through rocks and sand. I hear of wells going dry. The sun shines through a metallic haze – smoke from the wildfires in the west carried in the upper atmosphere. Even in rural Vermont, a haven in this pandemic year, we feel the world hurting. Fires, drought, violent storms – all seem fitting companions to the human turmoil of this year.

News comes that one of Mink's cubs has been hit and killed by a bus. One has been safely taken to Ben Kilham's bear sanctuary in Lyme, New Hampshire. The third is still out there somewhere.

A late-night walk with the dog before bed: stars muted by haze, we go from bush to tree by flashlight, checking out the messages of the day. Suddenly the cries of coyotes fill the dark, not singing but the frenzied howls I've been told signal the killing of prey, a coyote feast. The hair stands up on the dog's back.

On a snowy morning in early March, I met a coyote face to face. Walking up over a rise, I stepped into his path, and there we were, about the recommended six feet apart. "Hello," I said, hoping to sound casual. My growling dog crouched nearby, as if ready to spring. The coyote ignored him, but looked steadily at me. We regarded each other for several seconds before the coyote turned and trotted off toward the trees, in no hurry.

The encounter seemed a simple acknowledgment of our living in the same place, a nod of mutual respect. For me, it also marks the start of reckoning with a new disease that has revealed so much about our human lives, our first steps into unknown territory.

Even as summer turns to fall in familiar, reassuring ways – geese flying south, blue jays attacking the sumac, late tomatoes ripening as the vines die – we turn toward greater unknowns. Let us proceed with grace. —*Catherine Tudish*

# *Extraordinarily Dry*

The weather headline for almost all of September 2020: Rainfall needed. A prolonged dry spell from September 3rd through 27th kept things extraordinarily dry. According to a State report, by the end of the month, 23.35 percent of the state was abnormally dry, 47.26 percent was in moderate drought, and 29.39 percent was experiencing severe drought conditions. Several very dry months preceded September, contributing to lower water tables, which affected wells, as well as lakes, ponds, streams, and rivers. Luckily, a wavy frontal low pressure system tapping into the tropics and subtropics moved up the eastern seaboard with a full latitude trough of lower pressure and brought an exceptional day and a half of moderate to locally heavy rainfall on the 28th into the 29th. The rainfall was substantial enough, in fact, to set new records for the date. The catch-up on precipitation was just what the doctor ordered; it raised ponds, rivers, and streams, though not to the point that they were full.

Temperatures for the month of September ended about 0.4 degrees above normal, but a stretch of chilly, frosty mornings mid-month stood out. The first touch of frost hit cold valleys on the 15th. The nighttime cold intensified, and many places tied or

*This Killington ground fire burned for three days in mid-September.*

MURRAY MCGRATH

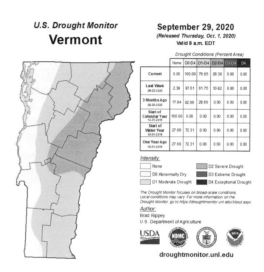

**U.S. Drought Monitor**
**Vermont**

**September 29, 2020**
*(Released Thursday, Oct. 1, 2020)*
Valid 8 a.m. EDT

*Drought Conditions (Percent Area)*

|  | None | D0-D4 | D1-D4 | D2-D4 | D3-D4 | D4 |
|---|---|---|---|---|---|---|
| Current | 0.00 | 100.00 | 76.65 | 29.39 | 0.00 | 0.00 |
| Last Week 09-22-2020 | 2.39 | 97.61 | 61.75 | 10.82 | 0.00 | 0.00 |
| 3 Months Ago 06-30-2020 | 17.94 | 82.06 | 29.60 | 0.00 | 0.00 | 0.00 |
| Start of Calendar Year 12-31-2019 | 100.00 | 0.00 | 0.00 | 0.00 | 0.00 | 0.00 |
| Start of Water Year 10-01-2019 | 27.69 | 72.31 | 0.00 | 0.00 | 0.00 | 0.00 |
| One Year Ago 10-01-2019 | 27.69 | 72.31 | 0.00 | 0.00 | 0.00 | 0.00 |

*Intensity:*

None
D0 Abnormally Dry
D1 Moderate Drought
D2 Severe Drought
D3 Extreme Drought
D4 Exceptional Drought

*The Drought Monitor focuses on broad-scale conditions. Local conditions may vary. For more information on the Drought Monitor, go to https://droughtmonitor.unl.edu/About.aspx*

*Author:*
Brad Rippey
U.S. Department of Agriculture

USDA   NDMC

**droughtmonitor.unl.edu**

set record lows each morning starting on the 19th and lasting through the 22nd.

Overall, oscillations in temperatures became more defined during September, with a warm period on the 9th and 10th topping out at 86 degrees. Cooler Canadian air settled in from the 10th through the 15th, just a bit ahead of the very chilly dry air mass that ended the growing season. After that shock to the system (human and plant alike), temperatures eventually moderated upward, maxing in the upper 70s on the 26th ahead of incoming moisture and the much-needed wet weather.

Like the month of August, September averaged more sunshine than cloud cover. With such a dry stretch of weather, there were no thunderstorms.

By late September, some areas were experiencing the best autumnal landscapes in memory, likely a function of the deciduous trees being stressed by the lack of rainfall. Leafpeepers were treated to vivid reds, oranges, yellows, and purples, which carried over into the month of October. However, some of those visiting the state may have missed part of the show because, overall, the fall colors were about one to two weeks early. —*Roger Hill, Weathering Heights*

# NATURE NOTES

**THE FINS AND BELLIES OF BROOK TROUT**, like the leaves above them, change color in the fall. This heightened color – triggered by shortening day length – is accompanied by aggression as males vie for the opportunity to be closest to an egg-laying female. Bright colors can be a disadvantage, of course, especially to an animal that must be constantly wary of predation from above. So trout have evolved a two-toned skin. The reds and oranges and pinks and silvers and blues on the side contrast with a dark back, engraved with an ornate camouflage called vermiculation. These speckled patterns break up reflected light, making trout almost invisible from above.

## *An Outpouring of Birds*

September 15, 2020. 6:02 a.m. 37 degrees, wind SSE 0 mph. Sky: last night, star-studded and bird-filled; this morning, pale orange wash in the east; haze from California wildfires does little to hide Mount Ascutney, forty miles away; my visibility yardstick.

The night sky holds far more than a billion stars. And this time of year, an equally unfathomable number of migrating birds. The unseen pageant moves south above the face of the continent, patterns established since the Ice Age, a watershed of feathers. Colorado State University's AeroEco Lab, a leader in the new science of radar ornithology, predicted that last night more than four hundred million migratory birds would be aloft over North America. Fifty million over the Northeast, which includes more than two million over Vermont. I think I heard seven thin peeps, chips, much softer than cricket chirps, an audio drizzle from a thousand – maybe ten thousand – feet. More distinctly at pre-dawn, when cold-stunned crickets fell silent. A friend, lying on her picnic table, claimed to have heard an ocean of sound, the soft woosh of busy wings, as though the entire flight of songbirds and cuckoos and whippoorwills and hummingbirds passed over her. A wonderful image... but more likely, she suffered tinnitus. I have suspicions.

Amid the noise of blue jays, crows, chickadees, and nuthatches, bands of warblers and vireos, mumbling incoherently and screened by yellowish leaves, pass through the canopy, refueling on numb insects. Too high, too indistinct to recognize. Four wood thrush, the first I've seen since late May, erect and synchronized like the guards at Buckingham Palace, patrol a neighbor's driveway. A clipped chorus of purple finches.

Every fall, most species of warblers fly more than a thousand miles to crowd into a fraction of the landmass they occupied during the summer. Upon arriving, they face a different suite of predators – bird-eating snakes and spiders, among them – and competitors – antbirds, manikins, and so forth. They must also adapt to a vastly different forest structure and climate. Take the lonely eastern kingbird, a hunter of bumblebees and dragonflies over pastures and marshes. A kingbird aggressively defends its summer turf against other kingbirds and robins and tree swallows, even bald eagles (their Latin name is *Tyrannus tyrannus*). But, wintering in a New World jungle, kingbirds transform into gregarious and peaceable berry eaters, a Fred Rogers among flycatchers. For me, the capacity to change, a repeatable lesson, a continuous striving. —*Ted Levin*

**ACCORDING TO GEOLOGIST PETER THOMPSON**, the layers you see in these southwestern Vermont rocks were sediment deposits in a shallow sea that existed at the eastern edge of the Laurentian continent, in the Cambrian Period, more than 500 million years ago. The rocks were on the leading edge of what has been dubbed the "Green Mountain Frontal Thrust," a fault that brought the seafloor westward onto the margin of the continent. The rock layers were folded by the same forces that caused the thrust faults.

**THE THREE-INCH-LONG TOBACCO HORNWORM CATER-PILLARS** *(Manduca septa)* that gobble up tomato plants are beautiful but somewhat intimidating. They'll bite you if you're careless, plus they make audible clicking noises with their mandibles when threatened. Hornworm caterpillars that are colonized by parasitoid braconid wasps *(Cotesia congregata)* never achieve such size, and they don't get to pupate. Instead, the pupal cases of the wasps emerge from emaciated caterpillars. They look like grains of white rice on the animal's skin. Some years they're hard to find; other years it's all too easy.

**SOMEWHAT GOOD NEWS, FOR A CHANGE:** The Asian long-horned beetle is still with us in parts of New York, Massachusetts, and Ohio, but it is thought to have been successfully dealt with in Illinois, New Jersey, the New York City area, and areas where more isolated infestations have occurred, such as in Boston and parts of Ohio.

AT HOME

※

# *Make Your Own Bear Grease*

Like many people, I've long been conscious about where our food comes from and what resources are required to get it here. At home in Bradford, we grow and harvest much of our own food, which covers our needs for produce, meat, eggs, and legumes. But often in the grocery store I'll notice myself shopping in two other categories: grains (rolled oats, rice, pasta) and fats (avocados, walnuts, coconut oil).

When I learned that bear fat is nearly always tossed aside and wasted, it didn't take long for me to reach out to the local game processor to establish a connection. The raw material is plentiful on bears this time of year, as they've eaten their fill of berries, plenty of corn, and acorns. Unfortunately, according to the local game warden I recently spoke with, as a whole, Vermont hunters are not especially resource-savvy when it comes to using all the bits of taken animals.

Enter me. As a self-proclaimed "resource manager," I'm keen on the idea of exposing friends, family, and anyone else who will listen to the idea of using local and affordable resources that would otherwise go to waste.

Bear fat has a long history of uses: from a dense source of calories to predicting the weather, it's really only recently that we've started NOT using it. It had a wildly popular phase from the 1600s–1900s, when it was touted as a cure for hair loss, and has myriad other uses, including leather conditioner, cooking and baking fat, burning as fuel/candles, relieving pain, and healing dry, itchy skin. The process of turning the raw animal fat into a usable and more shelf-stable product that would be used in those ways is called rendering. On the following page are some simple ways to incorporate bear fat into your life.

—*Amanda Narowski*

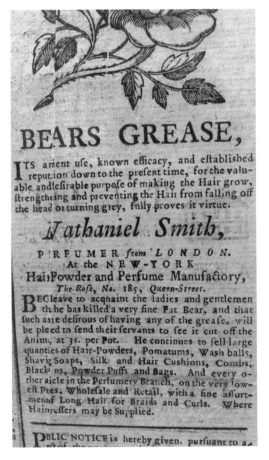

*An advertisement in a colonial newspaper for bears grease.*

## STEP ONE: GET THE FAT.

You have the option to go out and slay a bear yourself, but I prefer to use the resources available at the local game processing station. Most likely, you'll be able to source some on the cheap, while developing a connection with the animal, the butcher, the seasons, and what it means to be a human consumer.

## STEP TWO: CHOP AND MELT.

Now that you have your slabs of flab, it's time to begin preparing it. You could simply throw these chunks in a crockpot – I've done this. But it will yield more if you chop it into one-inch cubes before heating. It's easiest to cut at refrigerator temperature as opposed to room temp, which is messier because when warm the fat slips around. This is how I prepare it before dumping it in my crockpot.

Another version is to heat it in a stockpot on the stove with about an inch of water – the stove top temperature is higher than a crockpot, so the purpose of the water is to keep the fat from burning to the bottom of the pot. The water will evaporate as the fat melts, and you'll be left with pure fat.

## STEP THREE: WAIT, THEN STRAIN.

Now you have your one-inch chunks melting away – either very slowly in a crockpot, or rather quickly in a stockpot. In the crockpot version, I like to leave it on high (somewhere outside if possible – the smell can be overwhelming) for 24 hours. In a stockpot it will be much faster, as little as one hour if you're using high heat and a small amount of fat. Bear fat has a high smoke point, making it excellent for frying and baking (pies especially), but also making it easier to render

without ruining it. Once 50 to 90 percent of the solids have become liquids, it's time to strain. Use a double or triple layer of cheesecloth and a funnel to transfer your liquid gold into jars that you find suitable for your culinary enjoyment, leather application, or long-term storage. The solids, called "cracklings," can be fried, added to cornbread, or fed to chickens.

Bear fat is relatively stable once all the impurities have been strained out, but I like to store mine in the fridge or freezer to be on the safe side.

### SIMPLE BEAR FAT SALVE RECIPE
*100g bear fat*
*25g beeswax*
*10-20 drops of any essential oils (optional)*

Melt the beeswax in a double boiler.
Once liquid, add the bear fat.
When they are mixed, pour into a 4 ounce jar and add your essential oils if desired!
Apply to bruises, scrapes, burns, dry skin, eczema, nail cuticles, etc.

# My son just shot his first squirrel.
# Now how, in God's name, do I cook it?

First, get the hide off. Use poultry shears and cut off the feet and head. Then make an incision perpendicular to the spine in the middle of the back that's big enough to get your fingers in. Pull the squirrel skin in either direction – it should peel right off the meat. The sooner you do this after harvesting the squirrel, the easier it is. Any place it hangs up, use your fingers to separate hide from meat.

Once the hide's off, cut the legs off from the body with poultry shears. Cut around the shoulder blade and remove the front legs as well as any flap meat that's not attached to the carriage. At this point, you've got 95 percent of what you're after. It's possible to extract a bit more meat from the carriage, but that's squirrel butchering 202, which you'll get to once you've mastered this.

Squirrel's delicious – nutty and dark – but it's tough.

So as you cook, think low and slow. Fricassee is the go-to old-school technique. Melt some bear fat (or bacon or seed oil) in a frying pan. Dust the squirrel pieces with flower and jerk or Creole seasoning, then add to the hot pan.

When they're brown, remove and deglaze the pan with grated onion, stirring frequently. Add some minced garlic and sauté it for a minute, then sprinkle the whole thing with flour so it looks like a dusting of snow. Add some beer and chicken stock. Stir until it looks like melted ice cream. Add the squirrel chunks back in, cover, put on low, and simmer for a couple hours. Don't rush it. When the meat is falling off the bone, you're there. Adjust seasoning at the end – some coarsely ground black pepper and some parsley garnish is a nice touch. Add cream if you want to be authentically southern.

# Insight into Frost

Most places in Vermont experienced some unusually cold temperatures in mid-September, so let's take a closer look at frost.

There are two types of frost to watch for: advective and radiation. Radiation frosts are usually the first of the season and happen on clear, calm nights when warm air rises, causing an inversion with cold air closer to the ground. Advective frost forms when a cold front moves through an area, usually later in fall, and typically is accompanied by clouds and gusty winds. In these situations, cold air may reach a mile high.

Since there are often a couple weeks or more of the growing season after the first radiation frost, you can usually minimize the effects. The first step is to know what you're up against: a light freeze (29 to 32 degrees F) will kill only tender plants; a moderate freeze (25 to 28 degrees) will be widely destructive to plants and fruits; and a severe freeze (24 degrees and colder) damages most plants.

If you can't protect sensitive crops like tomatoes, harvest them early. Green tomatoes don't need light to ripen, and in fact ripening can be slowed by light. Keep tomato fruit between 55 and 65 degrees in paper bags or out of light for best ripening. Tender crops that can't withstand frost include tomatoes, eggplant,

*The year's first touch of frost on September 15, 2020.*

peppers, beans, cucumber, sweet corn, squash, and melons. Beets, carrots, lettuce, cauliflower, and potatoes will withstand a light frost. Cool-season crops such as cabbage, broccoli, onions, parsley, peas, radish, spinach, turnips, and Brussels sprouts will withstand a hard frost.

Of course the main prevention is covering plants. Woven fabrics are better than solid ones, such as plastic. Complete garden centers often sell floating row covers made of breathable white material. Whatever fabric is used, greater protection comes from not having the material rest directly on the plants. Apply covers in early evening as winds die down, and remove the next morning as the sun warms the plants.

Looking ahead to next year, you might consider cold frames for your garden, either portable or permanent.

*Dr. Leonard Perry*
*Horticulture Professor Emeritus*
*University of Vermont*

# A LOOK BACK

## *In Old Vermont*

I can remember when I was four or five years old, we were digging dandelions. We would take an old bushel basket, go down to the meadow, and start digging. We used a very dull butter knife. It would take us hours, and when we were done digging, we had to clean them, making sure there was no grass or other material mixed into the greens. This was a long process. It took a lot of greens to make a quart, and Mom would put up more than 100 quarts.

Often, we ate them with cider vinegar and salt. Another way was with potatoes and a slab of bacon, cooked together and served with homemade butter. There was so much iron in the greens that it turned the potatoes sort of a black color.

We raised large gardens; there were four or five different spots so the gardens could be rotated. Potatoes, squash, pumpkins, corn, and beans were in big plots. There was another one for onions and other vegetables that did not use up so much space.

Dad would drive his old doodlebug onto the sites and start to plow the ground up, and then take a harrow to make it smooth. The calendar was checked for the dates of the last full moons in May and June. This would tell him when to plant. The potatoes were one of the first to be planted. They were placed in a dug row and covered. Once the plants started to emerge from the ground, they were checked closely for potato bugs. If they got ahead of you, they could destroy your crop. My sister and I would take a can with some water and a bit of soap in it, pick the bugs, and put them in the can. This took some time since it was a large area to cover. The rows were hilled up two to three times during the summer.

They would flower late in the summer and the tops would die off. At this point, Dad could no longer wait for a taste of his potatoes. He would dig a hill up to see how big they were. He would go to the house, with supper in his large hands: golden beauties, called Green Mountain potatoes.

We always dug them on Tunbridge Fair weekend, unless it rained. Dad would get the doodlebug and plow under the rows, to expose the great gift. He would get the potato fork and go down the rows to pull out the ones that were hiding. He would say you don't want to spear the taters, you have to feel them and gently pull them out. It took a few times before you could feel the taters, but he was right.

The potatoes were taken to the cellar and placed in two very large bins about three feet off of the dirt floor. In the middle of the winter they were checked for sprouts, which we pulled off. Usually, the potatoes lasted until the new ones were ready.

Shell beans were one of my favorites. We would pick the shell beans and can them in quart mason jars. They were so good. Mom would open a jar, put them in a pan with milk, butter, salt, and pepper. She would heat it on the wood stove, and then they were served. One of the best dishes!

The rest of the garden was harvested and canned, dried, or frozen. The onions were braided or put in bins in the cellar. Apples were picked and vinegar was made. A couple of bushels of apples were to be eaten. Cabbages were hung from the rafters. Beets, carrots, and turnips were put in clean sand and a bit of water was added every so often.

Hunting season started in September. We ate a lot of raccoon – the freezer was loaded with them. Mom would place it in a cast iron pot with water and a bit of vinegar, and it would simmer on the back of the wood stove. After it was finished, she would put it in a cast iron spider and bake it. Spices and herbs were added. It was very good. Dad would hunt and usually got a buck. That was canned. My sister and I would hunt with our grandfather. Neither one of us ever got a deer, but we enjoyed going. I found an old license that I had, dated 1973, and that was the last time I went.

The family also harvested a pig and a beef cow. The pig was smoked in an old drum. When it was finished, it was put in the cellar, hanging from the rafters until we needed it.

We learned a lot through those years. I am grateful that my parents and grandparents took the time to show us the art of gardening and what it meant to work hard and to be proud of it. To realize that you can survive if there was a crisis. I look to the future, and I hope I can work with the children and teach them as I was taught. —*Chief Shirly Hook, Koasek band of the Abenaki nation*

*Chief Shirly Hook's parents, Clyde and Betty Ann Hook, with the doodlebug in Chelsea*

INDUSTRY

# Getting Started with Honey Bees

## A HANDFUL OF THOUGHTS ON A CHALLENGING ENDEAVOR

You'll often see them while driving the back-roads of New England, tucked in the corners of hay fields or backyards: towers of aged wooden boxes containing colonies of honey bees. To the uninitiated, these hives and the bees inside them may seem equal parts quaint and dangerous, and any-one who keeps bees must surely be insane (why else would anyone choose to endure the pointy end of a honeybee?). For those who can get past the prospect of some hard work and the occasional stings involved in beekeeping, it can be a rewarding hobby. Here are a few hard-earned thoughts on getting started:

### A BEEKEEPER'S MOTIVATION

The most important question to ask is why are you interested in keeping bees. If your goal is simply to produce honey for your own use, you are probably better off going to a store. While you may fill some jars in the fall, the unprepared beekeeper will likely find that their bees will swarm – or worse, die. But if you're looking for a wonderful window into the natural world, beekeeping will provide it. You must embrace the seasonal changes in order to be successful, and a beginning beekeeper should be ready to learn at every stage and to grow with their bees.

### ASSIGNED READING

One of my beekeeping mentors once told me that I should consider reading about bees for a full year be-fore I picked up a hive tool. This was excellent advice. There are thousands of books on beekeeping, but two that I found particularly useful as I got started were *The New Complete Guide to Beekeeping* by Roger A. Morse and Thomas D. Seeley's *Honeybee Democracy*.

### MENTORSHIP

Beekeeping has a long tradition of mentorship, and finding a knowledgeable beekeeper to work with can prove priceless as you strike out on your own. I still routinely call the beekeepers who mentored me with questions and to shoot the breeze about bees. Getting involved with a local bee club or state organization is also likely to be very helpful.

### BEWARE OF USED EQUIPMENT

As you get ready to welcome your bees you will need to buy or build frames, boxes, bottom boards, and covers to house the bees and their brood and honey. Don't buy used equipment. Build or buy new versions of everything you need. Wooden equipment can retain spores from pathogens like American foul brood for more than 40 years, and there's no way of knowing if those used boxes on the internet are fine or are going to kill your bees.

### BUYING BEES

You've read all the books, taken a hive tour or two with another beekeeper, and you're ready to get going. The next step is buying bees. The best piece of advice I can offer is to buy local bees. The genetics of your bees go a long way in determining whether they survive the winter, and buying cheaper bees from southern states won't do you much good in New England. Skilled local beekeepers sell nucleus colonies ("nucs" for short) with a queen that they've bred and that has survived a Vermont winter. Buying local bees also cuts down on the chances that parasites and viruses hitch a ride in your nuc from other areas of the country. It's best to buy at least two hives, so if you do lose one over the winter you'll still be a beekeeper in the spring.

### TREATMENTS

There's a lot of debate about whether or not to treat for varroa mites, but I tell people getting started that they should treat their bees. It takes a large apiary, an experienced beekeeper, and well-informed management to begin considering a treatment-free approach.

### HAVE FUN

Beekeeping at every level is rewarding and fulfilling. The bees and the environment are always changing and inspire the beekeeper to be adaptable and inquisitive. Things that worked one year might not work the next year. As your experience level increases, you can begin making your own new colonies by splitting hives, making nucs, or even raising your own queens. When done with thought and care, beekeeping can be a lifelong pursuit with sweet rewards.

*Ethan West*
*Owner/Beekeeper/Sugarmaker*
*Republic of Vermont*

## Honey in the Kitchen

When using honey in cake baking, the general rule is to reduce the amount of liquid by one-quarter cup for each cup of honey that is used to replace sugar. In a recipe, the liquid could be water, milk, coffee, eggs, or juice.

Substituting honey for the full amount of sugar may produce a heavy texture in baked goods. In recipes calling for a large amount of sugar, such as cakes or sweet breads, substituting honey for half of the sugar and reducing the liquid will produce a lighter product.

In a cake recipe calling for one cup of sugar, use one half cup of sugar and one half cup of honey and reduce the liquid by three tablespoons.

In some recipes the total amount of sugar can be reduced when substituting honey, because honey is sweeter than sugar. For example, in cookie recipes calling for large amounts of sugar, ¾ cup honey can be substituted for 1 cup of granulated sugar without reducing sweetness noticeably.

In breadmaking, honey can be substituted for all of the sugar called for, as most bread recipes do not call for large amounts of sugar.

For leavening, best results are obtained by using the directions on the baking powder can. A small amount of baking soda is needed to neutralize the acidity of the honey. When honey is substituted for sugar, add ¼ teaspoon of baking soda for every cup of honey. If the recipe calls for sour milk, baking soda, and honey, it is not necessary to add any extra baking soda for the honey.

Breads, cakes, and cookies made with honey will brown more readily than baked goods made with granulated sugar. It is good to reduce baking temperature about 25 degrees to prevent over-browning of honey baked goods.

For easy pouring and less waste, use a greased cup when measuring honey. Measure the fat first, then the honey in the same cup. Cooking oil, melted butter, or egg white will serve the same purpose. Likewise, when measuring tablespoons of honey, dip the spoon into oil and then fill with honey. The honey pours off to the last drop. —The Vermont Beekeeper's Cookbook, *published by the Vermont Beekeepers Association*

## *Switchel*

When working outdoors in the heat of the day, consider bringing some switchel along: roughly three cups of cider vinegar in three-quarters of a gallon of water, plus some honey and some ginger. Cider vinegar supplies potassium and the ginger helps potassium absorption. Honey both revives your energy and reduces the tartness. Variations of this concoction have been used by farm workers since before the Civil War. Sometimes black strap molasses, which supplies iron and magnesium, is added.

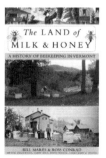

# Bees and Honey

The honey bee is one non-native widespread species that has largely, though not entirely, escaped criticism. As pollinators and producers of honey, these insects have been admired, cared for, and sometimes misunderstood for millennia. Honey bees were brought to North America by the earliest European settlers and have spread on their own or been spread by humans throughout all but the coldest parts of the continent.

In the early days, bees were a standard component of Vermont farms. The 1850 US census reported that nearly 250,000 pounds of honey were produced in the state that year and since that time this figure has usually been considerably higher: four times as much in 2019 according to the Vermont Beekeepers Association. Most of the larger honey producers now are in the Champlain Valley, most notably in Addison County. Bees continue to be an important part of the agricultural landscape in the state; as pollinators of apples, they are essential.

For as long as bees have been tended here, there have been problems: two kinds of foulbrood (an apt name for a bacterial larval disease), some fungal diseases, wax moths, weather too hot or cold or dry or wet. Tracheal mites were considered a serious problem when they showed up in the mid-1980s, but nothing compares to the varroa mite, which was first found in Vermont in 1992.

This little mite shifted its host from the Asian honey bee *(Apis cerana)*, where they are a minor problem, to the honey bee *(Apis mellifera)*, probably near Vladivostok, Russia, in the 1950s. Although varroa mites are blind and wingless, and can't crawl from one hive to another, they have managed to invade almost every honey bee colony in the world since then. Varroa mites are formidable foes, unlike anything else. Beekeeping around almost the whole Earth is in two categories: before varroa and after varroa. It's a bee pandemic, for sure.

Varroa mite reproduction is complicated and weird, but the short version is that they lay their eggs in the cells of bee honeycomb and the mites mature after feeding on the bee larvae and pupae. They then attach to and feed on the stored fat of adult bees. They spread to other beehives when bees mistakenly enter the wrong hive or when the honey in weakened varroa-infested beehives is robbed by other bees. Robber bees bring back mites as well as honey, mites that are highly likely to doom even a formerly strong colony.

Since varroa mites have become widespread, annual colony losses throughout this country have run close to 40 percent, as opposed to 10 or 15 percent in pre-varroa times. In the past year in Vermont almost 40 percent of the colonies died, nearly all because of varroa. The mites stunt the growth of bees and make them more susceptible to pesticides, among other things. Compounding threats, such as loss of nectar-producing plants, for instance when corn replaces clover-filled hay fields, plus pesticide exposure, also make life hard for these animals. Undernourished bees and those that have been exposed to pesticides are more susceptible to varroa mites.

Varroa mites bring an array of viruses with them, and these are even more harmful to the bees than the mites themselves. Nowadays, the worst is deformed wing virus, an affliction that's easy to see, but there are other debilitating viruses as well. Once a virus moves from a varroa mite to a bee, it can spread from bee to bee to bee.

Both organic and synthetic chemical treatments have been used to kill varroa mites but the mites have developed resistance to most or all of them in an appallingly short time. Mites that survive one chemical treatment, of which there are at first just a few in a hive, produce resistant offspring. Changing to a different treatment is useful in nailing the resistant survivors. Both rotating treatments of different products and using management techniques to reduce mite numbers are now essential for most beekeepers. Some treatments only kill mites on adult bees, not those inside cells. Others leave toxic residues. There's no one clearly superior product, and all of them need to be used with extreme care as they aren't good for people and easily can kill bees as well as mites.

The larger beekeepers in Vermont have a long history of mutual aid and, often through the Vermont Beekeepers Association, are continually working out methods to help bees. Approaches to the varroa problem go down two rather different tracks. Kirk Webster, of Middlebury, pioneered a no-treatment approach, and other strategies have been worked out by many of the other Vermonters who make most or all of their livelihood from bees.

Just in the 70 or so years since varroa has existed in honey bees, some managed colonies and some wild colonies have been able to survive without any chemical treatment. When colonies are treated with chemicals, the role of natural selection is lost. Accelerating natural selection by breeding mite-resistant queens and replacing less competent queens has been effective in producing bee traits, such as more fastidious grooming, that reduce mite numbers.

When varroa mites first arrive, they wipe out almost all feral honey bees, but in just the 30 years since varroa has been in our region, wild bees appear to be doing better than those in apiaries. In the wild, bees do what bees in the wild have always done; they form small, widely spaced colonies and swarm often, which results in new genetic variants, and results in colonies with no brood, thus disrupting mite reproduction. Under these conditions honey bees can sometimes keep mites to a manageable level.

Summer/early fall hive failures have been on the increase recently, perhaps due to viruses that have become more virulent. But it's in winter that most mite-infested colonies die. These losses can be offset by carrying many carefully selected queens through the winter in small nucleus colonies, called nucs. Conventional wisdom has long held that a bee hive needs about 60 pounds of honey to get through the winter, but small colonies in a small space, on top of and warmed by a larger hive, often come though well. Nucs that live till spring tend to be the ones that have some mite resistance, and they quickly grow into productive colonies. Many Vermont beekeepers use this strategy with good outcomes. However, coming up with a hundred or so top-quality queens and installing them into new quarters is not a simple matter, certainly not one for a beginning beekeeper.

Many people become interested in keeping bees as a way to make the world a better place, providing a helping hand to beleaguered pollinators, local food for themselves and their neighbors, and beeswax candles. This worldview often includes a strong distaste for pesticides of any kind, and when it comes to varroa mites, this is not likely to work.

Several management techniques can help. Giving bees wax that's imprinted with oversized cells encourages them to create drone brood, which the mites greatly prefer, and then removing it before the mite-laden drones emerge can slow mite population growth. Deciding what to do starts with a mite count, a procedure which has become standardized. Then, most beekeepers use several chemicals for mite reduction if mite levels exceed the treatment threshold and again before bees go into winter, depending on the level of infestation. Winter bees need to be healthy, since unlike summer bees, they live for many months. Carrying a weakened mite-infested colony into the fall could be compared to not wearing a Covid mask – your hive will spread bad trouble to your neighbors and then it will die.

Varroa mites have made beekeeping an expensive labor-intensive hobby for the small-timers and an almost insurmountable challenge when it comes to making a livelihood from bees. But in Vermont as elsewhere, people who tend bees are hopelessly fascinated and charmed by them. Somehow, a way will be found. —*Virginia Barlow*

# Making Honey with the Mraz family

Back in 1931, Charles Mraz founded Champlain Valley Apiaries, a family-run honey of a business that is now in its third generation of ownership. A New Yorker, he started tending his first beehives in Queens at the age of 14, and subsequently worked his way via New York's Finger Lakes region to Middlebury, Vermont, where he settled. By then, the state had transitioned from the collapse of sheep farming to dairy farming, and the Champlain Valley, and much of the rest of the state, had become milk country. Vast hayfields in the fertile plains around Lake Champlain were full of clover, trefoil, and alfalfa, creating a perfect symbiosis for beekeeping. Charles and his bees thrived in what was, quite literally, the land of milk and honey.

During his lifetime, Charles gained notoriety for his campaign to have apitherapy – the practice of having bees sting the area around afflicted joints – recognized as a viable treatment for arthritis. After successfully treating his own arthritic knees with bee venom, promoting the cure for this and other autoimmune disorders became his life's work. He never lived to see apitherapy get accepted by the medical establishment, but he did gain a huge following of people who came from around the world for his free treatments.

His belief in these curative properties led him to also figure out how to extract the bee venom in

OLIVER PARINI

quantities sufficient to supply any researcher or scientist who displayed an interest. Over time, apitherapy gained traction in alternative medicine for treating arthritis, MS, and allergies, but it still hasn't been sanctioned by any official body. And yet, the FDA has approved bee venom for desensitization, and nowadays, Champlain Valley Apiaries still sells pharma-grade venom for immunology drug production.

Charles also discovered that he could use carbolic acid fumes to drive the bees deep down into the hive while removing frames to extract the honey. With 1,000 colonies of 30,000-60,000 bees apiece, having a way to suppress angry bees was critical. The carbolic acid fume board was a game changer for beekeepers everywhere, enabling them to easily deescalate attacks. Then, when Charles's son, William, took the reins, he perfected the seal uncapper, which scrapes the wax caps off each honeycomb cell for easier extraction.

For 89 years, the Mraz family has minded their hives in the bucolic hayfields and orchards of Vermont, while breeding their own strain of mutt bees uniquely adapted to the mostly organic environment. Now, Charles's grandson, Chas, runs Champlain Valley Apiaries and has 1,000 hives in 30 different locations between Whiting and the Canadian border, producing about 60,000 pounds of honey annually. His bees forage over 450 square miles – an area three times bigger than Detroit.

Much has changed in this time, and the three generations of the Mraz men have adapted accordingly. Just 20 years ago, a hive could survive on its own, superseding new queens and making enough honey for themselves to get through the winter and for the beekeeper to sell. Back then, a hive could keep itself going for 25 years, no problem. Nowadays, it's more like three years, and then only if you manage them to protect against colony collapse disorder, the tracheal mite, the varroa mite, foul brood, and, most recently, murder hornets. Chas has had to develop a much more complex management system than did his father and grandfather, tweaking it according to how the bees are doing every season. "Work with the bees," he says. "They'll tell you what to do." Then he laughs about the murder hornet, says they're so big all you have to do is put a screen in front of the hive entrance. Still, it's just another problem in a bee business

that used to be able to take care of itself.

The super-villain now is the neonicotinoid, introduced in the 1990s. Although this pesticide has been banned in much of Europe, the German manufacturer still sells plenty to US farmers, who primarily use neonicotinoid-coated seeds for corn and soy crops. Neonics have been linked to colony collapse disorder, the declining ability of bees to endure the long winters, and massive bird and insect die-offs. Regardless, factory farms and monocultures like the immediate gratification.

This is where Chas gets all fired up, and rightly so. Neonicotinoids are like the classic comic book bad guy, so obviously evil, and yet they remain a multi-billion-dollar industry poisoning the world. These days, the voice Rachel Carson once used for the elimination of DDT would be drowned out by the static of lobbyists and big money that can only focus on immediate returns, not the possibly irreversible damage left behind for future generations.

"Neonics aren't necessary," Chas says. "They do not increase yield enough to account for the depletion and destruction of the soil. Neonics are hurting farmers, not helping them. They're more harmful than just pouring fuel onto the ground. We used to farm according to our own local knowledge. Now chemical companies are globally dictating the rules. That's why dairy farmers are going out of business. They don't even know about the coated seeds. They're just looking at the advertised end result, what to feed cows, how to get more food – while actually only four percent of the neonics get absorbed by plants and insects, and the rest goes into the dirt, the ground, the water supply. It inadvertently kills the soil that then needs more chemicals to re-amend it."

Ask Chas what he thinks about the future of beekeeping, and he says, "It's directly connected to the future of dairy farms. If they go, our hayfields are gone, and they are responsible for 70 percent of our honey production. It takes 15 years for a farm to turn back to a forest. Vermont is 85 percent reforested, which is why we have bears in the valley now. Never had them before. Now, we have bear fences around 90 percent of our hives."

Does he have an answer to this? "We're caught in a national market we're not part of anymore, can't compete with. We need to specialize. Vermont needs to get completely out of this national market and brand itself."

Made in Vermont already has cachet. Farmer to farmer, they know this, he says, but there's a disconnect between farming and Montpelier with their feel-good politics. For example, legislation was passed in 2019 mandating licenses for anyone using neonicotinoids. But, he says, it's useless – anyone can get this license.

"Let's get lobbyists out of the room, tell our representatives to get rid of neonics, do everything we can to save farming in Vermont. We can't say this is just another phase like sheep. Sheep were replaced by dairy. What will replace this? We need farming on a scale to keep fields open and productive, to keep bees productive, to keep vistas and landscapes we can see from the road – the aesthetics that keep tourists coming."

"To do this," he says, "we need to do better. Not organic, necessarily, but we need to focus on integrated pest management and innovative and value-added farming, which makes better food. We're in a good place to provide the Northeast with good healthy food. It costs more, but they'll spend the money for the better products.

"We make top-notch honey, maple syrup, cheese. There's huge marketing value in saying we're keeping Vermont farmers and agriculture healthy. We need that type of cooperation because we're getting to the point of desperation."

He laughs, realizing he's on a rant, but it's a passion borne of frustration with seeing solutions so clearly and feeling like a voice blowing across the disappearing hayfields.

Ask him where he finds inspiration, and he will tell you about his father and grandfather who taught him to question things, to avoid the rabbit holes, to be a practical environmentalist. He is inspired by stories of newer corporations who want to make corrections, those with conscience and common sense.

And he is hopeful. Champlain Valley Apiaries has gotten through incredibly hard times with the bees. They've survived colony collapse, they're managing mites, and he has faith in his bees and their genetic diversity. Breeding queens with different drones promotes evolution of the survivors and the ability to adapt, he says. The bees they have now are related to bees Charles Mraz started with over 90 years ago. They are Vermont bees, and with collective determination the land of milk, honey, and good food can survive. —*Tania Aebi*

# The Vermont Bee Lab

The Vermont Bee Laboratory at the University of Vermont opened in 2019. Funded in part by a Vermont Specialty Crop Block Grant and by the Vermont Beekeepers Association, the lab carries out research, outreach, and education with the goal of protecting insect pollinators. Samantha Alger, the director, and several undergraduate and graduate students, have been working as a group since 2013 when Alger herself was a graduate student.

Some of their research was underway before the lab opened, but having a home has been a big help. And Alger, now that she's a research professor at UVM, is able to mentor graduate students, apply for funding, and collaborate with external stakeholders to promote pollinator health.

During the beekeeping season, the Vermont Bee Lab offers free diagnostic services for Vermont bee-keepers with a focus on Nosema (an often-lethal fungal disease) and Varroa mites (the most damaging pest in modern beekeeping). Vermont beekeepers can send or deliver bees to the lab for analysis. You can find more information about diagnostic services at the VBL website (vermontbeelab.com).

The lab also manages several research projects focused on the spread and transmission of bee diseases. In a study published last year, Alger and her colleagues discovered that RNA viruses spread from honey bees to bumble bees through the shared use of flowers. Bumble bees near apiaries had the same viruses that the honey bees had. Bumble bees living far from apiaries, on the other hand, were virus-free. Only flowers located in honey bee apiaries harbored RNA viruses. Now, the lab is working to understand if different flower shapes are more or less likely to serve as bridges in viral transmission between bees. Results from this work could help people choose flowers that are best suited to pollinator-friendly plantings. This work also underscores the importance of maintaining healthy honey bee colonies to lessen the risk of disease spillover that is harmful to wild species.

To support honey bee health, the Vermont bee lab manages the USDA-APHIS National Honey Bee Survey for Vermont, a nationwide effort to gather baseline data on bee diseases and pests. Each summer, samples are collected from 24 apiaries throughout Vermont and tested for pests and pathogens, including exotic pests not yet known to exist in North America. Up to 10 samples of wax or pollen are also collected to understand how honey bees in Vermont may be exposed to over 170 different pesticides. This survey has resulted in Vermont's first standardized long-term dataset on bee pests and we are now able to see how Vermont compares to other states and national averages. Results from the survey can be found on research.beeinformed.org/state_reports.

Education is one of the major goals of the Vermont Bee Lab. In the summer of 2019, Alger began teaching UVM's first beekeeping course in over 50 years. She continues to teach two courses through the Plant and Soil Science Department and has begun offering both an online and hands-on version during the summer. The summer beekeeping courses are available for both UVM students and community members. Through this course, students learn the fundamentals of being responsible stewards of honey bee colonies and the skills to support good decision making in today's changing world of beekeeping. —*Virginia Barlow*

## COMMUNITY SUPPORTED PUBLISHING

Did you enjoy Volume 1 of the *Vermont Almanac*? Do you see the potential in what it could become? If so, help us create next year's edition by **donating or pre-buying today at vermontalmanac.org**.

The 20th-century model that supported publishing is broken. In the internet age, no publication can subsist on advertising revenue and newsstand sales. And so, like farmers who sell CSA shares to get money up front with which to grow their crop, our economic model relies in part on donations and pre-buys from readers.

Work on the second volume, covering October 2020–September 2021, is already underway. We've got a new weather station that's going to give us first-hand data with which we'll build stories. We've got a half-dozen talented new contributors lined up and dozens more we plan on reaching out to. We're already getting reader feedback to incorporate.

The goal is to publish a book each fall that people can collect. Your support helps make it happen.